"Seldom does one find a book that provides academics with textbook-clear explanations of project management/project delivery typologies which also challenges practitioners with visionary projections of possible evolutions of the complex, but fragmented profession/industry that designs and constructs buildings. From the unique perspective of decades of in-depth involvement as an architect and constructor, Thomsen tells the stories of how project management is morphing into program management, giving us experience-based insights into fundamental processes of how the built environment has been, and will be, shaped. The new models he proposes encourage cooperation. We will all participate in the exciting future that Thomsen describes as a multi-industry, multi-national, and multi-professional collaboration leading to better buildings. Well organized from concept through detail and laced with innovative diagrams and compressed histories, this book will benefit the architecture and the construction student as well as the seasoned CEO. Don't miss it."

—Tom Regan, Dean and Professor, College of Architecture, Texas A&M University

"In short, great work. My favorite part is the organizational behavior and people stuff at the end. The page on friendship is so on point that I intend to read it to our next all hands staff meeting. One of our major training initiatives internally involves spinning up newer people on exactly what really goes on in the industry and among its players. We should make this book required reading for every new FMI employee."

—Henry M. "Hank" Harris, Jr., cmc, President and Managing Director, FMI Inc.

"I've worked with Chuck on the country's largest building program, shared podiums with him and now have read his book. Read it and Chuck will profoundly redefine your construction world."

—Jim McConnell, Captain (Ret) U. S. Navy Engineering Command, former Chief Facilities Executive, Los Angeles Unified School District

"I found myself saying 'Yes, Yes, Yes, he nailed it.' In the fields of architecture, construction and construction management it will become an instant classic and a must read for owners who are involved in facilities."

—Dennis D. Dunne, FCMAA, Chief Facilities Consultant, California Department of Corrections and Rehabilitation

"In 'Program Management' Chuck Thomsen has written perhaps the most comprehensive and up-to-date book on the challenges facing owners engaging the building design and construction industry. Anybody dealing with this industry, attempting to create the buildings their organization requires, would do well to read Thomsen's book. Thomsen has worked with the most talented innovators in building design, construction and ownership for the last 50 years. With a clear, understandable writing style he has succinctly captured that incredible knowledge and insight in this very well organized book."

—Sidney J. Sanders, Vice President Facilities and Construction, The Methodist Hospital System, former head of Facility Planning, Design and Construction for the University of Texas System

"Chuck Thomsen's 'Program Management' is well written and a must read for owners planning major construction programs, program and construction managers, architects, engineers, builders, educators and students. I have had the good fortune of working closely with Chuck on a number of occasions and know first-hand of his keen mind and expert insight."

—George T. Heery, FAIA, RIBA, FCMAA, Chairman & CEO, Brookwood Group, Construction Program Managers

"Thomsen's 'Program Management' should be manna from heaven for owners launching a capital building program comprising multiple projects. Calling on his unique experience, Thomsen convincingly demonstrates how wise owners can sift out the repetitious aspects of their building programs and realize significant savings in time and money while enhancing the quality of their buildings. (My own university, engaged in constructing a second campus, would profit from his counsel.) But the book goes much further; in addition to his analysis of multiple building programs, Thomsen draws on his fifty years as a project delivery innovator to give the reader what is surely the most lucid and useful primer on project delivery available in this country."

—Carl M. Sapers, Professor of Studies in Professional Practice in Architecture, Harvard University Graduate School of Design

Although many organizations have traditionally managed their capital building programs, the concept of Program Management as a professional service is a relatively new approach to project delivery in the design and construction industry, and thus there are different ways of looking at it. In this book, Chuck Thomsen defines a program as "a capital building activity with multiple projects" that "usually serve a similar purpose and are executed by an organization with unique characteristics." Program Management involves taking the broad view, rather than a project-by-project view. Thomsen points out that this approach allows the Program Manager to identify the common aspects of multiple projects—processes, products, and people—and to learn from them to improve the cost, schedule, and quality of future projects in the program.

Thomsen gives his opinion that the building industry has entered an era when most building projects other than custom homes, museums and churches are constructed by commercial, government, or other organizations that continuously build new structures. He also discusses changes in technology that facilitate new ways of doing things in the industry, and emphasizes his belief that improvements in communications are vital as well.

Significantly, Thomsen (who is an architect) notes that architecture firms, engineering firms, contractors, CM firms, owners and other entities are offering Program Management services, often in teams. He is a strong advocate of industry collaboration, Integrated Practice and stresses the importance of design in Program Management practices.

Because Program Management is so new, the American Institute of Architects recognizes that other views of it may emerge over time. Chuck Thomsen acknowledges this, as well, describing the variety in the ways the many firms and individuals interviewed for this book engage in Program Management. The ideas expressed in the book can serve as a catalyst for considering this new way of approaching the work that architects do. They are the beginning of the discussion, rather than a strict path that all must follow.

—*The American Institute of Architects*

PROGRAM MANAGEMENT

Concepts and Strategies for Managing Capital Building Programs

CHUCK THOMSEN FAIA FCMAA

Construction Management Association of America Foundation
7926 Jones Branch Drive, Suite 800
McLean, VA 22102

Proceeds from the sale of this book will go to the
Construction Management Association of America Foundation

The cover design was donated to the Foundation by Mark Geer, Geer Design, Inc.

This book is dedicated to all the owners, architects, engineers, construction managers, contractors, subcontractors, manufacturers and educators who are creating new ways to work together to make better buildings.

Table of Contents

Systems to Manage the Detail

An Ability to Work with People

Author's Note

Most of the buildings built today are for owners with continuous building programs. Many of the men and women who manage these programs are improving the results by thinking of their work as a *program* rather than a series of individual *projects*. That's the subject of this book.

Program Management is not simply a technical undertaking. The processes and the results are profoundly influenced by predictable characteristics of human behavior in large groups. So this book deals with how different forms of contracts and different team structures will influence people, how goals will shape management processes, how the personality of leaders will control design and construction activities and how these conditions will affect the productivity of people executing the work.

This is not a technical reference. You will not find statistical techniques for risk analysis, a discussion of clash detection in BIM systems or detailed verbiage for contract language.

Rather, we (my colleagues and I) have worked hard to show how our design and construction programs are as varied as the personalities of the individual owners, managers, designers, builders and manufacturers that populate them—sometimes appropriately so, sometimes not. We've described many paths to success—and to failure. We've discussed the many yardsticks that owners and the public use to measure accomplishment and, consequently, how resistant it is to scientific measurement and engineering analysis.

I believe that the construction industry has quietly and without fanfare changed from a project industry to a program industry. And I believe many Program Managers have missed this change and the opportunities that programs offer for continuous improvement that are unavailable to us when we do single projects.

At this point I should explain what I mean by Program Management. I think it appropriate because people who are expert in a subject rarely agree on definitions. No group of architects would agree on a definition of architecture, nor would the best artists agree on the meaning of art.

Our world of management is no different. As I write this I know that men and women with as much or more experience than I will advance different meanings to these terms. That's fine. There's no official dictionary of construction terms. While many states have legal definitions for architecture and engineering, few have addressed these management terms.

But if I'm to use these words to communicate, I need to tell you what I mean. So here is an explanation.

As I use the term in this book, Program Management is the management of a portfolio of projects for a capital building program. A Program Manager can be a person or an organization. A Program Management organization may include project management and construction management responsibilities. Program Management may be provided by an in-house staff or it may be outsourced. Often there's a combination of both.

Many professionals use the term "Program Management" to mean the management of all the steps from financing and site selection through commissioning and occupancy of a single project. While that is certainly a legitimate and common use of our language, and while I have no objection to that usage, for the purpose of his book, I use the term project management for that function.

Therefore, on the following pages, a project manager is a person or an organization that manages a single project—perhaps part of the owner's organization or a consultant hired by the owner to represent the owner's interest. The term also has a second context. Each organization that has a body of work to do will likely have someone they call a "project manager" who manages that work.

A construction manager, as I use the term, is an organization that manages a single design and construction project replacing the need for a general contractor. Typically a construction manager is hired during design and contributes advice on construction cost and technology during design. Sometimes, a CM may be responsible for managing the AE. There are two common approaches.

1. A CM may work in an agency role for the client, managing multiple prime trade contractors. Some organizations call that CM agency or CMa.

2. A CM may hold the subcontracts. In this case the CM may or may not guarantee the final construction cost and schedule. This role is essentially that of a general contractor (GC) who has been selected based on qualifications and provides pre-construction services. Some organizations call that CMc, CMAR or CM-at-risk.

However, while these definitions are common, they are far from universal. Many owner organizations have people in-house that they call Construction Managers and the next construction professional may use all these terms differently. So it will always be wise to ask, "What do you mean by…?"

In writing this book, we thought about our own projects that had various degrees of success and talked to hundreds of people who managed other programs. And we pondered the matter.

Here is what we think.

Acknowledgments

We began by mixing my half-century of experience with a group of exceptionally bright young men and women who had almost none.

Jesse Wells made major contributions to the research and writing. He worked with me two summers while he was finishing his master's degree at Harvard. Then he joined us full time. He researched many companies and offered insight and observations that are remarkable for a young man just beginning a career.

Jim Avant, a graduate of Texas A&M, and Miriam Bentley Swift, a graduate of Rice University, were part of the team who also helped interview owners, collect information and discuss the ideas on these pages.

Jesse, Jim and Miriam made penetrating observations that people with more experience would not have thought of. They were unconstrained by the burdensome traditions of the construction industry and had no difficulty seeing the good sense in the innovative practices of the organizations we interviewed—often wondering out loud why everyone didn't do it that way.

Jesse Wells, Jim Avant and Miriam Bentley Swift

At the time we did this research, I was chairman of 3D/International. Prior to its merger with Parsons, 3D/I supported an R&D group that included Jesse, Jim and Miriam. Others who participated in the R&D group included Dr. Lee Burch, Chuck Dunham and Aidan Chopra.

The group did much of the research and investigation that triggered the concepts and data in this work. I need to thank my colleagues on the executive committee at 3D/I for supporting the cost of this effort: John Murph, Gary Boyd, William Turner, Alan Fleishacker and Ron Begnaud. I would also like to thank my colleagues at Parsons who, after our merger, generously supported this effort by letting me keep all the material I had written as part of 3D/I's R&D program.

3D/I was working on some of the country's largest Program Management assignments—hardly strangers to the subject of Program Management. Nevertheless, I was concerned that we might develop a self-appreciating, insular view of our Program Management concepts. So with this team of bright young people, we went to work to broaden our understanding. We felt that if we learned how other organizations manage programs we could improve our own work.

We interviewed many owners from different sectors: government, institutional and private. We talked to owners in healthcare, education, religion, retail, fast food. We interviewed developers and facility staffs. We interviewed Program Management companies and many members of our own staff.

As this book began to take shape, I imposed on some of my colleagues at CMAA to review it and offer their insights and criticism. They are:

Bob Fraga, AIA, CMAA, is Director of the Office of Contracting for the Smithsonian Institution. Previously, Bob was Manager of the Facilities Portfolio for the U.S. Postal Service. He was responsible for the upkeep of 37,000 postal facilities. We met Bob when we did the case study of the USPS. Then I watched his able leadership and wonderful sense of humor as President of CMAA in 2006.

Don Russell, CCM, FCMAA, at the ripe old age of 30, on 11 legal-size pads of paper, using two boxes of #2 pencils and a hand-held calculator, developed a multi-billion dollar budget for King Faisal University in Saudi Arabia. Don and I worked together at CM inc., in the 70s. We sent Don to California to lead a major state hospital project. It was California's first use of a CM firm. (Today they are one of the largest clients for CM companies in the U.S.) Don then founded Vanir and led its growth into one of the country's leading construction management companies. In so doing, he trained and mentored a measurable percentage of California's CM executives.

Bob Hixon, FCMAA, initiated GSA's Construction Excellence Program, managed the construction of the Capitol Visitor's Center for the Architect of the Capitol, and is now Senior Vice President with Hill International.

Bill Hoy led design and construction for 100 hotels for Marriott's five Limited Service Brands and is now Senior Vice President for Construction at the B. F. Saul Company. Bill is also on the board of the National Institute of Building Sciences (NIBS), a non-profit that facilitates the introduction of new technology into the building process.

Bob Wilson, FCMAA, had two construction careers. The first was with the Civil Engineer Corps, U.S. Navy. After retiring as a Captain, he spent 25 years with Gilbane Building Company. Then he managed the building market sector program for Parsons Brinckerhoff. Bob was the first chancellor of CMAA's College of Fellows—a symbol of the respect his colleagues have for his CM acumen.

Bruce D'Agostino is President and CEO of CMAA. Bruce has provided encouragement and the support of the wonderful staff he has built—particularly the support of John McKeon, who has more experience than I in this world of publishing.

I had a lot of help from my colleagues—in our company and throughout the industry. As we assembled this book, we gained invaluable insight from individuals throughout the building industry who spoke to us about their programs. I'd like to thank the many people who were generous with their time and candor for their contributions to this study. (See the list of people who gave us some of their time in the Appendix.)

I also had invaluable help from my family. I must thank my daughter, Melissa, and my granddaughter-in-law, Cory, for their careful proofreading, my grandson Shaun, another architect, for his insights into large-scale architectural practice and my son, Jeff, a general contractor, for many philosophical conversations about collaboration (and lack of) between designers and builders.

Jerre Paseur and Emma Kate Powell each took on the task of proofing the final draft. I am grateful to both for their painstaking, valuable work.

I will never be able to thank Lois, my wife, enough. She has helped edit proposals throughout my career. She became affectionately known at the office, alternately, as the hyphen harpy or the comma queen. She has read this material repeatedly; she provided her usual surgical criticism of grammar, punctuation, spelling, logic, idea structure and concept development. She also mastered the mysteries of computer graphic design and produced the print file for this book.

We were told far more than I've captured on these pages. So I've had a hard time completing this work. It's been more difficult than my previous books because there's so much information and because new revelations changed previous attitudes. I have been like an architect who can't quit designing a project.

But eventually, one must print. So Bruce D'Agostino and I agreed on an approach. We plan to produce revised editions in the future.

Now is the time to say the obvious. Despite enormous help from all these people, I must say that I'm the guy who wrote this stuff, so if there are mistakes, as I'm sure there are, it's likely that they're mine.

Chuck Thomsen
Houston, 2008, charlesthomsen@charlesthomsen.com

Foreword

by Don Russell

The time has come for this book. Or perhaps it's past due. If Program Management is understood by owners and accepted by the building industry it will result in cost reductions, shorter schedules, reduce review and approval agencies burdens, and increase the satisfaction of owners that are repeat-builders. Most important, it will result in significant improvements in the quality of the buildings we construct.

Our industry has gotten pretty good at figuring out construction problems and managing individual projects, considering the uniqueness of each project and team. During the last 30 years of the 20th century, we developed sophisticated, computer-based systems to help us control and manage everything from written words and decisions to line-item budgets. Communications between project teams became much faster with use of e-mail. A variety of delivery strategies were born to optimize an owner's unique needs to distribute risk. Four-year degree programs in construction management appeared at universities. The Construction Management Association of America has a formal program so individuals who demonstrate their qualifications and expertise can become Certified Construction Managers. Skill sets for managing individual projects have been significantly elevated. Using those project-level management skills as a foundation, it's now time to turn our focus to the next level—managing building programs.

Program Management is a term that has become popular in the building industry. Yet there is little in the industry literature that would indicate any kind of clear and precise definition of what Program Management is, or should be. Is it beyond definition? I think not. For purposes of this book, consider Program Management to be a disciplined approach that applies standardized management and project control systems to the design and construction process of multiple construction projects for a common owner or builder.

There are a number of purposes behind this practice. The primary ones are to control completion costs and schedules, find opportunities for continuous improvement and achieve those improvements, improve the owners' satisfaction with the design/building process, and improve the quality of the buildings produced. Opportunities for improving project performance can be found in each of the three fundamental components of any building program.

First, there are always some common components in an owner's buildings. Buildings all have roofs and foundations, so certain components can be based on standardized designs. Design costs can be reduced. They all have air handlers and control systems, so owners can secure preferred purchaser status with many suppliers. Maintenance departments love it when they don't have six different types of flushometers and can minimize bench stock. And the list of opportunities and benefits goes on. These opportunities are associated with the product.

Second, since there is a series of projects in a building program, the Program Managers have limitless opportunities to improve the delivery process itself. We all tend to get better at things when we do them repeatedly, whether it's a golf swing or touch-and-go landings. Same thing with delivery processes and systems.

Managing the third design-build project is a heck of a lot less scary than the first one. It's a lot easier to accurately forecast what the soft costs on a project will be when you have done two similar ones the previous year. It's also easier to collect and use data as the basis for forecasting future costs for your building program when the database is created from the history of your building program, not one on the other side of the country. These opportunities are associated with the process.

Third, the list of opportunities open to a smart Program Manager is only limited by that individual's imagination and the imaginations of her or his fellow team members. The key is to maximize the benefits of improvements in the design and construction process, without stifling a designer's creativity or limiting a project team's ability to satisfy the unique needs of the owner for a particular building. These opportunities are associated with the people.

Finally, a word about technology and communications. Advances in technology have created tremendous opportunities for individuals to increase their job efficiency. The use of web-based project information systems, e-mail and the trillions of pieces of information available on the Internet, can drive a manager's efficiency to new heights.

On the other hand, zealous reliance on these technological advances also offers tremendous opportunities for driving that same manager's effectiveness down through the basement. When we try to write an e-mail as fast as it can be transmitted, we get sloppy. Meanings get obscured. When we start believing the old saw that "a picture is worth a thousand words," that BIM presentation becomes an end in itself, instead of a starting point for discussions with the owner to nail down a comprehensive Project Definition, we miss the point.

We are constantly developing better and faster tools to help us manage building programs and projects. To maximize the benefits of those tools, we also need to focus on constantly improving our communication skills.

People...process...product—it's a great framework for thinking about what makes a building program work really well. It's also a good segue to say a few words about the author. Chuck Thomsen is one of the individuals that created our construction management industry, starting back in the 70s. As an architect, he has always been genuinely concerned about improving the quality of the products that our industry produces. But he started one of the first agency-CM firms because he was also concerned about improving the process by which our industry delivered its products.

While his companies were successful as businesses, I think that Chuck's greatest accomplishments are about people. He built a couple of hugely successful companies, based on people. He occasionally explained his success by saying, "I know I'm not the best CM in the world, but I sure know how to find them." And he did! The alumni of his companies are in leadership positions throughout our industry.

But time is precious, so let's move on to the matter at hand... Program Management. Now is the time for us to study and perfect our program management skills, much as we did on project management in the 80s and 90s. The opportunities are there. The time is now. Good luck.

Don Russell, CCM, FCMAA
Sacramento, 2007

Overview

The Rise of Serial Builders

Organizations with continuous building programs build most of America's buildings.

Do you believe that? Consider this. Our buildings are constructed by real estate developers; national and local governments; education and healthcare institutions; Fortune 1000 companies; hospitality, restaurant, entertainment and retail chains; military and defense organizations. All build continuously. Look at the buildings around you when you drive through your community. The majority are built by serial builders. These owners are creating our built environment.

Consequently, most design and construction projects in the U. S. are part of a program. (For the purposes of this book, we define a program as a capital building activity with multiple projects.)

The projects in a program usually serve a similar purpose and are executed by an organization with unique characteristics. The projects will have similar characteristics in process, will use similar service providers and have similarities in the product itself. The similarities offer extraordinary opportunities for

"Program Management" is a term that is often used to describe the management of the sequential steps (from site selection to occupancy) of a single project. However, for the purpose of this book, we use the term to refer to the management of a capital building program with multiple projects.

continuous improvement to shorten schedules, save money and improve quality.

This book is for people who may be employees of an owner's organization or people who provide their services to these owners.

This book is for the service providers: the people who work for serial builders. They may be the employees of the owner's organization or they may be the AEs, CMs or constructors who provide services or products to these serial builders. In either case it's about how they may manage the program to capture those opportunities.

The construction industry is rotating.

When I began my career half a century ago, I worked for owners who needed a single building. The project was a unique event in their life, perhaps the only time when they would have anything to do with design and construction. That's changed. Then, corporations that wanted a headquarters hired an architect and contractor to design and build their building; today, they will turn to a developer who has experience with many developments. Then, hospitals would add a wing every five or ten years; today, they're part of a network with a facility group that manages a continuous design and construction program. Shop owners no longer build their own stores; they lease space in a shopping center built by a developer. We are rotating from a project-oriented industry to a program-oriented industry.

And this program-oriented industry offers huge opportunities to improve. Here's a self-evident realization. When we do something for the first time, we make mistakes. Then we learn from our mistakes, practice and get better at it. That applies to writing a book, hitting a golf ball, designing a school, laying brick or playing a piano—everything we do. It also applies to managing design and construction. So Program Managers must focus on bundling companies and processes into contracts to achieve economies of scale in purchasing, establish standards for continuous improvement and set the stage for continuous learning.

Of course, there are still one-project owners who will build custom homes, churches and museums. But they're the exception, not the rule. Jet travel and Internet connectivity have enabled big organizations. Government, institutions and businesses are growing, acquiring and consolidating. They all have building programs.

Serial builders aren't new and some of the best ideas are old.
A century and a half ago, the railroads developed prototype
designs for train stations. The Carnegie Libraries had prototypes.
Nevertheless, for the better part of the 20th century, most
clients were one-time clients. They were lay people who came
to architects and engineers to represent them and guide them
through the dark tunnel of design and construction.

That's changed. Now our clients are serial builders with a staff
of construction professionals to manage their programs. As
Program Managers, AEs, CMs or constructors selling our
services, we find ourselves working for other Program Managers,
AEs, CMs or constructors who are the owner's employees and
are our clients. In many cases, the construction professionals
in the owner's organization know more about their project's
requirements and how best to satisfy them than those of us
who provide services to them. We often find ourselves simply
augmenting their staff and supporting their leadership.

*Our clients are serial builders with a staff of
construction professionals.*

Unfortunately, most construction professionals, both owners and
service providers, have grown up through the ranks of project
management, and, unfortunately, they still see their building
programs as a sequence of individual projects.

*There are enormous benefits that can be had by
viewing the program as a whole.*

RESISTANCE TO CHANGE

The very structure of our specialized, fragmented, enormous
industry offers much resistance to change. We knit hundreds
of companies together into an ad hoc organization to deliver a
project.

And laws, regulations, standard industry contracts, inflexible
procurement regulations, political influences or just plain
unquestioning assumptions about tradition affect our processes.
It's an industry that is singularly resistant to innovation.

The construction industry

One of the reasons change is so difficult is that our industry is
so big and messy. In 2008, it is the second largest industry in
the U.S., behind healthcare. It's $1.2 trillion, 28% of the $5.2
trillion world market. It's 8% of the gross domestic product—
one dollar out of every twelve spent in America is spent in
the construction industry. It's fragmented and specialized. A
hundred and thirty-thousand architects in 17,000 firms work

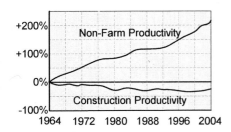

If the construction industry kept pace with the rest of our non-farm productivity we would build buuilings with half the people for half the cost.

Tradition is the glue that holds us together.

with 44,000 individual code jurisdictions. All told, there are 1,250,000 companies in the industry. Ninety-eight percent have fewer than 50 people. The average life of a subcontractor's business is 2.8 years.

If the construction industry had increased its productivity at the same rate as the rest of America's non-farm industries, it would produce the same volume of work today with half the people for half the price. But it has not, partly because it's a fragmented, labor-intensive, custom-made, project-by-project industry, executing its work out in the mud and the rain. Look at the next construction site you see. About half the workers will be standing around. Statistically, only 47% of construction workers are active at any one time. The rest are waiting for materials or equipment, directions or their turn at a task.

But managing a capital building program *as a program,* rather than simply a series of one-off projects, presents an imperative for managers to improve productivity. They can identify repetitive tasks and find ways, usually with technology, to do them more efficiently. That's exactly what's happening in the country's most sophisticated design and construction programs.

Tradition

Tradition is a barrier to change and improvement. However, our giant, complex, highly specialized, fragmented industry needs tradition to function. Hundreds of organizations come together to build the simplest project; thousands must work together for a major building. Contractors take verbal bids over the phone for hundred-million-dollar projects and don't have time to brainstorm, conceive original arrangements and write a management plan that defines new relationships for each new project. Architects, engineers, consultants, contractors, subcontractors, manufacturers, suppliers and regulators must regularly fit their services together into new, ad hoc organizations. Like the classic example of a supertanker that takes miles to turn, we find it nearly impossible to change course.

But tradition is not all bad. It's the glue that holds us together and informs our processes on projects. Winston Churchill said:

> *"A love for tradition has never weakened a nation; indeed it has strengthened nations in their hour of peril."*

So it is with our industry. The economy of the American construction industry is bigger than the GDP of most nations. Abandoning tradition is perilous. Organizations are justifiably circumspect about changing common practice. Consequently, many programs with multiple projects fail to change when the world changes around them. They think project not program. They fail to capture the benefits available in a continuous building program. They miss huge opportunities to save time and money and to make better buildings.

But, fortunately, there are increasing numbers of other construction professionals who see the enormous benefits that can be had by viewing the program as an integrated whole. They are striding out ahead of this project-oriented tradition. This latter group taught us much as we researched the industry.

In our research and in our experience, we met other owners with a team of construction professionals who use multiple projects for continuous improvement.

These innovative people identify the commonalities: processes, products and people.

These innovative people examine the workflow of their projects to identify the commonalities—whether those commonalities are processes in the project delivery sequence, products of construction or people with similar jobs. Then they rotate those commonalities from individual projects to the program. (If this important thought seems a little opaque, stay tuned. The first chapter, "Rotation, Repetition and Refinement" will fill a couple dozen pages with the concept.)

No two alike

All the organizations we've worked for and all that we've studied are different. They have different leadership, missions, constraints, politics, traditions, demographics, economics and so on. Some build nearly identical prototype buildings; others build unique facilities but develop standard procedures, standard building systems and continuity in their service providers. (There is that product, process, people categorization again.)

All the organizations we've studied are different and manage their programs differently.

The companies I've led have designed, constructed and managed tens of billions of dollars of construction in many countries. Every time we went to a new country, we realized they saw things differently. We also realized that if we kept our minds open, we could learn from them.

We interviewed the managers of 47 organizations with continuous building programs.

No one does it the same.

We have enormous experience. But one of the motivations for our research is that we also recognized the danger of "group think"—preaching our own convictions to ourselves, tuning out other points of view and succumbing to an intellectually insulated set of self-reinforcing, self-sustaining philosophies.

So my colleagues at 3D/I allowed me to staff a full-time research team to investigate how others manage their capital improvement programs. We interviewed the managers of many organizations with continuous building programs. They were in many sectors— education, healthcare, hospitality, defense, retail and commercial real estate development.

We listened. As the same message came up repeatedly, we noted it. When there was a unique or inconsistent message, we drilled deeper and usually found uniqueness driven by the individuality of the organization.

These conversations broadened our point of view. Through their experiences and ours, we purged some earlier convictions. No two do it the same. Different programs work for their different organizations. The leadership and their missions affect how the programs are run.

Consequently, we wanted to illustrate the extraordinary differences in Program Management with the experiences of real, warm-blooded people working in different kinds of organizations.

There were hundreds of small "best practices" that popped up during our conversations. Each of the organizations invented many little things to advance their interests. Hines held a "submittals workshop" at the beginning of construction. HEB standardized and procured one size of bar joist for multiple projects. Target developed on-line procurement of subcontractors, applying the technology that was part of their core business of procuring merchandise. Los Angeles Unified School District packaged mini-drawings of school components in their instructions to architects. Good ideas were abundant.

Some of these good practices were unique to the mission and not exportable to other programs. Standardizing bar joists wouldn't work for most building programs. But many practices were exportable. Everyone can have a submittals workshop. So in reviewing these practices, we searched for some principles—concepts that would enhance our understanding of our chaotic industry.

We looked for good ideas that would inform us about good ways to manage design and construction programs. We found many, but there is no universal best approach.

No common metrics

We had hoped to find metrics to test the value of different processes and project delivery strategies. That didn't happen. We couldn't find a common yardstick. There are too many variables.

Good comparative analysis normally requires a researcher to hold all variables but one constant to measure the effect of that variable. We can't do that. We can't build two projects at the same time, on the same site, with the same people and simply change one thing. We can't compare design-build to CM-at-risk by duplicating everything except the project delivery strategy. About the best we can do is to identify a practice and measure results against a large sample. Sometimes there is overwhelming evidence of the value of a good practice. An example is the statistical results showing the value of Project Definition. (See page 40.) Even then, there will be skeptics.

To compare different processes to determine the best, you must hold all the variables but one constant. We can't do that with design and construction.

"Good practice" is relative to the organization's mission. Each organization we talked to has different goals that influence outcomes. The classic triumvirate of cost, time and quality is usually there, but the emphasis—and the very definition of the terms—changes with the organization's mission. Cost might mean first cost, return on investment or life-cycle cost. Time might mean as soon as possible. Or it can mean a date certain—like getting a school open for fall classes or getting a store open for the Christmas shopping season.

And then there is quality—yes, there's that word again. That's the one that the industry has the most trouble measuring. Frequently, it's a personal, fuzzy definition. In rational organizations, quality in design and construction means "conformance to requirements." However, the requirements change and the emphasis changes within a given set of requirements. The requirements can be functionality, durability, aesthetics or any number of other things.

Different goals produce different products and different processes. Wal-Mart and MIT are extreme differences. But even similar organizations will have substantial differences. Texas A&M and the University of Texas do things differently, as do Wal-Mart and Target.

We learned more from the differences in the programs than from the similarities.

Other equally important issues affect the design or the process. One owner may be concerned with community relations, others care about using historically under-used businesses, providing jobs in a depressed market or building green.

Different goals undermine any rigorous attempt at comparative measurement. MIT wants to build an icon of contemporary architecture to advertise its image as an institution at the front edge of innovation. They will suffer the agonies of design and construction at the frontier of aesthetics and technology. Frank Gehry spent years designing the Stata Center and its cost increased steadily. Wal-Mart, on the other hand, wants to build stores fast with the same image and at the least cost. Bob Workman at BSW International says he can modify prototypical components and produce the design and working drawings for a unique Wal-Mart store in less than a day.

How do you compare? MIT would consider a building on its campus that looked like a Wal-Mart to be a failure, and Wal-Mart would consider a project that took even a tenth as long to design as the Stata Center to be a disaster.

Meanwhile, the personal values of my various readers will render similar judgments on the two projects. Perhaps the design-oriented readers will admire the Stata Center and the production-oriented readers will admire the Wal-Mart process.

That's an extreme example. However, even similar organizations will have major differences. Texas A&M and the University of Texas do things differently.

So it's a daunting task to make sense and produce useful information from this unbelievably diverse world of design and construction. We can't apply a consistent yardstick. While we amplified and broadened the convictions that we had about Program Management when we began our study, we were more impressed with the differences that emerged. Ultimately, the differences were more instructive than the similarities.

Of course, there are some consistent goals. Vitruvius, the author of the first printed work on architecture, wrote of "commodity, firmness and delight" in about 25 B.C.E. These three values don't change. They're valid today but usually re-expressed as form, function and technology. These same three principles seem to affect organizational structure. In a large program, there will be a group that specializes in functional requirements (commodity), a group that specializes in building technology (firmness) and a group that specializes in design (delight).

Another trio, "cost, schedule and quality," is always there. But both the interpretation and relative importance of these basics change in the environment of different organizational missions.

So while we found it hard to uncover universal best practices, many management teams developed practices that are unique to a multi-project program that produced improvements.

Here's a glimpse of what will come on the following pages.

FUNDAMENTALS FOR A PROGRAM MANAGER

We've heard people say that a good manager can manage anything. We've seen a few Program Managers without much experience in design and construction who were successful. But they did it because they surrounded themselves with good people who augmented their knowledge. They knew how to evaluate these people and how to listen. Indeed, most of the experienced people we met were wise enough to do the same.

Here is a mantra to live by. A Program Manager must have a clear view of the process, systems to manage detail and an ability to work with people.

So we wrote about the comprehensive, prerequisite skills for a Program Manager that seem to be consistent among all programs. We're convinced that to succeed, a Program Manager requires a clear view of the process, an understanding of the technical systems to manage detail and, finally, an ability to work with people.

There are a few people with all three qualifications. Usually it takes a team.

A clear view of the process

The team's collective brainpower must have a clear view of where they are going and how to get there. Leaders must have a cognitive vision of how things should unfold that includes knowledge of how building systems are assembled and who puts them together. They need to know how long design and construction tasks take so they can build schedules. They need to know what kinds of organizations do what kind of work so they can fit people and organizations together. They need a grasp of what things cost. They need to know what a contract should say and how to track, document and enforce it. They need to be

Leaders must have a vision of how things should unfold.

comfortable with computers and interested in the value of these extraordinary tools for collaboration and information management. Most important, they need to know how to evaluate the people and what talents and skill sets they need to help them with these tasks.

As they apply to projects, these bodies of knowledge have been taught to us in school, written about in many books and studied in owner, AE and construction organizations. There is much written on the subject. So we skipped technical detail about project management.

Classic project-related activities change when applied to programs.

But when applied to programs these classic project-related activities change. In a program, there are far more choices in bundling design and construction work than in a single project. Multiple projects change cost and schedule priorities. Documentation and reporting become more challenging.

So our purpose is to write about how these things are best done when they are applied to programs instead of projects. We identified five major issues that are particularly important in programs with multiple projects.

Rotation, Repetition and Refinement

A reoccurring message throughout this book is that we make mistakes the first time we do things and that reliable results and efficient workflow come from study and repetition. However, many serial builders never focused on the repetition in their projects. Conversely, the most skilled of the serial builders we talked to searched for things that reoccur in their projects and singled them out for standardization and continuous improvement. Then they rotated these items of project work-flow into program workflow.

Standardization is a springboard for continuous improvement.

The best organizations extracted people, processes and products from individual project assignments and applied them to multiple projects across the program. They standardized, but they didn't view standardization as a restriction but as a springboard to take the next leap to improved results. The result was continuous improvement in cost, schedule and quality.

Program and Project Definition

Repeatedly, we heard variations on the basic principle of "plan what you do before you do it, define requirements, get alignment" and "when you plan, get as much information as possible up front." Define the approval points from the constituencies. Then schedule and manage change tightly. When there is a program, a Program Manager should continuously enhance the definitions of requirements with each subsequent project. That will help to jump start the project teams and accelerate work.

Outsourcing Program Management

All programs we learned about had some construction professionals who were owner employees. Nevertheless, all outsourced some of the work. There were extreme differences in how much was staffed internally and how much was outsourced. Some organizations only had an executive running the show with everything else outsourced. Others had complete in-house staffs and only outsourced for specializations and peak loads.

All programs had construction professionals who were owner employees and all outsourced some of the work.

There were extreme differences in the way organizations set the rules of engagement with the outsourced companies. In some cases, owners integrated outsourced staff with their own employees. In other cases, an outsourced organization worked alongside or below the owner's facility management group but was an intact group.

Organization

There seem to be as many organizational structures as there are organizations. But the best find ways to accumulate knowledge and pump that knowledge back into the projects. The best organizations were characterized by:

There are as many organizational structures as there are organizations.

- a leader who could maintain a personal network with the users, the organizational governance and the leaders of the service providers
- an operational manager who could evaluate talent and then assemble and direct project teams
- an information group that organized the enormous amount of detail and kept the extended program team informed
- a group that understood the functional requirements of the parent organization
- a group that understood the building systems that best served those requirements and how best to acquire them

Project Delivery Strategies

During the last half-century, there's been bedrock change in the way owners buy buildings. We've seen the emergence

It takes a team.

of construction management, Bridging and the increased use of design-build in the public sector. We've watched the professionalization of general contractors.

Where once the AE was the master of construction technology, we've seen specialization develop to the extent that now there is no single source of knowledge and much resides among subconsultants, subcontractors and manufacturers. It takes a large team that includes designers, constructors and manufacturers. The AE's job has changed. Their primary job is not to design building systems, but to evaluate and integrate systems designed by manufacturers.

We've seen the number of subcontractors on a typical construction project increase from a handful to 50 or more, and we've seen AE firms that used to provide comprehensive services use 20 or more subconsultants on a single project. We've watched much building construction migrate from the outdoors to the factory floor.

If we limit these pages to current methods, the book will soon be dated.

Because of so much change in the construction industry, we're concerned that if we limit these pages to current methods, the book will soon be dated. So to understand where we are in the evolutions of our industry and to connect data points for a valiant attempt to extrapolate the future, we've woven a touch of construction industry history throughout the discussions of project delivery strategy. The design and construction processes we describe on the following pages frequently come with a small explanation of how they came to be what they are.

This book is about "how to do it, how it got that way, does it still make sense? and what's it likely to be?"

That means that we want this material to be a step beyond "how to do it." It's also "how it got that way" and "does it still make sense?" and "what's it likely to be?" If we understand the economic and technical environment that created our business practices, we can adapt as our business environment continues to change.

Technical systems to manage detail

A construction program generates enormous detail to communicate, absorb, document, integrate, store and retrieve. It's required to inform managers, enhance collaboration, improve designs, defend claims and report to governance. It cannot be held in a human brain and has outgrown the medium of paper and file cabinets.

During the last two decades, we've watched the enormous impact of computer technology on these tasks. It's a crucial tool and is rarely used well.

Controls

The classic functions of cost, schedule and quality control change when a project becomes a program. And presenting the program's vital signs for management action becomes more challenging.

Cost, schedule and quality control change when a project becomes a program.

Project management information systems

Good Program Management information systems provide executives with a window into their program—a method of grasping the entirety of their extraordinarily complicated landscape of activity. On-line, web-based systems to store project status information and provide collaborative support to the extended project team are fundamental management tools and BIM (building information modeling) is a fundamental design and communication tool.

Information systems provide a window into the program.

An ability to work with people

Since there are so many people involved in a design and construction program, the predictable characteristics of large-group human behavior on a multi-building program have much to do with success and failure.

Human behavior and interpersonal skills have at least as much to do with success and failure as technical competence.

Leadership

The leadership has a profound effect on the program. Executives, users, designers or a construction agent may lead a program. The leadership will affect the emphasis placed on the values of cost, schedule and quality in decision making and set the yardstick used to measure performance and success. The leaders may do so subtly or with precision. Their definitions will affect the tolerance for change and on-course adjustments. Leadership may change during the program, and if it does the yardsticks will change too.

Leadership will define the measurements for success—subtly or with precision.

Team behavior

We also need to understand the basic mechanics of inter-personal relationships, the predictable behavior of groups during periods of stress and the forces that influence the actions of people who work together. We need to learn how to create and manage collaboration—to understand the architecture of teamwork.

In the past, organizations were smaller; they built occasionally. Today, organizations are much larger; they build continuously.

Throughout America, there's a spectrum of these serial builders. At one end of the spectrum are the owners who build one-of-a-kind, iconic and sometimes inspiring works of architecture. At the other end are the owners who build repetitive, frequently ordinary buildings. These projects are the constructions of government, institutions and developers. They're changing the landscape of our country and setting the environment where we live our lives.

This change in process needs better understanding in the colleges and universities that train our design and construction professionals. It certainly needs better understanding from mature professionals. And perhaps most important, it needs better understanding by our clients.

This book is about program processes that will lead to better project delivery. By better project delivery, we mean less time and less money. We also mean better design—we mean sustainable, functional buildings that grace our environment.

Great design and great reliability rarely come as a set. Some of the world's most inspiring buildings, designed by our most hallowed architects, blew budgets and schedules and had leaky roofs. Frank Lloyd Wright was once quoted as saying:

> *"Of course it leaks. That's how you know it's a roof."*

Paradoxically, some of the most mundane buildings and frequently maligned works of ugly, repetitive architecture delivered the most reliable response to their functional requirements.

We don't need to accept that contradiction. If we focus on the techniques of Program Management, we'll be able to polish our processes and our products. And we'll improve both the aesthetic and the practical.

A Clear View of the
Process

Rotation, Repetition and Refinement

Program Managers have an opportunity that project managers don't have. They can examine their individual projects to find similarities. When there is a similarity, they can rotate the similarity from the project workflow into the program workflow. Then there is an opportunity for repetition and refinement instead of reinvention on every new project. The results can produce enormous benefits in time, cost and quality.

Rotation is a term used to describe the process of turning a custom, project-oriented activity into a continuous, program-oriented standard. Standard processes, standard products and standard human participation save time and money. But standards shouldn't be static; they should be a platform for continuous improvement.

People do better work as they gain experience. They improve their processes, their work products and the buildings. And the people themselves get better.

The amount of rotation, repetition and refinement that can be achieved in a program is a function of the number of projects, the similarity of the projects and the authority of the Program Manager to enforce standards and push improvement.

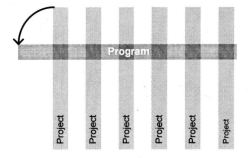

The process of rotation, repetition and refinement requires:

1. *analyzing projects in a program to identify the similarities*
2. *choosing the similarities that are the most repetitious and offer the greatest possibilities for standardization and continuous improvement*
3. *focusing on ways to improve these standards at the program level*

Think how poorly you perform when you do something the first time. It doesn't matter whether you try to hit a golf ball, play chess, play a musical instrument, work quadratic equations, lay a brick wall, ride a bike or design a school. How did it go?

We make mistakes the first time we do things. We get better with practice.

When we do things the first time, we are awkward and we make mistakes. As we practice, we learn and get better. Compare your first performance to what happens when you are experienced. Think how that level of improvement might apply to design and construction.

First of all, just getting it right each time takes practice. Every golfer's dream is a repeatable swing. And every golfer knows you don't need great shots to shoot great golf. You only need consistency. All you need to do to shoot par is to hit good shots—every time. So good golfers practice their swing endlessly.

With repetition, improvement can be enormous. It would take me half an hour to change a tire. With a little practice and a little technology, a tire shop can do it in a few minutes. With the pressures of competition, a pit crew at Indianapolis can change four tires in a few seconds.

That's an enormous improvement. It takes about 500 times longer for me to change that tire than it takes the pit crew. Are there tasks with 500X improvement potential in project delivery? We think so.

Improving one process stimulates improvement in related processes.

Furthermore, if you improve a process, it stimulates improvement in related processes. When the tire changers in the pit crews at Indianapolis began to finish before the tank fillers, the tank fillers had to devise a faster way to fill up.

Consider a single project. Usually experienced people do the work. Someone who has drawn door details before draws them this time. But they're slightly different. And someone who has laid bricks before lays them this time. Typically there are small, arbitrary differences from the last job for every task.

There's another issue. The team changes with each new project. Some of the people have never worked together. And, inevitably, not only are the tasks unique, the sequence of assembling them is unique. There's lots of downtime sequencing different groups in and out of the project. The uniqueness of the project, much of which is arbitrary, results in inefficiency and mistakes.

Of course, every project has unique parts. Bad things happen when a standard is applied to a non-standard requirement. However, within any program there are always similarities. They exist in the need for similar services, in similar processes and in similar products that are used to make the buildings. The challenge is to find the similarities and to eliminate arbitrary uniqueness. But to repeat myself for emphasis, it's essential to ensure unique results when there's a unique requirement.

Every project has unique parts. It's bad to apply a standard to a non-standard requirement.

When we talk about rotation, owners or facilities managers often respond that it won't work for them because they must build different buildings. So, let's get this notion out of the way. Capturing the benefits of rotation does not require designing a prototype and plunking down cookie cutter replications. In fact, in our experience, in all of our research—and in just looking around us as we drive through our communities—we found few cases where serial builders could use prototypes.

Of course, there are some. The fast food and big box retailers create prototypes and constantly work on the designs. Some create a prototype and roll it out for a number of editions. Then they develop a new model—similar to the automobile industry. Others just improve continuously. But even the owners who build the most common prototypes find that they must frequently modify them for unique conditions—like the Santa Fe edition of a McDonald's in the margin.

I'm sure the design team for McDonald's didn't have an adobe aesthetic for Santa Fe in mind when they conceived their prototype. But even the most common and ubiquitous prototypes are often modified to adapt to community requirements, indigenous aesthetics or unusual sites.

So there is a spectrum. At one end are the clients that can work with prototypes. At the other end are clients with a program of different building types, like a municipality. Perhaps they must build a police station, a fire house, a library, an administration building and a golf course. But even at that extreme, there will be many similarities in process, in the products and systems and in the people who execute the work.

We all grew up doing individual projects. The project mentality is strong in our industry. In our interviews with serial builders, we found many that continued to treat each project as an intellectual stovepipe that had little intersection with other projects. They had not made the mental adjustment to program thinking. They were still thinking project.

So when we got the typical response of *"All of our projects are different,"* we always took it as a challenge. We drilled down in the conversation. As we did so, it became clear that all the programs we reviewed had many similarities among their projects that were reinvented repeatedly.

ROTATION IN INDUSTRY

While we think about rotation, repetition and refinement, it's worthwhile to consider how rotation has occurred in other industries. Indeed, entire industries have rotated and capitalized on the repetition and refinement that became available.

Consider the automobile industry a century ago. Originally, a single team led by a master mechanic assembled an entire car. The car stayed in one place for most of the assembly and the workers moved back and forth getting and attaching parts. Just like a construction project, some stood around and watched while others did something that had to be done first.

Henry Ford's Model K (the predecessor of the Model T) cost about $3,000. Inflation since 1913 is estimated at about 2,000%! That means the cost of a Model K in 21st century dollars would be about $60,000 today. And it was a primitive machine: no starter, no top, no doors, no windows. Add the improvements and technologies that are part of a modern car and it might have cost half a million dollars.

After Ford rotated assembly, the cost of a Model T dropped to $300. The Model K had cost $3000..

When demand for cars increased, there weren't enough master mechanics to produce them. So a few of the best mechanics designed a process and trained unskilled workers to do one step in the process. They rotated the assembly process—the workers did one job, stayed in one place, and the car moved down the assembly line. The quality soared and the cost plummeted. After Ford rotated the assembly process, the Model T dropped to $300—10% of the cost of a Model K. That's a 10X cost improvement. And it was a better car.

Similarly, when General Motors acquired Chevrolet, Oldsmobile, Buick and Cadillac, GM rotated many functions (body design, engine manufacture, instrumentation) out of the individual companies and applied the best talents and manufacturing resources across all of the individual automobile companies.

One of the most spectacular examples of industrial rotation occurred in the computer industry in the early 1980s. Before that time, IBM, DEC and a few other computer companies enjoyed dominance over a vertically integrated industry. They designed the computers, made their own memory, processors, printers and card readers. They wrote their own software, sold, serviced and financed their computers.

The computer industry is a spectacular example of rotation.

Then affordable personal computers exploded on the market and demand increased enormously. The entire industry rotated. Intel made processors, Microsoft made software, HP made printers, Asia produced memory, Dell assembled parts for highly specialized manufacturers in a well-managed supply chain—and so on.

Again, the costs plummeted and performance increased. In 1978, the price of Intel's 8086 was 1.2 cents per transistor and $480 per million instructions per second (MIPS). By 1995, the Pentium Pro's introductory price amounted to 0.02 cents per transistor and $4 per MIPS. By the early 21st century, the cost per MIPS was $.42. That's a three order-of-magnitude reduction. And if you want to go back to the first electronic computers and project forward another decade, you can get five orders of magnitude. That's a 10,000X cost-benefit ratio.

The cost benefit ratio in the computer industry has exceeded 10,000X.

That extraordinarily rapid rotation nearly bankrupted the vertically organized companies like DEC and IBM. Compaq acquired DEC and was later acquired itself by HP. IBM restructured and sold services to its traditional customers to help them integrate the myriad products from multiple horizontal producers.

Of course, those industries produce highly similar products. It's unlikely that the construction industry will rotate to the extent that the automobile or computer industry did—at least not in the near future. Perhaps a model that's more relative to the U.S. construction industry is shipbuilding. The Construction Industry Institute, easily the country's most respected construction

The Koreans and Japanese dominate the shipbuilding industry. They lowered cost 20% and shortened schedules 30% by creating a database of standard components that could be assembled into custom-made ships.

think tank, funded a study on the global shipbuilding industry. Essentially, the Japanese and Koreans dominate. They have dramatically reduced cost and schedules by creating an "interim database" of standard ship "building blocks" that is complete with construction details and supply chain information. These building blocks are components of workflow that have been rotated from the world of custom construction. They can pull those standard building blocks (along with sourcing information) from that interim database. They then can shape them into a custom design and deliver results for about 20% of the cost and in about 30% of the time that the U.S. and European shipbuilding industry takes. That's about a 5X improvement.

Rotation increases with similarity and multiple editions and when leaders want to capitalize on specialization, economies of scale, consistency and continuous improvement.

There's a principle: production of a single product is a linear activity. As the number of reproductions increases, many project tasks, many products and many services can rotate into the program and be made available to individual projects without the need for re-invention or re-sourcing. The potential for rotation increases with the similarity and number of editions and when the producer wants to capitalize on specialization, economies of scale, consistency and continuous improvement.

The construction industry is rotating in baby steps. But it is happening. Drive through any city in America. Clients with multi-building programs build courthouses, schools, hospitals, hotels, colleges, fast food restaurants, grocery stores, universities and retail chain stores. Some of these clients are changing the way the industry works.

Organizations are getting larger; they have continuous building programs. They add construction professionals to their staff to manage their programs. Our clients are now construction professionals.

As our economy becomes global, corporations, institutions and even governmental entities are consolidating operations. Some have prototype buildings; some standardize systems and products; others build unique facilities but standardize processes. Most rotate and standardize management. We're moving from a project-oriented industry to a program industry. The owners of construction projects have construction professionals on their staff who are unbundling the project delivery process and rearranging the parts.

THREE CATEGORIES OF ROTATION

When I try to develop an orderly way to understand a subject, my first inclination is to set categories—buckets to receive related information. This matter of rotation is no exception. The best way to understand rotation opportunities is to categorize them into three broad groups.

People (services)
Owners hire construction professionals to manage their building programs—either an outsourced Program Manager, internal staff or a combination. Then they may hire AEs, CMs and consultants to work on multiple project assignments.

Process (activities)
Then the managers develop and standardize approaches for hundreds of procedures like team selection, approvals and communications.

Products (building systems and materials)
Typically the third step is to standardize products such as equipment, building systems, functional layouts and, sometimes, prototype buildings.

Let's examine these categories in more detail.

PEOPLE
Think of CEOs who are faced with building programs. They quickly learn that dealing with AEs and CMs takes time. They recognize that they can't manage a program and run their organization too. So the first thing they typically do is appoint someone to be in charge. They believe there will be better results with management continuity overseeing the projects—and if they have a manager who is a construction professional.

Then the person they appoint to be in charge builds a team—either with new employees or with outsourced companies. Program Management emerges. Management is the first rotated activity. People are rotated from an individual project workflow into a multi-project program workflow.

Here's a striking bit of evidence that supports the value of "rotated" continuous management. FMI, a large management consulting company that focuses on the construction industry, worked with CMAA, the Construction Management Association of America, to develop a survey of owners with continuous building programs. The FMI Seventh Annual Survey of Owners

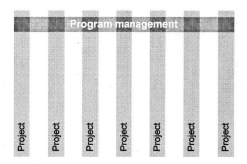

The first thing an organizational leader who has a building program typically does is to appoint someone to be in charge. A Program Management function emerges.

indicated that organizations that use a consistent management team (either in-house or outsourced) tend to lower their management cost by 30%.

A valuable body of institutional knowledge grows. The sum of the program experience accumulates in the heads of team members and improves their judgment. It can't be replaced by documentation and databases (although those things help).

Then the Program Management team begins to see that continuity provides value in other professional services. There's always a need for the same kind of brainpower and task execution on project after project. So they rotate many of the professional services required to execute the work. They may staff these services internally or hire organizations with evergreen contracts to work on multiple projects.

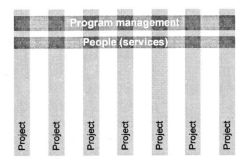

Continuity provides value in other services. So Program Managers rotate many of the professional services required to execute the work.

Perhaps, at first, they only stick their toe in the water and choose to do something simple like contract with one testing and inspection lab for all their projects. Or they may add other consultants such as roofing and wet-proofing, security, landscaping, data distribution, etc. Or, at the other extreme, they may put together an entire design team for all their projects.

There are some heroic-scale examples. Parsons is managing design and construction for renovation and new construction for the U.S. Post Office nationwide. Bovis Lend Lease did the same for British Petroleum worldwide. During our research, we met BSW, an AE firm working on its 4,000th Wal-Mart.

Hiring a single AE to design multiple projects is an economical thing to do and it will provide the opportunity for continuous improvement. That's easier for private clients than for public clients who must spread the work to different firms in their constituency. But hiring individual AEs for each project doesn't close the door on rotating services. AEs use a large set of specialty consultants. They must pass the cost of these consultants on to their owners as a reimbursable cost or include it in their fee. Most of the subject matter these consultants work with has program-wide relevance.

AEs, like GCs, have a surprising number of specialized subcontractors.

AEs are becoming more and more like general contractors that subcontract most of their work. AEs now have a surprising number of specialized consultants. They include roofing and wet-proofing, audio visual, data and communications, security, life safety, accessibility, sustainability, commissioning, testing and inspection, furnishing and equipment, acoustics, lighting, food service, landscape architecture, graphics and signage, civil and geotechnical engineering, transportation, parking and traffic engineering, interior design, hardware and locking and so on. Of course, not all of these consultants are required on every project. While all of them will have a roof, not all will have food service.

Owners can rotate these consultants. The consultants can be hired by a project-specific AE but be an owner's specified consultant and have program-wide responsibilities. The consultants can develop standards and prepare basic specifications and prototype CAD drawings on their first project for their normal fee. Then those standards and specifications can be provided to each subsequent project team. The consultant can review those subsequent projects for a much smaller fee. What's more, the consultant can review the results and improve the product with each subsequent project.

Many of the subconsultants that AEs use should be program-wide consultants.

To illustrate this concept, let's take roofing as an example. In our condition assessment work, we've walked through about 2 billion square feet of buildings. The most common problems are caused by water. It seems that in 4,000 years of architecture, we still haven't learned how to keep the water out. It's hard to think of anything in the world of facilities that deserves more attention for continuous improvement.

Now let's assume that the Program Manager selected the best roofing and wet-proofing consultant to be an "owner-nominated consultant." The roofing consultant would earn a full fee on the first assignment. Normally, it would be a reimbursable expense in the AE's fee. The roofing consultant would prepare specifications and drawings of standard roofing and flashing details. That package would then become the standard for that system.

Then each time a new project emerges with a need for that roofing system, the consultant would provide the AE with the standards, answer questions and review drawings. The fee for the repetitive service would be about a third of the full fee. [1]

1. In estimating this cost reduction, we spoke to Fred King at Inspec, Inc., a large and (in our opinion) highly competent roofing and wet-proofing consultant. Inspec provides services for the Minnesota Colleges and University System. Other consultants may work with other fee schedules but the conclusions will be the same.

Rotating consulting services would save significant amounts of the consultant's costs.

Rotating this consulting service would save two thirds of the consultant's cost after the first project. And it would increase cost predictability and shorten schedules a bit because the details are standard. Moreover, there should be continuous improvement in the roofing system—with a review of the standard details after each installation. There should be reduced maintenance cost and fewer errors. We might even have a roof that doesn't leak.

Of course, there can be variations on the approach. If there's political pressure to spread the work around, the owner could hire two roofing and wet-proofing consultants—one for flat roofs and one for sloping roofs. The economies would be similar. That's about a 3X improvement. Similar approaches can be used for other consultants.

Most things cost less in larger quantities.

Owners can usually get a better deal when they buy things in larger quantities. But the economies of scale are usually greater in the procurement of services than products. Buying windows for a dozen projects might save 10%, but buying the design will save a lot more than 10%. If one can develop a good idea, the implementation of individual editions may cost little or nothing.

Buildings are the only common product in our economy that must usually suffer 100% of the design cost. If the design cost of an iPod had to be amortized against a single unit, the price would be prohibitive, and we would all be poorer for it. When we deal with an individual project, we don't have the time and money to study many alternatives, research many practices and polish many processes. However, a Program Manager can amortize such an effort against multiple projects and reap the benefits repeatedly.

Process

Try this. Select several projects from a multi-project program. Diagram the design and construction activities. You will uncover many repetitive processes in contracting, requirements setting, communication, decision making, documentation, approvals, controls and so on.

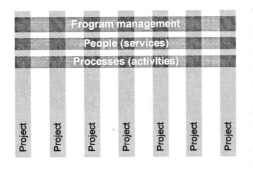

Since so many people are involved in delivering a building, designing a process for engaging the entire team— communication, collaboration, planning and forming agreements—is as important as designing the buildings.

So, in thinking about these repetitive processes, we asked ourselves if there were tasks we could rotate that would produce the 500X benefit ratio that the tire change example produced.

Here is one—a practice that many good program owners have already adopted. Normally it takes weeks, perhaps months, to negotiate a contract for design or construction. The owner's protective lawyer meets with the AE's or CM's protective lawyer. Each represents its client's potential risk—and, to be a little cynical, each is paid by the hour. They argue their points and then schedule independent interim meetings with their respective clients. Changes must travel through bureaucracies. Multiple meetings suffer the delays of calendar conflicts.

Some owners solved that problem by meeting with their service providers and developing fair standard contracts. They include them in their RFPs and ask responding firms to note objections. That feedback produces continuous incremental improvement in the baseline contract. Assuming the contract is fair in the first place, the final contract gets signed without a meeting. That process helps the project schedule as much as HEB's standard bar joist. That may be about a 500X improvement.

Serial builders usually develop project delivery processes that vary from industry standards. (Industry standards for project delivery are vanishing anyway.) Good Program Managers understand that to get people to work together effectively, they must set a clear vision, develop tools to extract the intellectual capital of specialists, install systems of information dispersal and find clear ways to describe the processes that must be followed for the hundreds of people who have to work together.

Program Managers need processes to make sure everyone knows what to do. In the 1990s, our company developed an electronic, web-based policy manual that we could customize for each client. It had on-line forms and instructions for many procedures. A contractor could go on-line and read the instructions for billing the owner. Then the contractor could fill out on-line forms for the money due. Many other organizations have done the same.

The art of getting information up front and defining a project quickly is a clear example of important process improvement. Hines has built hundreds of office buildings throughout the world. The Hines people hire internationally famous designers

There are many repetitive processes in contracting, requirements setting, communication, decision-making, documentation, approvals, controls and so on.

All the Hines office buildings look different. Nevertheless, there are many similarities in the building materials and systems that the Hines organization has refined over the years.

Rice University has rotated the aesthetic concept of the ultimate product — the buildings. Lovett Hall (top) was built in 1917, Baker Hall (below) 80 years later.

because they believe that creative, unique, world-class designs attract top-tier corporate clients as tenants.

Hines has arguably built more fine architecture than any owner in the world. If you look at a collection of Hines office buildings, they all look different. Nevertheless, despite the unique appearance of the buildings, there are many similarities that Hines has refined over the years. They're likely to have the same five-foot module. There will be MEP systems (mechanical, electrical and plumbing), ceiling lighting systems, elevators, door frames, structural bays, hardware and so on that they have used before and are refining on one more job.

There may be several different choices for each system with different price tags depending on the potential tenants and location. When Hines starts a project, there is a 45-page checklist of choices that includes things like finishes in the toilet rooms, lobby height, elevator finishes. Jerry Lea, who leads the Conceptual Construction Group, makes decisions on these items with the local Hines team and the AE team in the first few weeks of the project and refines the list on every new project.

Hines also uses a submittal review process that saves lots of hassle. Just before the start of construction, Hines holds a submittals workshop. Typically submittals trickle in over the life of a project. They delay the work because they're never first priority for anybody. Then, at the last minute, someone finally gets around to reviewing the submittal. And guess what? The submittal gets rejected. That precipitates several meetings to resolve the issue. With calendar conflicts, it takes weeks. So the project schedule is blown. Hines does it all at once before the project starts. They bring in the AEs and the key subs and review everything at one sitting.

Here's another example of product rotation. Rice University has rotated the aesthetic concept of the ultimate product—the building. The original design concepts were set by Cram, Goodhue and Ferguson. Ralph Adams Cram led the assignment and invented an architectural style for the school. The architecture is frequently called Neo-Byzantine or Byzantine Romanesque. It is unique and it reinforces the vision for the school.

Stephen Fox, an articulate historian on the Rice faculty, describes the beginnings of Rice:

"The architecture of Rice University represents an extraordinary assertion of will. It was designed to represent the identity of a cultural institution that, because it was newly created, had no identity." [2]

The point is that the architecture, as a representation of the new University, helped define the University. Although today Rice works hard at choosing world-class architects for the campus, Rice asks them to maintain aesthetic continuity with the original design. Nobody has to spend time deciding on materials and the visual vocabulary.

The University of Texas at Austin also has a grand architectural tradition set early in the 20th century.[3] The University has wisely decided that its architectural heritage is a valuable asset and should be preserved. So the University asked Cesar Pelli to develop a manual of aesthetic design guidelines. Providing architects with these guidelines accelerates the design process and maintains the aesthetic continuity of the environment.

PRODUCT

If programs are thought of only as a series of individual projects, each project is a separate intellectual smokestack executed by a separate team. One project fails to inform another. Sometimes the AEs produce good results; sometimes the next edition, done by a new AE, is not as good as the last. Always there are some good ideas that are not replicated and some bad ideas that are.

Even though an owner may require buildings with unique designs, hundreds of functional requirements will be common. For instance, an educational institution will want individually designed buildings for different disciplines (a math building, an English building, an engineering building, etc.). But the buildings will have faculty offices, classrooms, laboratories, toilet rooms and dormitories with identical requirements. And building systems are repeated: roofing, AV, data distribution, MEP, lighting, etc.

Although the buildings in a program may each be unique, many requirements will be common and many products may be used for multiple projects.

2. Stephen Fox, *Rice University: an architectural tour*, Princeton Architectural Press, 2001. p. 2.
3. Cass Gilbert, Paul Phillippe Cret, James M. White and Herbert M. Greene are considered the visionary architects who set the aesthetic style for the campus.

Each of these similarities can easily be a continuous improvement program—increasing performance and decreasing cost. The Program Managers can learn from the experience they accumulate. They can replicate the best functional layouts. They can refine building systems and choose equipment to minimize maintenance inventories. They can develop good architectural practices that are sustainable in a world of limited resources and increasing competition. Most important, they can build each project on the last set of experiences instead of reinventing a new and perhaps lesser product.

With standards, owners won't need to fight political battles with their users for capricious requirements on every project.

The life of the administrators will be improved as well. If owners have functional baselines and building system standards, they won't need to fight political battles with their users for capricious requirements on every project. Cost control will be easier and owner-initiated change orders during construction will decrease.

On a large community college program we managed, the president felt obligated to hire multiple AEs because multiple firms had supported the fundraising programs. The plan was to hire one AE for each of the five campuses. But after some thought, we realized that approach would have five presidents and their AEs competing for space, five different mechanical systems, five different kinds of faculty offices, five different kinds of classrooms and so on.

We suggested they hire one AE for "Program Definition" and then hire multiple AEs for execution. They took our advice. The Program Definition AE set finishes, accessibility standards, LEED requirements, IT communication guidelines, landscape and irrigation concepts, furnishing, fixture and equipment selections, security standards and an energy code. Then the Program Definition AE established standards for lighting, acoustics, thermal and air quality and designed common, reoccurring spaces like faculty offices. As the program moved ahead, the project AEs established specific requirements for their buildings. It worked well.

Here's another example of rotation that works without prototype building design. Starbucks must build its coffee shops in unique locations—airports, office buildings, bookstores, shopping centers. We managed the construction of about 30 of these shops. We quickly learned that no two could be the same—the shops went into different buildings. Occasionally Starbucks built a stand-alone building, but the shopping center design or whatever group of buildings that surrounded it would control the building design.

Therefore, Starbucks couldn't design a prototype building. But it could standardize the cabinetwork, equipment and finish materials. Starbucks bought these products in bulk, warehoused them and delivered them to construction sites. The standards saved design time, the bulk purchases saved money and the warehousing saved construction time. And they delivered a consistent environment that their customers came to expect.

Starbucks can't design a prototype building. But Starbucks can standardize the cabinetwork, equipment and finish materials and deliver the environment its customers expect.

HEB is a large grocery store chain in the Southwest and produced one of my favorite examples. Howard E. Butt set a policy that his grocery stores must respect the aesthetics of communities where they're built. (His son, Charles Butt, is now chairman and carries out the same policy.) So the stores have unique exterior treatments. As usual in a steel frame design, the shop drawings preparation, shop drawings approval, fabrication, delivery and erection were critical path items. So HEB decided to use a standard structural bay and only one bar joist size. HEB bought several years of bar joists in an evergreen indefinite quantity contract. They saved a little on the cost of the joists but saved months in the delivery schedule. Another grocery store builder, the Defense Commissary Agency (DeCA), builds at military bases around the world. Most of the bases have design guidelines (called installation compatibility guidelines) that require different exterior materials, fenestration and roof lines. Each base is different. Moreover, some bases are bigger than others, so they need bigger commissaries.

Like Starbucks, DeCA can't build prototype buildings. However, it can design prototypical layouts, structures, MEP systems, cabinetry, shelving, refrigeration, checkout facilities, framing, etc. DeCA has eight prototype layouts that can be adapted to individual base requirements. A Facilities Standard Review Board re-examines and updates the prototypes. Ideas come in via a website and an on-line chat room. Often DeCA varies the prototype. A change might be adding a fish market in San Francisco or New Orleans.

Many Program Managers hire individual AEs for each project. If the Program Manager doesn't inform the design teams with program standards, the AEs will design the building from

Many programs hire individual AEs for each project who then replicate each other's work endlessly.

scratch. They will study basic questions such as lighting, HVAC and structure no matter how many times other AEs have settled those questions satisfactorily on previous buildings. Often there will be an old design that was better than the new design. That's not continuous improvement.

Conversely, many of the serial builders we interviewed built buildings with similar requirements and abandoned the thought that each should be unique. They design unique components only when the requirements are unique. Then they use standards or try to improve on the last edition of a standard when the requirements are unchanged. Some have found ways to implement those standards with great efficiency.

The Los Angeles Unified School System has the largest building program in the United States ($19.2 billion as of 2007). LAUSD's policy is that their schools should fit into the architectural character of their communities. So each project is an individual design. And like many public clients, the LAUSD people feel they must pass work around to different architectural firms in their community. They also hire a few famous firms for trophy buildings.

In their first major round of school building, they gave the architects a loose-leaf notebook of instructions with three pages of general written descriptions of the characteristics of a good school. In the next round of school projects, several years later, they included a CD with specifications and CAD drawings of good examples of designs from the first round of designs that met those characteristics. The CD included everything from good site layouts to well-designed library checkout desks.

Buildings don't have to be prototypes to benefit from rotation.

Lesson: you don't have to think of the whole building as a prototype to benefit from rotation concepts. There are many ways to increase productivity by rotating standards for parts of a facility—leaving other parts available to satisfy a unique requirement with unique designs.

ALL TOGETHER NOW

The chance of success increases if all three— people, process and products— are rotated.

Often, if a Program Manager undertakes a rotation initiative, the chance of success increases substantially if all three categories— people, process and products—are synchronized in the effort, if all three are rotated together.

If not, there is a chance of failure. For instance, the Air Force decided to do "definitive designs" for dormitories. The Air Force people felt that the requirements should be consistent across all their bases and that a standard design would make sense. So they hired an AE, developed the design and sent it out to the bases. It gathered dust on the shelves. The bases hired their own AEs, who had their own ideas about what to design and build.

It would have worked if all three categories had been rotated at the same time and the following had been in place:

1. a policy with schedules to review the definitive designs as they were implemented (the process)
2. an enforced policy to implement the standard design (the product)
3. a contract for the AE of the standard design to oversee the site adaptation of the design (the people)

STANDARDS AND IMPROVEMENT

The benefit of rotation is not only the cost and time reduction. It's also the increase in quality.

As we begin to answer the question "what can we rotate?" the inclination is to establish standards: a standard process or a standard product. The General Services Administration (GSA), with its enormous building program, has a large notebook of standards they give to AEs. But when I talk to designers about standards, I watch troubled frowns appear. It's likely that the best and brightest AEs will cloud up. Their concern is that standards will build barriers to innovation or their own creative ambitions. The reverse should be true. An organization with standards should always view each one as a current working standard (CWS). A CWS is only there until someone has a better idea. But a standard eliminates the cost of reinventing wheels and reduces the possibility that the next edition will be worse than the last.

A standard should be a current working standard (CWS) that is subject to continuous improvement.

The Program Management culture should encourage project teams to view standards as benchmarks—a platform for innovation and improvement. Standards are good but improvements are great!

The best of the serial builders don't leave their standards alone. They constantly tweak them. Meanwhile, if there's not a better idea, they apply the CWS to current projects and gain efficiency in the current project delivery. That's sure different than reinventing every part of every project.

Most capital building programs have projects that are staged over a period of several years. But they must meet budgets and schedules. If Program Managers build projects with similar standards, the time and cost will be more predictable. Furthermore, Program Managers dealing with similar projects will find more economies.

The original cost of a facility is only a fraction (usually less than 10%) of the total cost of ownership. Post evaluation of energy consumption and operations and maintenance can be fed back into a continuous improvement program.

How much would we save if everything were done right?

I had a conversation with Barbara White Bryson, who's in charge of design and construction at Rice University. Barbara is unusually skilled at keeping some of the world's best design architects within schedules and budgets. She constantly questions traditional processes and searches for improvement. She repeated a conversation with one of the senior administrators at Rice. He asked her how much might be saved if everything in the workflow were done right.

Who knows how much can be saved? Maybe 5% or 10%. Maybe more. However, we discussed a couple of refinements to the question.

We make mistakes the first time we do something; we only get it right when we practice.

First, as long as each project is a set of unique tasks, it won't all go right. We make mistakes the first time we do something; we only get it right when we practice.

Second, if we rotate tasks and focus on them, the first stage is doing it right. That might gain the 5-10% improvement. But with practice, and sometimes some new technology, we can produce enormous gains—radically exceeding normal expectations.

So the better question is, "How much can we rotate? And what savings will that rotation produce?"

Must each building be a unique work of art or will we have better architecture with repetition and refinement?

Instead of designing a unique building with each assignment, can we have great architecture and still polish our work through repetition and refinement—making it better as we progress? We think so. And many of the people we talked to in researching the material for this book think so too. What's more, they're proving it by doing it.

BARRIERS TO ROTATION

Design and construction are traditionally project, not program, oriented. Tradition is hard to change. Tradition governs the relationships among hundreds of organizations that are involved in a single project.

Saving time and money and implementing continuous improvement requires change. It takes authority to implement change. No Program Manager is in complete control of the building program. (Indeed, there is never any one person in complete control.) A board, users and administrators all exert influence. AEs have opinions. There are myriad entitlement agencies that present their wickets through which approvals must pass.

The ability to rotate people, process and product from the project to the program depends not only on the similarity of facilities the organization builds, but on the Program Manager's authority as well.

To implement standards and continuous improvement throughout a program, a Program Manager must have the authority to push change and enforce standards. Each project will be executed in a broad-based constituency of intelligent people with independent ideas.

Clearly, no Program Manager will be able to prevail consistently. Strong people with capricious ideas or a whim of iron will cause variance from the standards. However, a Program Manager must identify those areas of continuous improvement he or she can affect, and perhaps be sanguine about the territory beyond his or her control.

One day, Sid Sanders sketched out a diagram similar to the box on the right. His point was that the degree of rotation is not only a function of the similarity of the buildings in a program but also the amount of authority the Program Manager has.[4]

To illustrate that point, he drew this diagram and we filled it in together. Our assumption is that fast food chains and big box

Tradition governs the relationships.

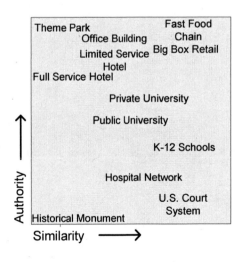

---

4. Sid was then head of Facilities Planning, Design and Construction for the University of Texas System. He is now Vice President for Facilities and Construction for The Methodist Hospital System, Houston, Texas.

retailers have considerable authority over their projects and the facilities have similar requirements. So they can achieve considerable rotation. A developer of an office building may have a lot of authority but the similarity of the projects will be affected by local markets and land costs. A limited service hotel will have more similarities than a full service hotel. A historical monument is apt to have totally unique requirements and many groups of people affecting its design. The U.S. courthouses have similar requirements but the local judges control the design. The Program Manager of a theme park may have a high degree of authority but the building requirements will be highly unique.

ROTATION AND DESIGN

A recurring message on these pages is that the first time we do things we make mistakes and perform slowly. Reliable and efficient results come from repetition and study. That inevitably triggers a concern among many architects who feel that architecture is an art and each building must be an individual creation.

The tradition of architecture is that every building should be custom designed. It should respond to the uniqueness of its site and the context of the neighborhood. No firm should ever copy another—and not even repeat itself. Basic design decisions for lighting, HVAC and structure need to be freshly examined for each project.

That tradition permeates the profession. Unquestioned, it sets the attitudes of many clients. And, indeed, many projects *are* unique and call for a unique response.

But, with few exceptions, the world's most sophisticated clients have abandoned those thoughts. The central question then is: "Instead of designing a unique building with each assignment, can we have better design by polishing our work through repetition and refinement—making it better as we progress?" We believe so, and we are seeing it happen.

Talented architects can leverage their skills across more of our built environment.

For many people who enjoy good design, there's a hope that talented architects can leverage their skills across more of our built environment. If Michael Graves can design tea kettles for Target, there is no reason not to have great architects designing great buildings for serial builders.

Whenever I am in Washington, D.C., I try to visit the Renwick Gallery. The Renwick focuses on crafts. There was a show of "Studio Furniture" that included wonderful chairs by George Nakashima, Tage Frid and Sam Maloof. I admire these craftsmen and their work. You can order a rocker from Sam Maloof now for about $7k—if you're willing to wait several years for it.

If you do that, you will have a wonderful, original, handmade product—but even at that price, it won't be completely unique. There will be others similar to it. Although I am in awe of the exquisite craftsmanship and would like to have one, I ponder my conviction that none are as functional or as comfortable as the Herman Miller mass-produced Aeron chair designed by Bill Stumpf or the many chairs designed by Charles Eames. Nor are they more beautiful. However, they sure are a lot more expensive.

Here is the arresting thought: during the 20th century our art forms became repeatable. Stage performances became cinema; paintings became prints; and music and photographs are now commonly duplicated. Maybe in the 21st century architecture will achieve that distinction.

During the 20th century, our art forms became repeatable.

❖

Clearly, no organization adopts every useful innovation that's available to it. While some quickly recognize opportunities for improvement and have the authority to cause change, most do not. It's understandable. There are lots of people involved in a building program. Regulations abound. Big money is involved. And these programs typically serve organizations with bureaucracies that don't understand construction and are inherently conservative. So it's hard to improve. And so we are antiquated.

Productivity is increased by applying technology to repetitive tasks. The reason the construction industry has not improved productivity is that it produces unique, labor-intensive, custom-made products. The great promise of Program Management is the opportunity to choose repetitive tasks, figure out how to do them efficiently, standardize them, improve them relentlessly, apply selective technology and make dramatic improvements in production.

Program and Project Definition

Managing design, minimizing change

A skillful Program Manager will determine the project requirements to achieve alignment among owners, agencies and constructors and then schedule the required wickets for approval.

Thorough Program and Project Definition for each of these three groups of constituencies improves design and minimizes change. It must include everything that concerns each of these constituencies and be tailored to the uniqueness of the program.

As a project advances, the bad consequences of change increase exponentially. Changes delay work, increase costs, generate claims and produce litigation. So projects with good definition cost less, finish faster and have less conflict.

There's an important opportunity to organize requirements and solutions from similar projects within a capital improvement program into extensive checklists to be applied to individual projects. These checklists will support

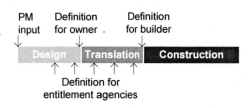

continuous improvement and jump-start the Project Definition process. This is one of the many opportunities for adding value that a Program Manager has over a manager of an individual project.

Approvals will be more likely to stick if the approving group fully understands the design and the design implications of cost, schedule and function. So documentation for the owner must be in language the owner understands.

After owner approval, the AE must translate that presentation language into the technical and legal language of construction. Approval agencies may have special language requirements as well.

Here's a self-evident observation. There are lots of people and lots of organizations that must agree before a project can be built. What's not so evident is that viewing those agreements in a *program* context instead of a *project* context can save extraordinary amounts of time and money.

Great efficiencies can be achieved by using Program Definition over Project Definition.

Traditionally, on an individual project, the architect's job is to get the project requirements nailed down. But for the repetitious aspects of the project, the Program Manager should do the nailing. To the extent that the requirements in a program repeat themselves from project to project, 10X efficiencies are possible.

The reason we define requirements is to explain the job to a large team so they can produce a body of work that meets those requirements, unhesitatingly, efficiently, without change.

We will always have frustrating changes in our projects. But we can minimize them. Establishing disciplined definition processes is the best approach to do so.

Two organizations that study design and construction have given much attention to the role of Project Definition.

Poor Project Definition increases costs substantially.

Independent Project Analysis, a Virginia-based construction consultant, has a large database of project histories—primarily dealing with petrochemical and pharmaceutical projects. Ed Merrow, the president, told us the company's database indicates that projects that begin construction with excellent Project Definition cost 17% less than the average. Conversely, projects that begin with poor Project Definition cost 20% more than the average. That's a 37% swing. Said another way, his statistics indicate that a project that starts construction with poor Project Definition is apt to cost about 50% more than one that starts with good definition!

The Construction Industry Institute (CII), the highly respected non-profit construction industry research organization, has invested many research dollars into the study of Project Definition. CII has developed the Project Definition Rating Index© (PDRI).[1] The PDRI is a method for measuring the degree of documentation at various stages in the development of a design. It's useful in highlighting missing information and consequently highlighting potential areas of risk.

The PDRI is a checklist with 64 weighted scope elements to guide definition. It standardizes terms, highlights potential risk, monitors progress and helps establish alignment with the extended project team. The PDRI also encourages the team to question and think about whether it's the right project (why), the right scope (what), and the right project delivery strategy (how).

Program Managers need the power of PDRI or a similar tool.

Building the wrong project is obviously bad for the owner, not having the right scope will produce uncertainty and change, and skipping a definition of the project delivery strategy will invariably delay the project. Section 1 of the PDRI is the why, Section 2 is the what and Section 3 is the how.

The PDRI is a powerful tool. All Program Managers should understand and should use it—or something similar of their own invention, perhaps built on the PDRI. GSA, NASA and others have used the PDRI and found it useful in ensuring that the entire owner project team is aligned.

Edd Gibson,[2] formerly on the faculty at the University of Texas, now at the University of Alabama, guided the development of the PDRI through many generations of development.

---

1. A document describing the Project Definition Rating Index for building projects (Implementation Resource 155-2, 2nd Edition) and many other insightful research papers may be purchased from CII at http://www.construction-institute.org. CII has also published a PDRI for industrial projects. The CII recommends that the PDRI tool be used with the Implementation Resource 113-3, *Alignment During Pre-Project Planning*, also available from CII.
2. Edd Gibson can be reached at egibson@eng.ua.edu.

Interestingly, CII has found that an outside facilitator (someone not directly associated with the project) helps greatly in making sure that a detailed and honest PDRI assessment of the project occurs when key project stakeholders are involved.

A survey of CII membership determined that 43 of their organizations (both owners and contractors) use the tool. CII compared 108 building projects worth $2.3 billion using the 200-point PDRI score for acceptable definition. Projects with a score under 200 (lower is better) constantly outperformed the others. The projects with scores over 200 averaged cost overruns about three times higher, schedule overruns about four times greater and change orders about a third more.

A DEFINITION OF DEFINITION

Program Definition and Project Definition are both processes and products. They are:

Program and Project Definition are processes.

- The processes of gathering facts and working out solutions to establish a meeting of the minds with the groups who play a necessary role in project execution and who must agree to do their job or provide their permission

Program and Project Definition are products.

- The product that describes that meeting of the minds in terms that are meaningful to the parties, in language that the parties understand and with the detail required for the parties to understand what they're agreeing to

At the *program* level, the groups who must agree may be a board, a legislature, a donor or another financial source. The document that describes Program Definition may be called a Capital Improvement Plan. (See *The plan,* page 206.)

At the *project* level, the groups who must agree may include some of the owner's extended groups mentioned above but will also include entitlement agencies and constructors. The documents that describe those agreements may be 3D design representations for the owner, an environmental impact study for the EPA or Contract Documents for the constructor.

THE ACCELERATING COST OF CHANGE

PDRI concentrates on front-end planning.

Part of the beauty of the PDRI is its concentration on front-end planning—a time when analysis and change is cheap. The

PDRI tool is rooted in delivering an individual project, but the powerful concepts behind it can easily be extrapolated for a capital improvement program where there are similarities among projects.

A Program Manager can create an extended checklist identifying the elements that are consistent from project to project and those that are likely to vary. (See *Rotation, Repetition and Refinement*, page 28.) It's not my idea. We were told that Wal-Mart has an 1800-item checklist that they use on every project and that Hines has a 45-page checklist.

Furthermore, while the PDRI tool focuses on establishing agreements with the owner in the early stages, the same concepts and methods can be applied to establishing agreements with entitlement agencies and constructors as the project moves forward. (Anyone who has worked through approvals with the Fine Arts Commission in Washington D.C. or the City Planning Commission in Santa Fe understands that obtaining agreements to build with entitlement agencies can be a significant challenge where the Program Manager is in bad need of a comprehensive checklist.)

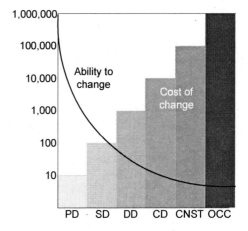

The idea is simply this: get the requirements nailed down and make changes when it's cheap and easy. Early in a project the alternatives are infinite and the cost of studying them is low. As the project progresses, the number of alternatives narrows and the cost of changing a decision increases.

The price tag for a change goes up roughly an order of magnitude as the project changes its "medium of existence." The reason is two-fold. First, the medium that defines the project becomes more costly to modify. Second, more building systems, more processes and more people get involved in the change. Consider the following:

At the start, the medium for describing the project is alphanumeric—words and numbers. Change is cheap. It typically requires nothing more than modifying a spreadsheet or a word-processing document. The team is small so few people are involved. This is the time for testing alternatives; much can be decided before a line is drawn. If the Program Manager has done a good job of collecting requirements and solutions from previous projects, the project team will get a jump-start.

Change is cheap at the start.

When the project moves into design, one change affects other aspects of the design. Changing the size of a room may ripple through plans and elevations. More work is required and the team has grown, so more people need to make adjustments. Furthermore, irritation emerges. People don't like the cost and frustration of redoing work. Maybe there is a change order for the AE and some delay.

Modifying the construction documents is another 10X cost increase. A change may affect floor plans, reflected ceiling plans, elevations, MEP, structure and specifications. The extended project team of engineers and consultants are involved. There is also a step up in irritation and certainly a change order for the AE.

Change becomes exponentially more expensive as the project moves through each medium: alphanumeric, design, construction documents, construction and post-occupancy.

Construction is even more expensive to alter. Tearing out concrete costs much more than deleting and reworking a CAD drawing. Furthermore, the unit cost of construction in a change order is invariably higher than in the original price. Lots of people—AEs, contractors, subcontractors and workers—are involved. There are usually disagreements about the price for the change order and irritation may rise to anger and litigation. Lawyers, administrators and boards join the fray.

After occupancy, the cost increases again. Typically the cost of occupancy is less than 10% of the cost of an organization's operation. If it's necessary to shut down operations, the interruption may cost 10 times as much as the bill for the construction. Now the friction of construction hampers the owner's core business and frustrates employees as well as the AEs, contractors, subcontractors and workers.

So it's sure important to get it right at the start. A change that costs pennies when the medium of existence is alphanumeric may cost millions after occupancy.

There are often people anxious to get started. They argue that it doesn't make sense to do another study. Their mantra is to start design and *"get after it."* But a costly and time-consuming event lurks in the shadows when a project team, in an effort to shorten a schedule, skips adequate definition. The inevitable result is retracing steps and doing things over—waste and delay.

A rush to construction causes delays in the long run.

A rush to construction is a common cause of change and delay. *People confuse motion with progress.* (That is one of my favorite lines from Sid Sanders, director of facilities for The Methodist Hospital System in Houston.) No matter how tight the schedule, defining the requirements rigorously and obtaining alignment on the best solution—with owners, agencies and constructors—produces the fastest result.

Lesson: Start with the most comprehensive checklist possible and expand it with as much intellectual energy as can be generated among the extended project team. Gather as much information as possible as early as possible. Then study the alternatives when change is cheap and the alternatives are many. Make sure to define everything that's possible at each medium of existence before progressing to the next.

Then document the decisions and items for the next checklist for the next project in the program. That's the surest, cheapest way to produce predictable results.

Fast-track projects

At this point, many people have blown the whistle with a comment like:

> *"That's fine if you have the time for it. But we have a crash schedule and we have to fast-track the project. We have to get going before we can define everything."*

But the reverse is true. Fast-track requires more, not less definition if there is to be any semblance of cost control. But the definition is done in packages congruent with the construction. In other words, each package of construction work requires excellent definition or it will suffer cost overruns.

Fast-track projects should be defined and documented in stages. Obviously, you can build the foundations before you know all the cabinet details. However, upstream construction creates inflexibility in the downstream design—or it triggers costly construction changes. So the Program Manager must know that the floor plan is final to be confident that the foundations are in the right place. A final floor plan becomes a fixed given in the foundation Project Definition package. If the requirements that shape the floor plan are poorly defined, there will be a foundation change or a floor plan that doesn't meet requirements. Meanwhile, the cabinet detail can be put off. It won't affect the foundations.

Fast-track projects require more, not less definition, but done in packages.

Said another way, to fast-track a project, the design team must think through the thread of downstream design variables that are constrained by early construction packages. Fast-track requires adequate definition of the downstream dependencies to ensure that upstream work will fit the eventual designs.

We have seen some projects that were so unique (such as a cutting-edge technology research facility or a thrilling show and ride at a theme park) that the designers and the owners got important new ideas and continued to refine the design as construction progressed. In these cases, the changes drove the project well beyond the original budget, but the owner accepted the cost overrun as the price tag for worthwhile improvements.

Sometimes the Program Manager knows there will be changes and puts together a team and plans for it.

THREE CONSTITUENCIES FOR AGREEMENTS

Think of it this way. The purpose of both Program and Project Definition is to establish agreements with everyone who participates in project delivery—no more, and certainly no less.

So Project Definition and its medium of documentation must communicate with and produce agreement with three broad constituencies:

- owner (and the extended owner organization)
- entitlement agencies
- constructors

Each must agree that the documentation of the design is adequate and the documentation satisfies their requirements. Owners must accept that the design meets their goals. Entitlement agencies must agree that the design meets their regulations. Constructors must agree that the documentation properly describes the work and the contract terms are acceptable.

If definition is incomplete for any of these three groups, there will be changes that will increase the project cost, cause delay, reduce quality and ultimately reduce everyone's satisfaction with the project. The trick is to do the work required for the first two groups—owner and entitlement agencies—thoroughly and deliberately. Then do the work for the third group, the

PM input | Definition for owner | Definition for builder

Design | Translation | Construction

Definition for entitlement agencies

There should be a point when the AE delivers full documentation—3D drawings and reports to the owner that demonstrate that the design satisfies all the owner's requirements. The documentation must respond to "everything the owner cares about in the owner's language." When it's approved, the AE translates it into a language that is technical and legal to communicate with the constructors. Meanwhile, the AE must satisfy entitlement agencies.

constructors, as fast as possible before anyone changes their mind.

Individual projects in a continuous building program should have definition documentation and approval similarities. A Program Manager must plan this documentation and decision-making with rigor and manage it with discipline. The database of Project Definitions and approvals should expand with each new project in the program.

The Project Definition database should expand with each new project.

The plan describes how the project team will seek out and extract the requirements from the groups who must agree. It then defines the information that the owner and the entitlement agencies require to make their decisions. Finally, the plan defines the form of documentation for the Contract Documents (CDs).

The CDs define the requirements in legal and construction terms. They can be a full set of construction documents with specifications, they can be design concepts and performance specifications for a bridging project, or they can be alphanumeric requirements for a design-build project. But they don't define the owner's requirements in a language that most owners understand, nor do they necessarily satisfy the requirements of the entitlement agencies.

Construction is production intensive. Design is decision intensive. The responsibility for planning this approval process is a major difference between a Program Manager and construction manager. During design of an individual project, an AE typically schedules approvals. A construction manager follows the AE's lead. However, in a continuous building program, the Program Manager (who may be an architect or engineer and may be an owner employee or outsourced) should establish prototype schedules and checklists to pump-prime project delivery and save time and money on downstream projects.

The Program Manager establishes prototype schedules and checklists.

This business of managing the collection of requirements and scheduling approvals is a fundamental difference between Program Management and the management of an individual project.

THE OWNER

Clients cause lots of changes in CDs and construction. Often it's our fault and could have been avoided with rigorous definition.

Owners have become multi-headed and may have conflicting interests.

Managing the client's decision-making is a high-value art for Program Managers[3] who need to manage the owner's extended team as tightly as design and construction. Moreover, owners have become multi-headed, usually represented by a governing body (such as a board), executives, administrators, users, facility managers and Program Managers. Each has responsibilities and, consequently, each will have biases and an agenda. And there will be conflicting interests. Perhaps executives will care about the budget and schedule, and users will want as much commodity as they can get. So there must be consensus seeking to obtain alignment.

Bob Hixon[4] tells an apocryphal story to drive home the importance of alignment with a multi-headed owner. During the initial PDRI meeting for setting the project budget submission for Congress, the team was asked if everyone understood the project's financial goals. The portfolio people said "yes." Everyone else was clueless; the financial analysis hadn't been shared. It assumed that the occupant would pay rent of $40 per square foot based on an upgraded mechanical system, renovated lobby and modernized elevators—items reflected in the scope of work.

The building manager blew a whistle and explained that the building needed a new roof and electrical panels. The security people asked about improved security systems.

The portfolio people responded that the ROI (return on investment) couldn't support that added work without more rent. But the tenant wouldn't pay more rent for building maintenance and couldn't afford the added security costs. The team realized they didn't have alignment. Of course, that was the right time to uncover the problems instead of during CDs or at a bid opening.

Problems uncovered early are the easiest to solve.

Bob's point is that this particular situation would probably end in an easy resolution since the issue was uncovered early. The scope of work, the rent and the ROI could be negotiated, and if some of the players didn't get all they wanted they could understand,

3. Clients with building programs usually have employees who are construction professionals. Of course, they are Program Managers. So when I refer to "the Program Manager," it may refer to the client's employees, an outsourced Program Manager or a combination of the two.
4. See Acknowledgements.

feel involved and accept compromise. If the problem had surfaced during CDs or after bidding it would have required deletion of scope to stay in budget or a request for additional funding that would cause delay and more expense.

The same multi-headed issues exist in a program, except there are more heads and more issues. Which building will be done first and with what scope? What infrastructure needs to be put in with the first building that will serve future buildings? How will the first facilities be operated with only part of the eventual operating structure?

With a program, these decisions and the processes for making them don't need to be invented repeatedly. (However, the processes may be updated for lessons learned along the way that will limit future hiccups.)

The Contract Documents mark a well-recognized milestone when the documentation of legal terms and construction technology must be complete. The CDs mark the point when the AEs have Project Definition for the constructor in the legal and technical language of construction.

Contract Documents are a legal milestone.

Unfortunately, there is no equally well-recognized milestone in the classic, traditional processes where AEs define the project for the owner in the owner's language. Far too often, Project Definition for the owner is a fuzzy by-product of the march to complete the CDs. Without a clear point of Project Definition, there is review and change all along the way. And it gets expensive.

A Project Definition milestone for the owner is fuzzier. An explicit point of approval is needed.

A wise Program Manager will set an explicit point for final approval with the owner rather than waiting for an implicit point when the constructors agree with the CDs.

Project Definition for the owner is that crucial moment when the owner's team understands and agrees with what they will get, what they will pay and when they will get it. It's the moment when the owner and the AEs agree that the design satisfies the requirements and the decisions that concern the owner are final. That moment should occur before the translation to CDs begins and can rightly be described as:

> *"Everything the owner cares about, described in a language the owner understands."*

Owners care about everything they use and see.

So there is no Project Definition with an owner until all the things an owner cares about are complete.

So what do owners care about? Of course it varies, but typically they care about everything they use and can see: site development, finishes and elevations, the functional relationship of spaces and the equipment. They care about the cost and the schedule. Usually they don't care about things they can't see—the duct sizes, the electrical runs, the re-bars, the foundations, although they certainly care about the performance of these engineering systems.

Each owner has different concerns. The Program Manager's job is to map these decisions so the AEs can focus on this decision-making process and set a point when they're done.

George Heery and I spent considerable time working on a graphic to express this idea. A hypothetical example is in the margin. The light gray areas are an alphanumeric description of the requirement. The medium gray areas represent design drawings. The dark gray areas describe specifications that could be performance, prescriptive or product based.

Project Definition for an owner's agreement may have little to do with the classic phases of SD, DD and CD.

Forget about fitting this set of concerns to the next program. This is only a hypothetical example. The next program will be different—different degrees of interest and different categories. So the Program Manager should concentrate on mapping these areas of the owner's interest (in a lot more detail than in this example) so the team can concentrate on addressing them. If the Program Manager leaves something out, it will trigger a change. The land mines are in the white areas in the graph. The map needs to be done before design and improved on each project. Digging out the owner's areas of interest as design progresses, exploring as you go along, like a Lewis and Clark of design, is not the way to do it.

Just to drive the point home, think of doing the opposite. Say the AE simply works steadily toward finishing the design, worrying about all the things that must be considered to get to a complete set of CDs with no particular focus on the owner's specific set of concerns. The drawings are developed with technical details that the owner doesn't care about.

The overabundance of documentation obfuscates some of the owner's areas of interest, but more important, when the owner makes a change, it ricochets through the entire body of work. The delay for rework and the cost of change is higher.

Things to consider for inclusion in the owner's Project Definition package (and put in a graphic like the one in the margin) might include the site development, space program, affinities and functional relationships, furnishing, fixtures and equipment, elevations, renderings of the exterior and interior, material selections, colors, budgets, estimates, operating cost, income and expense, cash flows, project team organization, project delivery strategy, contract terms, systems performance, telecommunications, smart systems and user's operating systems. That's a short list. A complete list will run multiple pages.

Program Managers must identify the various owner groups and meet their individual requirements.

Of course, there are chapters in the evolution of Project Definition as different owner groups review the design as it develops. A Program Manager must identify the owner groups that make decisions and then define the content these groups require. For instance, a board may require a budget, schedule and aesthetics; users may want to review room sizes and relationships, equipment and aesthetics; the facilities group will want to know about MEP and other building systems. Without clear focus on the individual interests and the ensuing requirements, these reviews and the subsequent modifications continue through CDs—a phase where change is painfully expensive and time consuming.

But nothing's perfect. Although we may be rigorous in defining the owner's interests, change will be inevitable. New people with strong views may join the user group or the organization's administration. External events may affect requirements. And then there are matters that require owner agreement that continue to trickle in until the facility is occupied and operational. These matters may be trivial, but the consequences of inattention can be significant. A delay in a no-cost decision, like picking paint colors, may delay the project and trigger a high-cost result. If we maximize the number of these decisions made early in the project by using our Project Definition checklists and milestones, we can minimize change.

Change is inevitable.

We've seen some owner organizations make this definition activity difficult. A common problem is not wanting to spend the time or money to do it thoroughly and, therefore, negotiating limited service in AE contracts. Not understanding the consequences of late changes in the project and delaying decisions is always costly.

Additionally, retrofit or repair and alteration projects, particularly in occupied facilities, pose a difficult challenge when it comes to changes. Even in the best planned projects, tenant and user needs will require a change in the project sequence.

In our conversations with serial builders, we didn't find any who claimed they could build without change.[5] Some had bureaucratic processes in place to review a requirements change during construction, but would tolerate the change if they felt it was worth it. Only a very few of the fast food chains or big box retailers tried to have cast iron points of *"no subsequent change."*

Project Definition for owners must be in a language that lay people can understand.

The language of Project Definition for most owners must be one that lay people understand. While some users are fully capable of understanding technical plans and specifications, most are not. So users who simply misunderstand drawings cause change. A Program Manager must be watchful to identify those misunderstandings and correct them before needless changes are made.

The drawings and specifications, particularly the Contract Documents, are in the language of construction technology—not a language that lay people use. We have all experienced the dismaying experience of a user who begins to see the final construction, is unpleasantly surprised and asks for changes.

AEs fully understand how to define a project in the legal and technical language that constructors understand. We need to be equally as good at presenting design to users in a language that users understand—and doing it early in the process.

Extracting owners' requirements is an art.

Some AEs are masters at it. Bill Caudill, the C of CRS, was a master at using the charrette process many years ago to extract an owner's requirements. He would lead a week-long work session in the owner's facilities and paper the walls with little 5 x 8 "snow cards"—each with a statement of an owner requirement.

5. One of the more revealing stories came from the Las Vegas School District. They build prototype schools. We were told that they typically suffer with change orders that amount to about 4% of the construction cost on the first edition of a prototype. Then they correct the documents. After that, the change orders are less than a quarter of a percent.

It was a great process for projects. It can also be adapted to programs by Program Managers. Every project in a program has both unique and common elements—be they people, processes or products. It's extraordinarily helpful to the design teams for the Program Manager to build a catalog of common requirements and then facilitate the development of unique requirements in a project-specific workshop. While some AEs are expert at extracting owner requirements, others need coaching. They may think of the CDs as their ultimate work product and be inclined to work with drawings that they can continue to develop until they complete the CDs. It seems the efficient thing to do. But if users don't understand these technical drawings, there will be changes and they will wreak havoc with the production of the CDs. We are smarter when we use rendered drawings with plain English descriptions instead of technical specifications to communicate with the owner's extended team.

THE ENTITLEMENT AGENCIES

It's hard to get permission to build. There are more approvals required—more wickets—than ever before. Environmentalists, fine arts commissions, historic preservationists, zoning boards, the EPA and planning agencies restrict or deny construction. Citizens groups influence public and private projects. Public opinion will sway public employees who control design.

The number of approvals required before construction continues to increase.

Many Americans no longer believe that construction is necessarily a good thing; many believe we are overbuilt and some communities have vociferous no-growth civic groups. Clean air, clean water, mobility, historic preservation, sustainability and urban design are public issues. We have eliminated tax incentives for development; states have no-growth movements; and cities have restrictive development codes.

These requirements can trip up serial builders. It's easy to fall into the trap of rolling out a prototype design to multiple locations just to find that agencies require unique modifications. Even when there are individual designs, the Program Manager will have to test the standards—the rotated people, procedures and products—for applicability with these agencies. Do AEs have the right licenses? Do fine arts commissions require special consideration? (Just try to build the same prototype design in downtown Santa Fe and Washington, D.C.) These agency

Agency agreements can be as crucial as owner requirements.

agreements are as crucial to define and schedule as the owner requirements.

And if a capital improvement program includes projects in different jurisdictions, as most do, the codes will vary. There are 44,000 code jurisdictions in the United States. Sometimes the jurisdictions change when you cross the street. Some will run through the middle of a project site. Even those clients who believe they can build identical prototypes will have variations imposed on them by the communities where they want to build.

THE CONSTRUCTORS

Years ago, I sat with about 50 construction industry CEOs through a presentation on productivity in erecting steel. The presenter compared three approaches. The steel was delivered and:

1. Laid willy-nilly on the site
2. Laid on the site in the order needed for erection
3   Picked off the delivery truck by the erection crane without ever touching the ground

Sitting next to me was the president of one of the county's largest construction companies. I don't remember his exact words, but at the end of the presentation he muttered something to the effect that:

> *"I don't ever want to listen to another presentation that shows planning saves money. I know that. What I want to know is how to get everybody to do it."*

There must be thorough definition of what is to be built and a meeting of minds with the constructors to have an enforceable, viable contract that will not be riddled with change as construction progresses. Without such a document, the constructors are not able to plan.

AEs have much to learn from the construction industry.

There are far too many construction professionals who approach their work with arrogance and a deaf ear. It costs their clients a lot of money. Every year more of a building is manufactured indoors instead of custom-made outdoors. Manufacturers and subcontractors have become more expert on construction technology and cost than architects, engineers or CMs. The industry is struggling to devise project delivery methods that pull their expertise into a collaborative design process and still maintain competition.

Despite our best efforts to complete Project Definition as early as possible, some need for definition invariably leaks through to downstream activities. So Project Definition is a journey over the duration of design and construction that continues until the project team arrives at the final destination of occupancy.

Project Definition is an ongoing process.

Even when we have a set of Construction Documents and begin to build we are not through. Submittals trickle into the offices of the Program Manager and the AE up to the day the users move in.

We've rarely had a conversation with contractors or sub-contractors when they didn't complain about AEs who sat on submittals and delayed the work. And I have frequently seen AEs who are frustrated by the incessant, random, irritating but necessary drip, drip, drip of these chores through their offices. So the role of the Program Manager to manage decisions hardly ends with the beginning of construction. It continues through commissioning and occupancy.

Decisions continue through occupancy.

Wise AEs have developed workshops to accelerate design. They bring together the key decision makers from the owner's organization with the AE team for a multi-day, intensive work session. It's an effective approach to jump-start decisions and build project momentum. The same technique works with submittals.

At the start of construction, the Hines organization brings the AEs and constructors together to review submittals and make many of the decisions that typically pop up randomly and are fumbled throughout construction. Just as design workshops build rapid momentum and accelerate design, these submittal workshops accelerate construction.

Some of the big box retailers, the hospitality chains and fast food chains have their Project Definition package so complete that it includes such downstream decisions as paint colors and fabric selections. But that's impractical for most owners. As much as it makes sense to make early decisions, sometimes it's a bad idea. With some owner groups, an early decision may simply be changed.

Not all decisions can or should be made early.

A classic example is a government or an institutional office building. It's not uncommon for these clients to ask their AEs to do complete interior layouts as part of a CD package. Then over a year or two of construction, new people enter the owner's organization or unplanned events trigger new requirements. Dozens of changes frustrate the project team and erode the contingency. It would be far wiser to imitate a spec office building developer, do allowances for build-out and then do the interior design at the latest date.

Even if we made all the decisions at the start of construction, and even if they were all good decisions, there would be change. User groups would have new players who would assert their will, and technology advances would make new equipment available.

So it's simply practical to delay some of these decisions until they're needed. Some, like paint colors, have no cost implications. Others may anticipate unknown events, so there may be allowances to cover the unknown availability of plant specimens for landscaping. The important point is that if Program Managers know enough about the decisions to know they can be delayed, they can plan around those decisions—and adjust the decision checklists for the next projects accordingly.

BIM

BIM (Building Information Modeling) will help a lot with Project Definition as it becomes more common. It will help to establish agreements with all three of the broad constituencies—owner, entitlement agencies and constructors.

BIM is a graphic and alphanumeric database.

Since BIM is essentially a database describing the entire project, it will be easier to produce reports for specific groups with subsets of information in the different languages required by owners, entitlement agencies and constructors. The 3D characteristics of BIM software and the data associated with the drawings will help owners and users to understand the design. Since reports that describe specific subsets of the BIM model are available, it will help the project team tailor appropriate content for the entitlement agencies. BIM enables collaboration with constructors during design, and the promise of integrating shop drawings into Contract Documents will help form better agreements with constructors.

For most of the 19th and 20th centuries architects and engineers described their designs with drawings and specifications—usually graphite on paper and an alphanumeric booklet. But with the emergence of economical computers, hand drawings could be replaced with computer-generated drawings.

The first generation of computer aided drafting (CAD) replaced graphite and paper with an electronic file that had formulas for lines, circles, arcs and polygons, plus coordinates that would locate those geometric figures in electronic space. The resultant array of single-discipline 2D images could be plotted at different scales and provided greater accuracy, ease of modification and were the first clunky steps to 3D representations. However, the drawing file remained "dumb."

At first, CAD was an electronic file with formulas for lines, circles, arcs and polygons, plus coordinates to locate them in space.

A new generation of CAD included the same basic geometric forms. But a startling new concept emerged. Added to the geometric lines and curves were 3D smart objects: windows, doors, walls, stairs and roofs. The objects had some internal rules to guide behavior. A user could grab a window by the corner and stretch it. The window would extend the length of the jamb and sill but not increase the jamb or sill section. It might know its size limits and add additional panes as it got bigger. If a stair was stretched, it would automatically add treads and risers at the right proportions.

The second generation of CAD included smart objects.

But there was a giant additional advantage. Data could be added to the object: specifications, warranty, cost, replacement parts, manufacturer's contact, supply chain, delivery date, tracking data, maintenance instructions—whatever was useful.

It was only a short conceptual step to BIM—the idea that the whole building could be a smart object. Like the window, intelligence could be built in. And BIM software could allow additional software to be plugged in—like one would plug a CD player into an amplifier. If mechanical intelligence was added, the design could calculate heat loss and gain if windows were added. If structural intelligence was added, the BIM model could calculate the increased building area if a room was stretched. Since the drawings were 3D, and since the structural and mechanical drawings were part of the model, "clash detection" routines could uncover situations where a beam and a duct occupied the same space.

Although it's a short conceptual step, it's a humongous undertaking. BIM moves far beyond enhanced design practices. BIM processes hold the promise of a quantum leap in how buildings are delivered and how the industry communicates and collaborates. Vast quantities of data can be added to a file for construction, for contractual purposes and for the management of the building after occupancy. Rather than communicating a building design with various single-discipline 2D drawings, integrated, interdisciplinary graphic images can be taken from the BIM modeling data.

BIM is no longer CAD or merely a 3D computer model. BIM is a comprehensive, integrated graphic and alphanumeric database—and a huge warehouse of related information. The 2D—or 3D—drawings plotted from the BIM database are only one form of available report. Obviously, specifications can be integral.

The construction sequence and duration can be added to elements of the building so a user can analyze assembly processes, enter a date to see the stage of completion or watch a movie of the planned construction activity. Many call that "4D" (3D plus time). And some add cost to the building elements and call it "5D."

The greatest promise of BIM is enabling collaboration.

Perhaps the greatest promise is that BIM enables a collaborative process—it is a tool that enables broad collaboration within an industry that is currently vertically structured and compartmentalized. It provides the same opportunity for design that web-based collaboration software provides for management—a means for an industry to pool its intellectual capital to improve a project.

BIM has great potential to solve many of the problems in our current processes. BIM, to be effective as a collaboration tool, will require fundamental changes in the way the industry normally contracts for construction. To get the full benefit of BIM the subs have to be working with the designer as design begins. We will have to contract with them before design is complete.

Getting builders involved in how to build things is a good idea. What could make more sense? If you were to land on earth from Mars and were told that the people who build things in the world's largest industry have little to say about how they're to be built, you would think that Homo sapiens needed more evolution.

Today much of the technical knowledge of design and construction resides with specialty subcontractors and manufacturers. Much of a building is built the way the subcontractors and manufacturers, rather than the AEs, think is best. Roughly half a set of CDs are replaced by shop drawings. If the CDs are 40% of an AE's fee, and half of it's discarded, that means 2-3% of the total cost of design and construction is discarded. That's a big waste.

Obviously, as contractors, subcontractors and manufacturers develop BIM capability, they will be able to provide both alphanumeric and graphic information in electronic files that replace the traditional 2D paper drawings. Integrating these drawings in a BIM model eliminates the stupid and costly redundancy of shop drawings replicating a large portion of the bid documents. And, of course, the collaboration of a large team reviewing the construction drawings uncovers errors before construction begins. If a manufactured product doesn't fit in the 3D space properly, the problem is obvious.

When we use project delivery strategies that include these manufacturers and speciality subcontractors during design, we will have better designs. They will be able to upload 3D shop drawings into a BIM model—producing an integrated set of CDs that can be used for construction. Currently, the constructors have a plethora of sets of drawings to sort through during construction. Look in any construction trailer. There is the set of AE drawings hanging on a rack. Then there is another rack with dozens of independent sets of shop drawings. Pity the superintendent. Think how wonderful it would be if there were one set of integrated drawings for construction.

New project delivery strategies will be required to fully enable the potential of BIM.

BIM is far from full implementation. Meanwhile, the Program Manager's job is to figure out, to the extent possible, how to extract this intellectual capital—this insight into construction cost and technology—and insert it into the design. (See comments in *Concepts of Project Delivery*, page 179.)

BIM processes require new participants on the project delivery team. Since there is so much programmed relationship between the building systems and data components of a BIM model, an addition of bad data or bad geometry can wreak havoc, ricocheting among the building components. So, just as is required in any process that requires data exchange between responsible groups, someone—perhaps called the BIM model manager—must monitor, coordinate and react to contributions to the BIM modeling database. That's not a surprising concept. When you think about it, it's no different than other data transfer procedures. For instance, although a Program Manager will operate accounting routines in their PMIS software, no Chief Financial Officer would allow that data in their general ledger without review.

Our traditions lag our technical advances.

Legal, professional and insurance practices lag behind these technological advances. Many state laws govern the architect's drawings and specifications. Elimination of redundancy is a goal of BIM processes, but licensed architects and engineers may only seal drawings or specifications prepared under their direct supervision. And insurance companies worry about providing Errors and Omissions insurance if architectural or engineering deliverables are used in subsequent BIM processes in unanticipated ways—ways that may benefit the project but add substantial risk to the design professionals.

Of course, these problems are a result of the archaic assumption that architects and engineers design buildings and contractors build them—assumptions that are institutionalized in standard form contracts. As I say repeatedly in this book, architects and engineers now must often evaluate and integrate building systems designed by manufacturers and specialty subcontractors rather than design the systems themselves.

Of course, one implication of the law is that the architect must assume some level of responsibility for the appropriateness of products he or she incorporates into the documents—a duty that is impractical in many situations. What architect can evaluate the effectiveness of a brake mechanism in an elevator?

The solution will include means for each contributor to electronically sign and assume responsibility for their contributions—just as subcontractors must assume responsibility for elements of the designs they supplement through shop drawings and building elements they construct. And, of course, Alliancing as a project delivery process will sure help.

BIM is developing through stages. In the early phases BIM is simply a 3D drawing tool, replacing previous versions of CAD for construction drawing production—with the inclusion of data associated with drawings of building components. Then it is a reasonably easy step to integrate drawings from the usual cadre of design consultants, principally the MEP, structural and civil engineering disciplines.

But a great promise is the step that integrates the shop drawings and specifications from specialty subcontractors and manufacturers. At that stage BIM is a vertical collaboration tool: a complete building model, an integrated set of construction drawings with built-in intelligence, with the ability to estimate and build electronically and provide a wealth of comprehensive information to the builder and the owner after occupancy.

This last stage is not technically difficult—but it will demand different project delivery strategies and a rearrangement of the contract structures common in design and construction.

Meanwhile, we must find temporary solutions to these long-term problems. One interim approach, suggested by John Hawkins (John is a skilled and knowledgeable construction lawyer with Porter and Hedges, LLP in Houston, who is relied on by many architects, engineers, CMs and contractors), is that the use of, and responsibility for, BIM processes affecting others be temporarily limited to enhancement of traditional quality control measures until wider use and practice define appropriate legal parameters. Collaboration is also encouraged when each contributor to the building design (architects, engineers, consultants, subcontractors, manufacturers) produces and retains ownership of its own portion of the BIM modeling data but grants other participants the licenses necessary to use the data for the common cause.

PHASES OF DESIGN

For building projects, design is typically divided into Programming (P), Schematic Design (SD), Design Development (DD) and Contract Documents (CDs). These traditional phases are set by a profession focused on getting to a set of Construction Documents and specifications that define the project in technical and legal terms. The purpose is to make an enforceable deal for construction and provide direction for construction assembly.

The documents are focused on only one of the three groups that must agree on the design. Unfortunately, too many AEs use these phases of work to extract, review and gain approval of the owner's requirements. It's a clumsy approach. Let's look at each of these classic phases.

Programming focuses on obtaining user requirements for space and functional affinities and project performance. Project Definition requires far more information to satisfy *"all that the owner cares about."*

Schematic Design or Design Development won't do the job either. At the least, Project Definition for an owner must include equipment schedules, material and finish selections and a management plan—none of these typically part of SD or DD. But Project Definition is not Construction Documents either. CDs are full of legal and technical details that don't interest the owner and are not in the owner's language.

Project Definition for the owner should be a clear inflection point in the process. If owner reviews are only a by-product of the march to CDs, it's likely that there will be fumbling and costly rework. Like the classic phases of SD, DD and CD, Project Definition for the owner should be a project milestone and be associated with a portion of the AE's total fee earned. It should be highly institutionalized with documentation and approvals tailored for each constituency. It's the point in the process when the AE says:

> *"Is this what you want? Do we have it all right?" If the final answer is 'yes,' the AE can say, "We have defined the requirements in your language. Now we can retire to our office and translate those requirements into construction language. And we don't need to bother you anymore."*

When that wonderful moment arrives, there is alignment. The project, as conceived and documented, is agreed to. After the owner approves all the components of Project Definition, the AEs should be free to produce the CDs with no further interaction with the owner. Although the owner's construction professionals and/or the Program Manager may review the production of CDs for compliance with requirements and for a general quality check, there should be no further need for a review of the design or the requirements.

Part of the problem in establishing a clear Project Definition point for the owner is that the traditional phases of design don't focus on that issue. There is no point of final approval that is defined as "everything the owner cares about in a language the owner understands." It's usually a by-product of the march to Contract Documents.

Sounds good but it's unlikely. New people will surface on the owner's team, a designer will have a late-arriving epiphany, new technology will emerge, demographics—or something else—will change. I suppose there have been projects for high volume serial builders that have had such a point of "no subsequent change" but I haven't seen it.

The future always brings the unexpected. A drop-dead date that cuts off all subsequent change is unrealistic and precludes the best result. The process should not prevent the inclusion of a valuable new idea, use of new technology, a response to a new research grant or some other valid requirement—even at the cost that downstream changes incur.

Some changes will be valuable. But capricious ones should be avoided.

But setting a clear point of final definition will at least get everybody's attention. After that point, a good manager will put a process in place to prevent capricious change. Perhaps there will be a committee to examine the benefit vs. effect on cost and schedule.

Most of the entitlement agencies have technical definitions of their requirements and the documentation they need. And AEs have plenty of experience preparing CDs for the contractors. But the information required to satisfy owners varies with each owner. The AE may not clearly understand what's needed to produce alignment. Indeed, the owners may not fully understand the scope of their interest either.

So a high value act in a capital improvement program is for the Program Manager to define the scope of the owner's interest. What's new here?

What's new is rigor. It takes a disciplined and comprehensive process to uncover and think through all the issues before they become trip-wires and land mines during CDs and construction.

What's new is media. AEs typically start drawings too early. Much of this information can be covered in the first few weeks with inexpensive alphanumeric documentation.

What's new is the Program Manager's role. The Program Manager, who has the benefit of experience from multiple projects with the owner, should have most of the fundamental decisions outlined at the start of the project. Then the job is to manage decision-making.

The Program Manager manages decision-making.

Go slow at the start so you can go fast at the end.

What's new is budgeting. Some clients still believe they must design a project before they can get a price. Yet it's not necessary. For most projects, particularly similar projects in a program, we don't need a design to know how big it should be, what systems it should use, how long it will take to build and establish an achievable budget. A Program Manager must methodically pull the knowledge together, understand and define the relationships, anticipate the hurdles and place each issue and each body of knowledge in its proper place in the schedule. But you go slow at the start to go fast at the end.

Planning and scheduling definition

As I have frequently repeated—there are lots of people and lots of organizations involved in design and construction. Presenting a clear picture of the sequence of tasks and the desired outcome sure helps everybody get it right.

Repeatedly, during our research of continuous building programs, we heard variations on this simple theme: *plan what you are going to do before you do it.*

The most skillful Program Management groups looked for techniques to pull as much information as possible into the beginning of a project, make decisions as early as possible, deliberate on them carefully before they become inflexible in detailed drawings, ensure consensus among the stakeholders and then get the work done quickly before anyone can make a change.

In our research, the best Program Management groups tended to learn extensively from themselves. They built reservoirs of historical data to pump prime new projects. In a continuous building program, having good information at the beginning of one project can show that someone recorded information at the end of a previous project.

These groups developed extensive checklists of the systems, procedures and functional requirements. They used the checklists to kick off projects and build immediate momentum. When they didn't have ready-made decisions, they listed the decisions that needed to be made. In other words, in their instructions to AEs they not only listed what they knew they wanted, they also listed what they didn't know—the information voids and the issues that had to be decided. They then worked toward resolving the open issues as quickly as possible, concluding with Project Definition.

There is an old saw to the effect that there are three categories of knowledge:

1. what you know you know
2. what you know you don't know
3. what you don't know you don't know

The third category is the one that bites us. The objective is to use each project to move #3 to #2 and #2 to #1.

What you don't know can hurt you.

KICK-OFF INSTRUCTIONS TO AEs

A Program Manager should have a "requirements checklist" tailored to the program (similar in concept to CII's impressive PDRI tool) that documents the requirements for each of the three constituencies. The requirements checklist should be part of a general "Instructions to AEs" given to AEs at the start of a project.

Extreme examples of requirements checklists that we learned of in our research were used by Wal-Mart and Hines. (Wal-Mart with its 1800-item checklist and Hines with its 45-page checklist.) They spell out at the start of the project the decisions that must be made. Having such a simple tool is a huge benefit to Project Definition.

Of course, most projects are more individual than Wal-Mart or Hines projects. It's unlikely that the AEs or owners will be able to anticipate every decision that must be made. The process won't be perfect. However, the Program Manager can work with each AE on each project and continue to improve the instructions. Such a process is far more efficient than waiting for issues to surface, one at a time, as design progresses.

In addition to minimizing change and its cost, a clear Project Definition package produces two additional benefits:

Work is more efficient. People and organizations, the extended project team, will work more efficiently when they have a clear, comprehensive view of the project and they're free to produce CDs—and then construction—with all the decisions in hand.

A clear view makes work more efficient.

Quality begins with Project Definition.

Quality will increase. In design and construction, the only meaningful definition of quality is "conformance to requirements." So quality begins with Project Definition—if, and it's a big "if," we are precise about identifying all of the requirements. And it only works if we make sure that the extended project team understands.

In the best of worlds, Project Definition defines quality—owner requirements, entitlement agencies and construction technology requirements. Since quality is conformance to requirements, by necessity, quality is conformance to Project Definition.

METRICS FOR MEASURING SUCCESS

So the role of Project Definition is, among other things, to establish goals and consequently the criteria for measuring success. But one of the reasons there is so much argument about the best processes for design and construction is that there is so much variation in the goals. Indeed, leadership may change during a multi-year program. If so, the goals will likely change too—maybe in subtle, unwritten ways.

Setting goals, detailed and clear criteria for measuring success, in the initial instructions to AEs is a great way to mitigate the disruptions that are the result of inevitable change.

CATEGORIES OF CHANGE

Setting goals mitigates the disruptions of change.

Throughout my career, we've dreamed of doing a project without a change. We've not come close.

There are several different kinds of changes, not all are undesirable.

Owner-initiated changes

Sometimes owners changed their mind or perhaps they added or subtracted something. Perhaps their markets shifted, new technology came into being or new leadership had new ideas. Sometimes new users or tenants have new requirements that are conflicting. We've seen clients who simply didn't make up their mind about what they wanted until late in the game and the Program Manager didn't lead them to decisions and simply didn't explain the costly effect of changes that occur late in a project.

Incomplete documentation

Sometimes we've started construction with incomplete documentation or were tripped up by an entitlement agency that had requirements we missed. Sometimes the documentation for a construction contract was incomplete or flawed.

Errors and omissions

No AE has ever produced a flawless set of contract documents—even in the delivery of the most repetitious of prototypes. Maybe the AE has rushed to design, not spending the time or money for adequate definition up front. Sometimes the owner's Program Manager has negotiated harsh terms with the AE and the AE, in order to minimize loss, has understaffed the job.

External events

Sometimes weather, technology, economics, politics, markets or some other unforeseen event affected our projects.[6] In excavating for the foundations of the Santa Fe Convention Center, we exposed a lot of bones and were held up for months by a large team of archeologists. Retrofit, repair and alteration projects, particularly in occupied facilities, pose difficulties. We uncover unexpected conditions. Even in the best-planned projects, tenant and user needs will require a change in the project sequence.

A number of years ago, I was at a school board meeting, selling our services. A board member pounded the table and declared that they would not tolerate change orders. I explained that it's unreasonable to expect to deliver a building without changes. We didn't get the job.

We must accommodate change—and it's the Program Manager's job to think about the issues mentioned above (and a plethora of others that are unmentioned), evaluate the potential for change, plan and budget accordingly.

The Program Manager must be the one to plan for change.

6. The most extreme example of an unplanned event in my career was when we were moving back into Wedge 1 of the Pentagon after two years of renovation—on September 11, 2001.

Even the best Project Definition will not completely eliminate change. The Clark County School District in Las Vegas built prototype schools. They were able to reduce change orders from about 5% on the first edition, to less than one percent on subsequent projects. But they were never able to get to zero. Even though they were building on flat land in the desert with common soil conditions, there were inevitable differences in site conditions—and the project team added refinements to the documentation on each new project.

A STRATEGY TO MINIMIZE CHANGE

So here are some thoughts for minimizing change in a program.

Design flexible buildings

If the design of a building is flexible—adaptable to the unknown future—it will be more adaptable to changes that occur during design and construction.

Design flexible buildings for the unforeseeable future.

Over my career, I have often observed that our crystal ball is pretty cloudy. During design we are never able to forecast with much precision how we will actually use a building. Yet we constantly design inflexible buildings that are hard to adapt to the future.

Although we think we know what lies ahead, the future always surprises us. I can't think of a building more than five years old that is used exactly as it was planned. The most common mistake in building design comes from the user's belief that they know how it will function.

Many years ago, we reviewed a study of change in higher education facilities for a state university system. The objective was to see when a building was most apt to be remodeled. We thought that we would get a bell-shaped frequency pattern indicating that the most likely time for remodeling might be seven or ten years after initial occupancy. It wasn't. The most common time for remodeling was in the six months *before* initial occupancy. It took so long to design and build the facility that users figured that as long as the contractor was on site, they might as well make the changes that represented fresh thinking.

Wise clients avoid inflexible buildings.

Wise clients recognize that their crystal ball is cloudy as well and constrain their user groups to prevent requirements that would create inflexible buildings. But a Program Manager must help most clients to arrive at that realization.

Define requirements cumulatively and exhaustively

Over multiple projects, a Program Manager can build deep reservoirs of knowledge about the facilities to be constructed. And then they can develop logical and effective decision-making processes for the definition of individual projects. That process will call up the common project requirements from the reservoir and then clearly identify the unique requirements.

These processes can become abundantly detailed, focusing on extracting information and obtaining agreements from three multi-headed sets of organizations—the owner, the entitlement agencies and the constructors. The mission is to ensure that there is a meeting of minds, requirements are met and approvals are as complete and final as an imperfect world will allow.

These agreements, and the information and decisions they depend on, are not matter: you can't weigh them. But scheduling these weightless activities is as crucial as scheduling the assembly of tons of construction material. And this weightless, intricate process doesn't end until the project ends.

The efficiency of obtaining these agreements is the result of an accumulation of knowledge about the product to be built and the decision-making process of building it. That deep knowledge of product and process clearly accounts for the 37% cost swings that Ed Merrow reports and that we discussed at the beginning of this chapter. (See page 40.) And this efficiency produces remarkable time savings—exceeding 37%—and reduces that angst of wasted effort.

The opportunity to gather relevant knowledge from similar projects and organize the decision-making process is at the heart of Program Management. It's a contribution to design and construction unavailable to clients who view their building program only as a series of individual projects. And it's unavailable to CMs and AEs retained for a single project. It requires a Program Manager (perhaps the same individuals or companies that might otherwise be an AE and CM) who has the responsibility for multiple projects and has the wisdom, vision and insight to see the repetitive patterns available for continuous improvement in a building program.

The decision-making processes are all aimed at reaching agreement for requirements and approvals.

Gathering relevant knowledge from similar projects and organizing the decision-making process is the strength of the Program Manager.

Establish approval set points

The Program Manager must establish a process. Many design teams manage a project as an eyes-straight-ahead march to Contract Documents—with milestones for Programming, Schematic Design and Design Development along the way. It's a blunt process for defining requirements and obtaining approvals. A better and more realistic approach is for the Program Manager to define each of the many approvals that are required from each of the constituencies and provide that information to the design team at the project's start.

Then, when changes appear after an approval, it's the Program Manager's job to define the cost and schedule implications for the owner—quickly. It may also be wise for the owner to have a small committee or a well-placed executive to resist capricious changes from a user group.

Imagine this. You are Program Manager for a multi-building program. You pick the AEs for a project and give them a complete set of requirements from your database of previous projects that the owner has reviewed and agrees with. Then you give the AEs a detailed schedule of meetings for every approval that will be required. The schedule identifies points where each of the approvals is final. Then you pick the construction team and do the same.

Meanwhile, the subcontractors and manufacturers review all building systems and suggest improvements. They provide shop drawings to be integrated into a BIM model so the final construction documents are fully integrated. And all the submittals are part of the BIM model and approved on the day construction begins.

Well, we can't achieve perfection—but we can try.

Outsourcing Program Management

Some companies have in-house Program Managers. Others outsource the work. Many combine in-house and outsourced resources. But all need a smart, experienced and responsible executive who knows how to choose good firms, interlace the processes of design and construction with the owner's organization and evaluate the work products.

Some owner organizations become entrenched and inefficient, but so do permanently outsourced organizations. The solution is twofold: first is an in-house executive who can evaluate performance; second is comparative competition—for either an in-house or for an outsourced organization.

There are four classic approaches to outsourcing work that we nicknamed layer cake, ham and eggs, fruit salad and blue plate. Each strategy has its pros and cons. But there is much to be gained when an owner's organization collaborates with outsourced companies. Each will learn from the other.

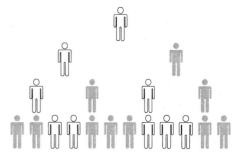

More school superintendents lose their jobs over a failed building program than a failed education program.

Dr. Nolan Estes, a good friend and advisor, has probably trained more school superintendents in his post-graduate curriculum at the University of Texas than any other educator in history. So he knows lots of school superintendents and has watched their careers. He told me that more school superintendents lose their jobs over a failed building program than a failed education program. With just a few changes in names, that story can be repeated for many organizations—public, institutional or private.

Organizations with building programs must control them with capable people or live with debacle, fiasco and calamity.

So this chapter is about the issues owners and Program Managers should consider in setting policies to get those people in place and produce happy results.

There was a day when many organizations—public, institutional or private—had large in-house AE and construction capabilities. The U.S. government used its own employees to build all projects until the early part of the 20th century and continued to build many projects with its own forces until mid-century. In 1941, it was government employees who designed and built the Pentagon.

The same was true for corporations: DuPont had an in-house construction company for most of the 20th century.

Some organizations manage their programs with in-house staff; some outsource the work; others combine in-house and outsourced resources.

Today, in-house design and construction organizations are uncommon. All the U.S. government organizations we interviewed, or worked with, outsource their construction. Most outsource their design.

But managing the program is a different matter. Some organizations have complete in-house groups of Program Managers. Others outsource the work to AEs, CMs or companies that specialize in Program Management. Many combine in-house and outsourced resources.

THE ARGUMENTS FOR OUTSOURCING

Remember Harry Truman's classic comment?

> *"Every time I ask an economist a question, the answer is 'on one hand, etc., etc., but on the other hand, etc., etc.' What I need is a one-armed economist."*

We carry the dismal science's guilt on this matter of outsourcing. So we'll present the arguments for both sides—and then drop a few convictions of our own.

Ed Feiner led the Design Excellence program at the U.S. General Services Administration (GSA). Ruminating on his career, he thinks it's not a good idea for an owner to outsource much Program Management. He says there must be people—employees of the owner's organization—who understand what they're buying and will ensure that the work is done properly, at a fair price, at the right time.

Bob Fraga was Manager of the Facilities Portfolio at USPS. He believes you can outsource everything—all Program Management services—except the fiduciary responsibility. There must be smart, experienced and responsible people on the owner's payroll who have the confidence of the owner's executives and understand how to buy services, evaluate the work products and interlace the processes of design and construction with the owner's organization.

It's hard to outsource fiduciary responsibility.

These two points of view sound different but there's no disagreement that these "smart, experienced and responsible" people need to understand how to buy and evaluate the services for the owner.

We agree. Strong in-house managers are invaluable—worth far more than they cost. If a manager has the full confidence of the owner's leadership, he or she is also worth a lot to outsourced design and construction teams. I can personally testify that weak client Program Managers who can't control the capricious whims of their leaders produce costly and troublesome projects. Furthermore, the design and construction companies that work for them lose money and deliver compromised results.

A strong in-house manager with the full confidence of the owner's leadership is valuable to outsourced teams. The weak in-house managers are bad clients.

GSA, the Corps of Engineers and the Naval Facilities Engineering Command have complete Program Management groups in-house.

Target has 600 people developing designs and managing construction. They have a powerful desire to control their brand and drive continuous improvement, but they like a balance of about 50/50 in-house/outsourced for design. Wal-Mart, a similar business, outsources considerably more than Target and is successful with its approach too. Both have impressive execution strategies.

Target does most of it in-house. Wal-Mart outsources.

Hines runs a lean organization. Hines manages a project with a strong regional Program Manager with an on-site Construction Management team backed up by fewer than a dozen people in the Conceptual Construction group.

So what's right? We struggled with this question and caved in on finding a universal best approach. Invariably, a unique approach was driven by a unique organization. A discussion of the various points of view is useful to raise the questions that may be examined for an individual program. And there were common concepts that reappeared.

CORE BUSINESS

The common argument for outsourcing is that an organization should stick to its core business and outsource to companies whose core business is managing construction.

The most common argument we hear for outsourcing is that an organization does best what it knows best. Executives should stick to their core business and hire organizations whose core business is managing construction. Managing in-house design and construction groups sidetracks the owner's executives. It takes time and adds to administrative chores. If a group isn't essential to the company's core business, it's a distraction. Furthermore, if an executive, no matter how smart, is unfamiliar with the technology and processes of design and construction he or she will make poor hiring choices—the you-have-to-be-one-to-know-one theory.

Many design and construction professionals want to be in an organization focused on their profession with opportunities for ownership and entrepreneurial rewards.

The argument continues that a core business shapes a company's culture: its reward mechanisms, its authority structure, its network of industry colleagues, how it deals with suppliers, customers and employees, and the things its executives think about at night. If its business isn't design and construction, its culture won't be appropriate for designers and constructors. The best professionals are inclined to gravitate to a company that has their profession as its core business. The cultural environment—the intellectual ambience of their profession—is important to them. They want to be in an organization where the conversations are about design and construction. They're interested in leadership in their own field, opportunities for ownership and entrepreneurial rewards.

So some owners cherry-pick top-notch consultants or sub-contractors that prefer the culture of a design and construction organization. It's unlikely that Michael Graves would have wanted to abandon the design-oriented culture of his company to be an employee of Target. And it's unlikely that Target would have much continuing use for him in their company. But Target could hire him to consult on prototype studies for their stores and design some of the products they sell—to the benefit of both.

Herman Miller has an enviable 50-year record of long-standing, mutually rewarding relationships with great designers such as Charles Eames, Bob Probst, George Nelson and Bill Stumpf. However, these designers would probably not have been comfortable as employees in a corporate manufacturing culture—even Herman Miller, a company that is extraordinarily committed to excellence in design.

Great designers would probably not be comfortable in a manufacturing environment— or any large bureaucracy.

Designers are likely to prefer the intellectual stimulation of a large urban environment to Zeeland, Michigan. But it seems that no observation on this matter is consistent. Herman Miller did attract some outstanding designers as employees. Alexander Girard was a permanent, long-term employee. (However, Girard came up for cultural air from Zeeland by spending considerable time in the artistically rarefied air of Santa Fe.)

These are all good arguments. However, this core business question isn't as slam-dunk an issue as the rhetoric above would have it.

But the core business argument isn't a slam-dunk issue.

First, part of this subject depends on the role a building plays in a core business. Although a company's core business may be retail, healthcare or education, its buildings may be crucial to success. In many cases, such as housing, a pharmaceutical lab, a restaurant or a theme park, the building makes a material, sometimes a crucial contribution to the success of the enterprise. The construction professionals may have a satisfying sense of higher purpose and a fulfilling career participating in the organization's mission.

An organization's buildings may play a vital role in its success.

Second, during our research we met (and during our careers we've worked with) many Program Managers who were permanent employees of their owner organization and were as good as they come. Often, repetitive projects gave them more expertise with their building type than any outside Program Manager they could have hired.

Third, some construction professionals have discovered that businesses other than design and construction can offer larger

Some businesses offer larger rewards, more stability than is traditional in the construction industry.

rewards and more stability than is traditional in the construction industry. And they may offer wonderful opportunities for personal achievement. While Michael Graves didn't join Target, Rich Varda, a talented architect and a Fellow of the AIA, did. And Jerry Lea may have more professional satisfaction at Hines than he ever would have had if he had remained a superintendent for a general contractor.

Continuous improvement

Owner is apt to staff internally if they are looking for a long-term program of continuous improvement.

Speaking of Lea, if an owner wants to keep polishing the result, even though it's a common building type, the owner is likely to staff internally to do so. Lea runs Hines' Conceptual Construction Group that has the responsibility to consolidate their project experience. Early in Hines' career as a developer, he decided that he wanted his company to learn from every project. What could make more sense? Most people would agree with that; few organize do it. But Hines has. Lea's mission is to make the next office building better than the last. And although there are millions of office buildings in the world, and Hines has built about 700 of them, they keep making them better.

Like so many ideas in Program Management, there are many paths to success. There are cases where an owner has had a continuing relationship with an outsourced firm to push continuous improvement. The Mayo Clinic has worked with Ellerbe (now Ellerbe Beckett) for nearly a century. However, most owners believe that having direct control over at least a small set of in-house employees to keep polishing the product is the best strategy for continuous improvement.

Compensation for managers who control large expenditures

Some owners outsource Program Management because their compensation policies won't allow them to hire the adequate expertise in-house.

Construction professionals control millions, perhaps billions, of dollars. Competent construction professionals get paid well. Some owners have an internal problem with that. We've seen this problem repeatedly in school districts that typically live with taxpayer scrutiny and paltry pay scales.

Consider a school district that suddenly has a large building program. A seasoned Program Manager who is experienced with big construction risks is likely to be able to demand more pay that anyone in the school district's administration—

including the superintendent. Yet the school board would be hard pressed to pay a director of facilities more than the superintendent. So they sidestep the problem and outsource to a company with the right talent. (As an aside, it's not uncommon for a university to pay their football coach more than their president. We may see some wise school board do the same for their construction leader—or better yet, pay the superintendent what he or she's worth.)

Some owners simply don't recognize how much money and risk their in-house Program Managers manage. The owners underpay and the managers underperform. One of the saddest spectacles is an organization with a low salary schedule that hires low-paid construction professionals to manage big construction projects. To save thousands of dollars in salaries, they mismanage millions in construction.

Another sad spectacle is a company that values the executives who serve the company's core mission and views construction professionals as second-class citizens. So the company hires second-class professionals. The second-class professionals hire second-class firms and produce second-class facilities for first-class prices.

A sad spectacle is a company that views construction professionals, who manage millions, as second-class citizens.

Our own industry isn't free of this kind of internal prejudice. AE, CM and construction organizations are apt to pay their construction people well and then make similar mistakes in underpaying in-house lawyers and accountants.

COMMODITIES AND PROPRIETARY PROCESSES

Some owners outsource because they think it's cheaper than building their own staff. If a professional service is a commodity, easily available, it's likely they will be right.

If a design, construction or management task is common, it's unlikely that an owner can build an in-house group that will be competitive in cost or quality with what is available from the marketplace. So organizations that watch their bottom line are inclined to outsource a commodity service.

It's unlikely that an owner can build an in-house capability for common tasks as cheaply as what is available from the marketplace.

But if owners have proprietary processes, or if they must do something unusual, or if they must be prepared for an emergency, or if they have a mission-critical function, they will likely build their own staffs.

Owners with proprietary or unusual processes will likely build their own staffs.

Clearly, the proprietary nature of the production processes in a competitive industry is one of the motivations to have in-house capabilities at a company such as DuPont.

And when Disney builds a theme park, there is a powerful desire to have creative control. Of course, there is a lot of specialty construction—fake rocks; aged wood; walking, talking, furry mechanical creatures; thrill shows and rides. People experienced in managing the design and construction of these things don't grow on trees. But even if they did, Disney probably wouldn't outsource to them. Their commitment to creative control is too deep.

So Disney manages it themselves. They build shops to make their creatures and assemble designers and engineers to design their shows and rides. And if something on one of the rides were to break and children were left in a tunnel or up in the air, Disney couldn't wait for an outsourced crew from town to be available, so they have their own emergency construction crews.

When Disney built Disney World in Florida, they retained Tishman Construction to manage the program, but there was always an on-site Imagineering management team managing the manager.

In Orlando, with Disney as a core attraction, other theme parks came to town. They didn't have the in-house design and construction capabilities that Disney had, so private sector companies formed to do specialty construction.

Soon there were several companies around Orlando making old wood and fake rocks and building attractions. But Disney's overriding culture of maintaining absolute control of creative work was too strong to let much work out to non-Disney companies. They kept the work in-house.

Disney Development managed the roads, power plant, utility construction, hotels and administration buildings, but Walt Disney Imagineering designed and managed the construction of the theme parks. They kept the shops that did audio animatronics, skins, furs and feathers and character heads, and they husbanded the unique and specialized talent to design its shows and rides—those wonderfully creative skills that are core to Disney's success.

DELEGATING RISK

Some owners have said that delegating work to an outside Program Management firm minimizes risk. Well, probably not.

Ultimately, an owner owns all the risk of project delivery and it's fiendishly difficult to delegate management risk. Here's why. A Program Management company must always act in the interest of its client—must sit on the owner's side of the table. If an owner assigns risk (cost or schedule guarantees) to its Program Manager, it moves the Program Manager across the table—at least a little bit. The collaborative transparency clouds up.

An owner owns all the risk of project delivery. No way around it.

Furthermore, if an executive assigns risk to a Program Manager and the Program Manager fails, how do you think the organization will view the executive who made the assignment?

However, it's certainly sage strategy for an owner to farm out work to a Program Manager with greater expertise and experience in managing design and construction risk than the owner has in-house.

RESOURCE LEVELING

There's a convincing argument for outsourcing to level peaks and valleys in staff requirements. All organizations, particularly public organizations, have difficulty trimming staff when work slows. One public owner told us:

> *"I want people I can fire if I need to."*

Conversely, finding good people, training them and getting them in a functional position always lags the demand when the workload grows. So outsourcing is often a good idea.

LEARNING FROM SPECIALISTS

Another argument is that an in-house Program Management team can learn from outsourced consultants. Any smart owner will realize that it's a good idea to bring in highly specialized talent to deal with specialized problems. Since our company frequently learns from competitors when we work in joint-venture or from consultants who work for us, and since we frequently learn from our clients, we buy this argument wholeheartedly.

Outsourcing for learning also makes sense.

Entrenched in-house groups can build empires, become calcified and inefficient.

CONTINUITY AND COMPETITION

Throughout this book we stress the value of continuity in people, processes and products to a building and maintenance program. But many owners feel that entrenched in-house groups, untested against the hard anvil of competition, will build empires, become calcified and inefficient. We've certainly seen some groups that fit that description. The solution to that problem is an owner executive who can judge the productivity of the in-house organization. And the best way to judge is comparison. That means outsourcing some of the work.

Government agencies, institutions, consultants and self-appointed civic action groups often do studies comparing the cost of in-house Program Management to the cost of outsourcing the work.

In our experience, if the study is done by the owner organization, the real overhead cost of the institution isn't properly included. If done by an outside management consultant, the complications of governance are ignored and the compared services are unequal. The evidence is so inconsistent and ephemeral that the conclusion typically favors the researcher's point of view.

But, clearly, continuity is beneficial. The FMI study mentioned earlier reported that owners who concentrated their service providers into a few continuing relationships tended to lower their management costs by 30%. (See page 23.) We suspect that if FMI had measured performance, it would have improved as well.

Outsourced relationships can get cozy and inefficient too.

However, continuing outsourced relationships can get cozy and inefficient too. So here is the big question: how do you keep a Program Management group, in-house or outsourced, sharp?

The first requirement is to have those "smart, experienced, responsible" owner executives who can judge the productivity of both their in-house and their outsourced organizations.

Second, combining in-house people with outsourced people tends to keep both on their toes.

Third, some owners staff their team with people from more than one Program Management company. They all know they will be judged by the others. One owner said:

"We want the fewest possible organizations working for us as long as we still have competition. That means two."

INTEGRATING AN OUTSOURCED STAFF

So if you buy the argument that there is value in combining in-house with outsourced staff, the next questions—often overlooked—are these:

If you outsource work to a Program Manager to help manage your building program, and if you have people in your organization who do that work too, what is the relationship between your employees and the employees of the outsourced staff? Who is the boss? Do they work together or are they separate? If separate, how do you divide up the work? If together, how do you arrange teams?

There are four classic approaches for outsourcing Program Management. We gave them nicknames.

HAM AND EGGS

An owner can retain an outsourced Program Management company to assume part of an owner's program, leaving another part of the program to the owner's in-house staff.

Assume the owner simply carves out a portion of the building program and contracts with a Program Management company to manage it. Perhaps a school district assigns new construction authorized by a bond program to an outsourced company and assigns continuing remodeling and repair to its internal staff. Or perhaps a retail chain that is accelerating its roll-out of new stores gives the accelerated portion of 10 stores to the outsourced company and 10 that are part of a continuing program to an in-house group.

A nice characteristic of this approach is the clarity of responsibility. The Program Management company can accept specific assignments and report directly to an executive in the owner's organization. The Program Management company can use its own systems and procedures and get started quickly. Since the owner's Program Management organization is separate from the outsourced firm, the owner doesn't have to worry about integrating different cultures. Each organization can keep its own ground rules and habits.

Who is the boss? How do you divide up the work? If together, how do you arrange teams?

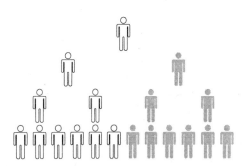

An outsourced Program Manager can assume responsibility for a set of projects while the in-house staff manages the rest.

Dividing the work between in-house staff and an outsourced company has clarity of responsibility.

The separate organizations are intellectual silos.

However, the separate organizations are intellectual silos—stovepipes that don't learn from one another. The owner will get different formats for their status reports and leveling contingency funds across different projects will be harder. The benefits of rotation will be fewer (see *Rotation, Repetition and Refinement*, page 17), and the ability to make program-specific checklists for Project Definition will be reduced. (*See Program and Project Definition*, page 43.)

There will probably be some responsibility overlap in the program. And it's likely that someone will compare the performance of the two groups; it's more than likely that the owner's group and the outsourced group will get competitive and cause some grief.

LAYER CAKE

An owner can retain an outsourced Program Management company and assign its management to the in-house Program Managers.

Many organizations with internal Program Management groups simply ask them to increase their staff for a peak load by contracting with an outsourced company for some of the work. The outsourced company reports to someone at the grass roots of the owner's group. Sometimes the owner's organization retains multiple Program Management firms.

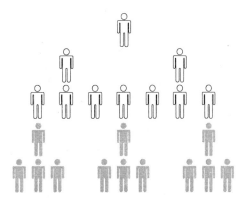

An outsourced Program Manager can assume responsibility for some projects and report to the in-house project managers. An in-house Program Manager can retain multiple outsourced Program Managers.

There is clear responsibility for the assignment. However, the outsourced company is likely to be buried in the client's organization and micro-managed by people in the owner's organization who are project managers themselves. They may expect the outsourced program managers to use the owner's procedures and standards and the owner's control and reporting systems (although they may be inferior). Because the outsourced company is unfamiliar with them, it's likely that the owner's staff will feel the outsourced company doesn't perform as well as the owner's own organization.

It is hard to define the division of responsibility between the in-house project manager and the outsourced company. And there will be finger pointing when the inevitable problems arise. Of course it *can* work—if the owner's group understands best practices and has the experience and capabilities that are better or at least as good as those of the company they're managing. But we've seen organizations with a board that said something like this:

> *"We haven't done much building in the past so I don't think our facilities department has the experience to run our big new program. Let's go out and hire the best firm in the world to manage it. Then they can report to our facilities department and we won't have to worry about things."*

Fat chance! They'll have plenty to worry about. It's nearly impossible for a professional service company to exceed the competence or the vision of its client. It's unlikely that the best firm in the world will do any better than the inexperienced facilities department would have done by itself because that firm will be taking direction from inexperienced people with narrow concepts who will make the wrong decisions.

Layer cake as an outsourcing concept will perform no better, and perhaps worse, than the bottom tier of people in the owner's organization that controls the services. Of the four approaches, it's apt to be the most troublesome. But like most of the points I make in this book, there are always exceptions. An organization with a highly competent facilities group with highly competent managers is likely to use the layer cake approach. If the owner's senior project managers who control the outsourced firms know their business, are willing to teach the outsourced firms the owner's procedures and create continuing relationships, it's apt to work.

Layer cake will perform no better than the bottom tier of people in the owner's organization would have performed.

The Los Angeles Unified School District program is, as of this writing, the largest building program in the U.S. LAUSD combines fruit salad and layer cake approaches. They cherry-pick talent from a number of companies that are working under evergreen contracts and sprinkle it among the Program Management staff who are LAUSD employees. Then they assign the design and construction management of some of their projects to individual firms.

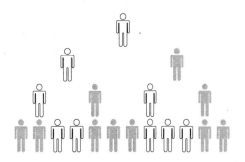

FRUIT SALAD

Some organizations with internal Program Management groups outsource part of the staffing by simply selecting key jobs they need to fill and contracting with one or more companies to

Some owner organizations cherry-pick talent from one or multiple outsourced companies and integrate the people in their own organization.

provide individuals to fill the spots. They rent people and take the responsibility to lead them. The Program Management team is a mixture of the client's employees and the outsourced company's employees.

It's successful with the right leadership. The Los Angeles School District program ($19 billion and counting) and the Pentagon renovation ($1.2 billion including the reconstruction after 9/11) both use this approach. When it's time to fill a new slot, the owner provides the job description to several firms that have evergreen contracts. The firms reply with resumes and the owner picks the best candidate.

The fruit salad approach works well but requires outstanding leadership at the top of the organization to integrate in-house and outsourced staff. Of course, this wouldn't work with an inexperienced facilities department as the leader. The Pentagon and LAUSD have great leadership.

Blue plate

There are some owners who don't have an in-house Program Management group and have no intention to ever have one. They believe in the stick-to-your-core-business argument. They choose to keep out of design and construction management entirely. So they simply out-source the whole show to a Program Management company that takes complete responsibility for the program.

Nevertheless, the owner still needs that "smart, experienced, responsible" employee with the confidence of the owner's leadership to manage the outsourced effort. Such a manager doesn't necessarily have to be an experienced construction professional.

Lee Evey was the manager of the Pentagon renovation before and after 9/11. He had master's degrees in public administration and education. We've never worked with a better leader from an owner organization. I once asked him if he felt that his lack of technical education was a problem. He said:

> *"My problems are people problems. If I can fix them, they will fix the technical problems."*

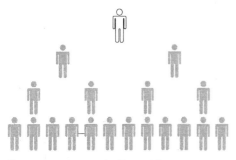

Some owner organizations outsource everything but the leadership.

We also agree with Bob Fraga that an organization shouldn't outsource its fiduciary responsibility. An organization needs its own respected employee to judge and report if the Program Manager is doing a good job or messing up—someone who, as Bob says, "knows how to buy services, understands how to evaluate the work products and knows how to interlace the processes of design and construction with the owner's organization."

A key manager who knows how to buy talent when it's necessary and do without it when it's not required, is likely to be far more valuable to an organization than the head of a big in-house department who wants to build an empire.

BRASS TO BRASS

These arrangements sound easier than they actually are. Unfortunately, fitting people and organizations together is a lot harder than fitting buildings together.

Things go wrong. Jealousy and politics emerge. People in the owner's organization get crosswise with outsourced people and there are inevitable project hiccups that stir dissension. The owner's organization changes policies or modifies a plan and the redirection causes frustration to the outsourced company.

In all of these cases, there's a crying need for the owner's executives to have a personal relationship with the leadership of the outsourced company. The relationship needs to form at the start of the program when no one is defensive about a problem. It needs to be a friendly, trusting, brass-to-brass relationship between the leaders of the owner's organization and the leaders of the outsourced company. Here's why it's necessary and why it needs to form at the start.

Somewhere along the line, something will go wrong. It always does. When problems occur, teams will point fingers. That corrodes collaboration. If there is a trusting relationship between the leaders, they can get into the problem and set a direction rather than let a problem fester down in the ranks. (See *Problems Can Polarize Organizations*, page 287.)

As the program progresses, there inevitably will come a time when someone on the team becomes a problem. Maybe he or

An organization shouldn't outsource its fiduciary responsibility.

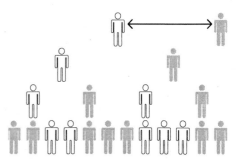

The owner's executives must have a personal relationship with the leadership of the outsourced company.

Something will go wrong. It always does.

Collaborative brainstorming will inform both executives.

Employees from the outsourced company need to feel a continuing relationship with their own company.

All of these outsourcing approaches work with good leadership.

The worst arrangement of all is when the concepts get mixed.

she won't be getting the work done or maybe he or she won't be collaborative. It could be the outsourced company's employee or the owner's employee. Chances are that if it's the outsourced company's employee the message will get to the owner's brass first—and vice versa. The two bosses need to know each other well enough for one to get the other on the phone to discuss this or other similar sensitive problems of human resources. No matter how "smart, experienced and responsible" the program leader is, the leaders of the outsourced company will have another set of experiences. A little collaborative brainstorming will give the owner's executive insight into lots of additional experience—and vice versa.

Meanwhile, the employees from the outsourced company need to feel a continuing relationship with their own company. If they think they have been rented to the project they may not see a career path beyond the program they're assigned to. They see people in their company climbing ladders that are unavailable to them. As the program winds down, they may start looking for another job. The owner's leader will be wise to make the outsourced company leaders visible and influential in setting strategy and policies. That will give the seconded employees continuing contact with their company leadership—and will likely improve the program strategy.

All of these approaches (ham and eggs, layer cake, fruit salad and blue plate) can work when good leadership from both the client's organization and the outsourced Program Management company is aligned.

The worst arrangement of all is when the concepts get mixed and the outsourced company leadership is ignored. We had a project where a client gave our company specific assignments for a set of buildings (ham and eggs), told us exactly how to staff the projects (fruit salad), and then we got directions from everyone in the client's facility organization (layer cake). Nobody in the owner's organization had any time for our executives. It was not a pretty sight.

Conversely, wonderful professional experiences come from well-led, clearly organized collaborations between owner organizations and outsourced companies that share the same vision.

WHERE'S THE BALANCE?

So, what do you do in-house and what do you outsource? Like all theories in the construction industry, the right decision is invariably situational and individual. None of the arguments about what should or should not be outsourced are consistently true. With a little research one can find examples to support either side of the question.

Repeatedly, we stumbled up against a fundamental realization. There are similarities among programs but there is also infinite variability. In deciding an outsourcing strategy the trick is to have the good sense to take stock of the human resources available on either side of the fence—and then figure out what is right for the program. It won't be the same as any other program.

However, after all the argument, there is clear value in combining in-house staff with outsourced resources. On one hand, the owner must have a trusted "smart, experienced and responsible" manager to consolidate and control the owner's many demands for design and construction services and to select, contract and manage the needed services. There can be in-house staff for continuous improvement, proprietary processes, core specialties and for services that aren't readily available on the market. On the other hand, the owner may be wise to outsource for commodity services and products, resource leveling, highly specialized talent that isn't needed on a continuing basis and high-paid talent that would upset internal pay scales.

And, finally, most owners can search out the best firms in the industry and learn from them as they work together.

The decision is invariably situational and individual.

There is clear value in combining in-house staff with outsourced resources.

Organization

An organization that manages a design and construction program should have at least five key functional areas. It should have people to:

1. *Work with the owner organization to understand its needs and translate them into a capital program*
2. *Set project delivery strategy, select the project teams and control project execution*
3. *Develop and monitor budgets and schedules, develop procedures, maintain documentation and inform the Program Management and parent organization of the program status*
4. *Collect and improve institutional knowledge of functional requirements for buildings*
5. *Collect and improve knowledge of the best building systems and construction technology to support the facility requirements*

Those five classic functions may be performed by a small or a large team. They may be done by the owner's employees, by an outsourced company, by several outsourced companies, or, as is usually the case, by combinations of in-house and outsourced companies.

There are probably as many management structures as there are programs to manage.

This is a risky subject. Few issues create more discord than a discussion of organization. It's likely that owners invent as many organizations to manage their capital programs as there are owners with programs. And many different versions produce good outcomes. So it's hard to take a rigid position about the right way to structure a team of construction professionals.

The right organization will change if the people change; organizational structure should be influenced by the unique set of individual talents that populate the group.

And, of course, many organizations assign other functions such as real estate acquisition, leasing, legal reviews and accounting to their Program Management teams. We leave those functions out of this discussion of a generic organization, not because they are unimportant, but because they are not the subject of this book. Nevertheless, there are basic requirements for an inclusive Program Management organization.

PROGRAM MANAGEMENT FUNCTIONS

An organization's structure is analogous to its mission.

Think of it like this. An organization is a human analog to the mission. Said another way, the mission's requirements are defined, categorized and assigned to people. Then the people are assigned to boxes in an organization that have the responsibility to satisfy one of the categories of the mission. So an organizational structure starts with a clear understanding of mission. Seems obvious, doesn't it?

Although missions vary with different programs, there are commonalities. They are to define the functional purpose and deliver facilities that satisfy the user's need; open for operations when planned; respect the economics of the organization with cost-effective execution; and maintain an image or grace a community with their presence.

And the Program Management group must accomplish these missions within constraints and social pressures such as environmental and sustainability commitments, concerns about energy consumption, myriad overlapping code restrictions, accommodation for the handicapped and pressures to use small or minority businesses. All this is going on in a world of changing technology that affects the way we manage information and execute construction.

The Program Management organization will have groups of people who specialize in these common missions and respond to these common constraints and pressures.

We will invent titles too. We will call them:

- Facility Executive Officer (FEO)
- Facility Information Officer (FIO)
- Facility Operations Officer (FOO)

I like these titles because they relate to the classic corporate titles that are recognizable and understandable. A classic American corporation has a trio at the helm: a Chief Executive Officer (CEO), a Chief Financial Officer (CFO) and a Chief Operations Officer (COO).

Although there's a lot of variation with different companies and individual personalities, typically the CEO sets strategic direction, drives change and represents the organization with the major clients, the public, the board and the shareholders. The CFO stays on top of the details of performance across the total operation and the COO sees to it that the organization is doing its job. It's a useful categorization of responsibility that has evolved with many companies over many years.

These leadership team concepts may be successfully exported to a Program Management group. Similar functions exist in managing a design and construction program.

Unfortunately, there is no common pattern of titles as there is for the key officers in a corporation; they seem to be invented for each program. But the next writer on this topic will probably use different titles that will be just as good. Probably the title "Program Executive Officer" might be used in an outsourced company while an in-house group might use the title "Facilities Executive Officer."

In addition to this tripod of leadership, the program should have three other positions:

- project managers who organize, monitor, control and document project delivery
- a building systems and equipment officer who defines the best construction technology
- a facility requirements officer who defines the functional requirements to serve the owner's requirements

A program may well be run by a tripod of leadership much like a corporation. The FEO networks with users, administrators and leaders of the extended program team. The FOO staffs, trains and manages the project managers. The FIO minds the store and keeps everybody's attention on the program status.

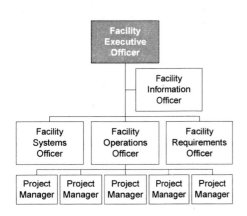

The FEO is the boss but must spend much time with users, administrators and leaders of the companies that work for the program—outside of the day-to-day program activities.

Here is a generic description of these officers and the supporting groups:

The Facility Executive Officer (FEO)

The FEO is in many ways similar to a corporate CEO. He or she is the boss and the primary officer responsible to the owner's parent organization.

The FEO must have a trusting relationship with the owner's key administrative officers and must spend priority time maintaining those relationships. If he or she is to be effective in the mission to develop suitable facilities for the organization, he or she must learn to interpret the signals from the owner's leaders, users and administrators; add specialized judgment from the construction industry; set strategy and guide in the development of the capital plan.

The FEO will also spend time with the public and will cultivate brass-to-brass relationships with the leaders of the AEs, contractors, major suppliers and subconsultants. These crucial roles are time consuming. Because of these command performances, ceremonial occasions and interpersonal networking responsibilities, the FEO needs someone who minds the store all day, every day.

To fulfill the FEO's primary responsibility for the success of the program and to exercise appropriate judgment in directing the operations, the FEO must know what's going on. He or she must have timely and accurate knowledge of the operations. That requires a staff of reliable people and reliable systems.

People

Much of the FEO's time will be spent simply talking to people—the owner's users and leaders and the key professionals in the Program Management organization. To a large extent, he or she will count on personal insight to stay informed. So the FEO must have a clear, uninterrupted chain of command and a reliable flow of information from project managers in the field.

Systems

Twenty-first century managers also have information systems to augment human interaction. These information systems allow leaders to turn around in their chair at their desk, punch a few keys and open a window into their program. Then they can review the vital signs or drill down to fine detail if there is a need. They can look at raw facts, un-spun by layers of management.

Furthermore, these information systems are tools that leaders can use to structure and bring order to the extended program team. So, in addition to the personal networks, the FEO must have an accurate, comprehensive management information system to provide near real-time facts on the status and projected outcomes of the projects.

But the FEO must make the systems work. These systems require input from project managers (or the project manager's staff). And there are precious few project managers who will maintain their input chores without regular executive encouragement. (How many times have I heard, *"I'm too busy managing the job to fill out those forms."?*) So the system will fail unless the FEO instills discipline throughout the organization to maintain accurate data input.

In addition to the free flow of information from the project team, and from a system, FEOs must have someone at their elbow who is monitoring the entire program information store and can get the FEO's attention to potential problems. That person is the Program Chief Information Officer (FIO).

The Facility Information Officer (FIO)

The FIO minds the store. He or she must monitor the details of the entire enterprise, note the hiccups and find the ticking bombs. He or she crunches the data required for the capital plan and reports on the progress as it is being executed. The FIO must manage the cost and schedule control groups who have the responsibility for such crucial matters as cash flow projections, controls and reporting on budget transfers within a program, contingency control, cost forecasting, contract tracking, payments, auditing and project close-outs.

Sid Sanders, who led both the University of Texas and the Methodist Hospital billion dollar programs, said:

> *"Simply put, in a program of multi-$100 million projects, aggressive schedules, multiple GMPs, early starts with a limited amount of the project budget 'locked,' the financial monitoring is vital. If I let a major project get out of financial control I will possibly be looking for another job."*

The FIO stays on top of the entire program and keeps the program team and the owner informed about the status.

The problem is the FEO doesn't have time to do this crucial job. The FEO's hide depends on the talent, commitment and skill of the FIO. The FIO's responsibility doesn't stop with the financial responsibility. While the FEO is dealing with the outside activities and the FOO is focused on the operational specifics, the FIO is looking across the entire landscape of activity and reporting on the status.

The other key leaders are regularly distracted by their special obligations. The FEO may need to be working with the owner organization's leaders to help adjust the development strategy, or there may be a ceremonial ground breaking to attend, a political knot to unravel or an employee problem to solve. The Program Operations Officer may be busy pulling a project out of the ditch, training or recruiting.

The FIO is the person who should maintain a detailed, current, comprehensive review of the program's vital signs and present it to the key leaders regularly.

So the FIO is the flag waver, the person who should maintain a current, comprehensive review of the program's vital signs. Then the FIO must get the attention of the entire Program Management organization and the owner's administrative staff and present the status of the capital plan and possible threats to success. The FIO should also understand the fine details of the program and report to the FEO on a regular basis with personal insight.

The job calls for a heavyweight. The FIO must be part of the triumvirate of leadership that runs the show. He or she must have a status in the Program Management organization comparable to a CFO in a corporation. Unfortunately, it is seldom so.

The crucial importance of the FIO's job is often ignored or understaffed with technical rather than managerial people.

Most Program Management organizations fail to recognize the crucial importance of this position. Burdened by limited vision inherited from project management traditions, the job is often titled "Controls Manager" and staffed by a technician experienced in CPM (critical path method) scheduling and project cost accounting or a computer jockey who is facile with one of the packaged project management control systems. These technicians lack the managerial clout to demand accurate and timely reporting from the project managers, and they lack the experience to anticipate the problems and interpret the status of the program.

Or worse yet, it may be that project managers keep project information on spreadsheets tucked away on personal computers.

When quarterly reports are due to a board or some other governing body, there is a donnybrook of information gathering and long weekends of preparation. Meanwhile, the program leaders don't know what's going on.

So there must be a person to maintain the program facts, make sure the vital signs are in view and understood, and make sure the executives react quickly to emerging trends.

There must be a person to maintain documentation and report on vital signs.

This is also the person who can push "print" on a computer when it's time for a report to the board so the team can spend their time managing the delivery of projects. This job is similar to that of a Chief Financial Officer in a profit-making corporation. Let me explain the analogy.

- Profit is the core mission in a typical for-profit organization. It's prerequisite to existence. The CFO's responsibility is to use financial data as an analog of corporate activity to report on the organization's condition. The CFO uses information technology that relies on accurate financial transaction inputs from people throughout the organization. In any good corporation, there is regular and consistent discipline in maintaining this flow of financial information. If the discipline fails, the organization is at risk—moving ahead in the dark, like sailing at night without radar.

- Delivering required facilities on-time and in-budget is the core mission for a Program Management organization. Like profit in a profit-making organization, this is prerequisite to existence. Just like a CFO in a for-profit corporation, the FIO should use information on the original plan, the current status and the forecast outcomes of cost, schedule and scope to report on the condition of the program. And just like financial data in a corporation, there must be regular and consistent discipline in maintaining this information flow. And once again, if the discipline fails, the organization is at risk.

To meet this mission, the FIO must have staff that includes people capable in the following areas:

Controls
The FIO's organization must maintain and report on the status of the capital plan, produce and maintain the master schedules,

prepare conceptual estimates and budgets, establish and monitor schedules.

Program Management Information Systems

The FIO should maintain a web-based Program Management information system (PMIS). It should inform the extended program team on the state of the program. It should include on-line, web-based central filing, document control, information processing and an on-line policies and procedures manual. (See *Program Management Information Systems*, page 203.)

The PMIS should have checklists of the owner organization's compliance requirements and the regulatory approval programs that control the individual projects. These requirements change frequently. A web-based system makes it easy to update the policies for everyone—there is only one place to make the change. The FIO should continuously review the data that flows in from the field for completeness and accuracy and blow the whistle if project managers produce flawed or incomplete input.

Project accounting

As project and Program Managers approve requests for payment and enter them into the PMIS, the project accountant will check them against contract provisions and previous and projected payments and pass them on to the owner organization's accounting department for payment. They will report on the financial status of the program.

The Facility Operations Officer (FOO)

The FOO recruits, trains, monitors and manages the project managers. He or she studies the process and drives continuous improvement. But like the FEO, the FOO will be distracted by special opportunities or problems. He or she will be engaging in a firefight one day, attacking a schedule overrun the next, recruiting the next and managing a crash start-up the next. Without the regular monitoring of the entire program by the FIO, problems may go unnoticed.

In some programs, the #2 person is called the deputy. That's a mistake, for two reasons.

1. The term "deputy" implies a person with similar responsibilities in an assistant role. The jobs of the FEO and FOO are different.

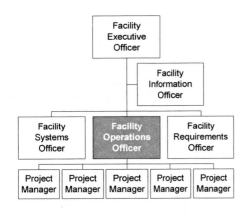

The Facility Operations Officer is responsible for recruiting, training, monitoring and managing the project managers.

2. Although the FOO reports to the FEO, he or she is not an assistant. And the FOO is not necessarily the #2 position. The FOO and the FIO are both #2.

The core mission of the FOO is to build a strong team, to develop a cadre of project managers and guide them in managing the execution of the capital plan. Although the FEO may select key employees from time to time, the FOO should direct recruiting, training and mentoring of the project managers.

Additionally, the FOO absorbs information from the entire program, develops good institutional judgment and then turns that judgment into documented procedures.

The FOO and the project managers should identify common aspects of projects to define best practices in project workflow. They should also modify and maintain descriptions of the design and construction processes, continuously improve the documents and forms necessary to implement these processes and advise the FIO on how to update the policies and procedures manual.

The FOO (with support from project managers) manages the project delivery strategies and the selection of project teams (AEs, consultants and CMs). Certainly, the FEO, the FIO, users and administrators may participate in these activities and may influence outcomes, but the FOO should manage the process and have much to say about the project team members.

The Project Managers
In general, the role of a project manager is to:

-   Manage the project team selection process with guidance from the FOO
-   Coordinate the interaction of the project team (designers and constructors) with the users, administrators and the FOO during design and construction
-   Participate in contract management—negotiation, execution and modifications such as change orders, RFIs, punch list control, close-out, etc.
-   Document and communicate project goals, requirements, budgets and schedules. Monitor the progress toward these goals and report on these vital signs. Assume responsibility for the accurate input of this information into the Management Information System

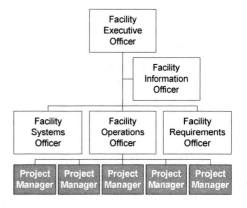

The project managers help assemble and organize the project teams, run the projects and keep the Program Management organization informed about the details of execution.

- Alert the FOO if projects vary from stated goals (cost increases, schedule delays, etc.)
- Lead the on-site project team in activities such as inspection and clerical functions

Project managers are responsible for the accuracy and completeness of project information input to the PMIS.

Project managers (or their support staff) are the primary source of project information input to the PMIS and responsible for accuracy and completeness. To make sure there is a reliable flow of information and reporting, project managers must be employees of the Program Management organization, not employees of some decentralized functional part of the organization. For instance, if the Program Management group is a university system, the project manager may be located at a remote campus but should not be a member of the remote campus staff. If it's a hospital system the project manager might be on-site, but should not be a member of the hospital staff being served.

If program managers do not report directly to the Program Management organization—with their compensation and promotions controlled by the central Program Management organization— it's unlikely that the data will be accurate and timely or the project managed in compliance. Reports to the owner organization will be flawed.

The Building Systems and Equipment Group

The capital plan offers an important opportunity for continuous improvement and economies of scale in the design and purchase of building materials and systems. The Building Systems and Equipment Group has the responsibility to capture that opportunity.

The Facility Systems Officer has the responsibility to determine and continuously improve the best building systems and materials for the program.

The Group should establish and continuously improve standards and guidelines for building systems and equipment they determine to be best for the owner organization's facilities. They should consult with program and project managers and review project plans and specifications for consistency with the standards. They would maintain and update policies for safety and risk management and provide forensic support after substantial completion.

The Group has a clear opportunity to become more expert than the AEs they retain for individual projects. They can collect and assemble experience from the project teams (architects, engineers, contractors, specialty subcontractors and manu-facturers) and then define the most appropriate building systems and materials for the facilities to be built. And they have an opportunity to work with the facility managers at many locations to evaluate the buildings they produce. They should conduct peer reviews during design and post-occupancy evaluations. It would be sad to neglect learning—and documenting and passing on that learning—from this wealth of experience.

The Group may function as the owner's manager for some rotated professional services that set standards for building systems. For example, a project design team may include many consultants for specific tasks that are common for many buildings, such as roofing and damp-proofing, network data distribution, security, audio-visual, life-safety, food service, hardware and acoustics. (See the discussion of People in *Rotation, Repetition and Refinement*, page 23.)

Although these consultants are paid by the AEs, the source of funds must ultimately be the owner. It would create economies of scale, continuous improvement and better buildings if these consultants were hired directly by the Program Management organization. They can develop system-wide standards and provide those standards to project AEs to be incorporated into project plans and specifications and to review designs for compliance with the standards.

The overwhelming tradition in design and construction is to focus on projects. Each tends to have unique requirements and teams.

Yet, as we have said repeatedly, there are many similarities to be found across the program that can produce economies and better buildings. To neglect them, reinventing much of the work for every project, is to miss an opportunity for enormous savings in time and cost. The Building Systems and Equipment Group is the group that helps the FEO and the FOO drive this process.

The Facility Requirements Officer

This generic Program Management organization should develop a thorough understanding of the owner organization's functional requirements for facilities. And they must understand how best to maintain adaptability for future change. In many cases, part of their job will be to apply objective evaluations to the requests of

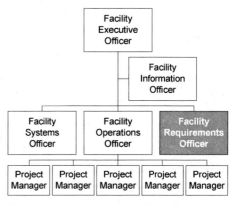

The Facility Requirements Officer has the responsibility to learn how best to house functional requirements of the owner's organization.

many decentralized operations, avoid capricious initiatives and balance building programs for the benefit and equity of the total organization.

Just as the Building Systems and Equipment Group should learn the best practices in building technology, the Requirements Group should learn the best way to configure buildings and equipment to satisfy the functional requirements of the owner organization.

The Requirements Group should gather the experience from each AE on each project. (In our interviews with serial builders in the private sector, we met many construction professionals who were far more knowledgeable about their building type than the AEs they retained to work for them.)

Many of the users will have good ideas about their requirements that need to be shared with other users with building projects. Some will have bad ideas that need discouraging. The same will be true of the AEs that execute the projects—there will be both good and bad ideas. So the Requirements Group should spread the good ideas and discourage the bad ones.

The people in the Requirements Group should have specialized building type expertise.

The Requirements Group should be composed of people with special building type expertise to support owner-wide projects. The Group should conduct peer reviews for projects that are under design, learn the best approaches from each of the projects and return to completed projects for post-occupancy evaluations.

The Requirements Group should have databases (eventually integrated into the PMIS) that record space and equipment requirements for the owner's building types. These databases should provide support in evaluating functional and space requirements for capital planning, master planning and for programming future buildings. They would set standards for space and equipment use.

CENTRALIZATION VS. DECENTRALIZATION

Many capital building programs have projects that are geographically dispersed. A state university will have projects spread across the state. A government will build at multiple locations across its jurisdiction. A retail chain may build nationally. A developer may build internationally. In these dispersed organizations that have strong user groups (such as a university system, a branch of the military or a healthcare network) tension will be inevitable. The users at decentralized locations will want to control their projects. But the administrators at the parent organization will want program control and accountability.

If the program is centralized, the regional users will usually have a low level of dissatisfaction. The regional groups will complain about their inability to get what they want. And indeed, there may be a danger that the centralized operation will be insensitive to regional needs.

A centralized program will have low levels of dissatisfaction at the local level.

A local leader, whether a college president, a base commander or a hospital administrator, expects service and wants to control the territory. Meanwhile, the centralized Program Management group must ensure compliance with policies and standards and must control schedules and budgets across the entire program. So the centralized Program Management function limits the autonomy and constrains the initiatives of the decentralized groups. That rankles the local leaders.

They will complain—and will do so effectively. The design and construction process is so fraught with unpleasant surprises that if someone wants to list mistakes, it's not hard to do. A central Program Management group will inevitably bear the brunt of many well-documented complaints. The local leaders will inevitably want a decentralized program.

So some organizations decentralize the program execution to avoid conflict and keep peace in the family. It is not a good idea. There will be cost overruns and idiosyncratic design. The organization will lose economies of scale and the accumulation of intellectual capital. Standards will vary and wheels will be regularly reinvented.

Some organizations decentralize the program execution.

Furthermore, the executive who wanted to escape conflict with decentralization will face a new problem. Each of the regional leaders will appear with their design and construction people arguing for needed resources. The executive will not have a centralized group to help analyze need and determine an equitable distribution of resources. Decisions will be political.

A Program Management organization should be centralized.

Despite the probability of some conflict, a Program Management organization should be centralized. The overriding reasons for centralization are inherent in the tasks. The organization's job is to:

- Assume single responsibility for results, ensure compliance with policies and report on the program status to the governance of the owner organization
- Establish program-wide controls for cost, schedule and scope
- Develop a thorough understanding of functional requirements and how best to maintain adaptability for future change
- Glean continuous experience from architects, engineers, contractors, specialty subcontractors and manufacturers and define the most appropriate building systems and materials for the intended use
- Build good judgment from continuous experience with the program, develop the best procedures for project delivery strategy and apply that judgment to capital expenditures
- Capture the benefits of resource leveling, specialization and economies of scale in staffing and in the procurement of goods and services that are inherent opportunities in a program
- Apply objective evaluations to the requests for facilities, avoid capricious initiatives and balance building programs for the benefit and equity of the total organization

So the right balance is to centralize Program Management and decentralize project management. Locating project managers close to the projects improves relationships with the users, develops a better understanding of user needs and will likely be more effective in managing the day-to-day details of design and construction activities.

However, the project managers must report directly to the Program Management organization, not to the regional leaders, or the Program Managers will not be able to get the facts and control results.

Design-Bid-Build

Often called the traditional process, design-bid-build isn't very traditional. It wasn't common in the U.S. until the late 19th century. But for most of the 20th century, for institutional and public projects, it was the blindly accepted, blithely unquestioned and predominant project delivery method. Why do so many owners, AEs, Construction Managers and Program Managers at the beginning of the 21st century shun it? Will it disappear?

Perhaps if we want to look forward, we should look back. It helps to understand where to go if we know where we are and how we got here.

❖

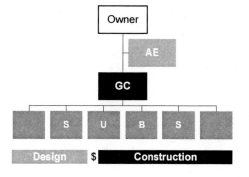

Design-bid-build is a compelling idea: design and specify what's wanted and ask contractors for a fixed price. What could make more sense?

However, when a product is as complicated as a building, a description of what is wanted requires expertise. And it takes expertise to make sure that the building that's delivered is what

The design-bid-build process requires an AE who is the agent of the owner. There weren't many professional AEs in America until the mid-19th century.

was designed and specified. Of course, architects and engineers provide that expertise. But there weren't many architects and engineers until the mid-19th century. AEs who are separate from construction organizations are a modern business arrangement. Except for the Renaissance, when many architects were artists, most of the architects in the history of Western civilization were also the builders. Design-bid-build didn't become common until independent firms of architects and engineers were common.

The early roots of training architects as a profession separate from builders can arguably be traced to 1648 with the founding of the Académie des Beaux-Arts in Paris (changed to Ecole des Beaux-Arts in 1816). Like the artist-architects of the Renaissance, their programs focused on understanding the classical architecture of Greece and Rome, not on building technology.

The Ecole des Beaux-Arts was the place where many American architects went for education well into the 20th century. It was two centuries after the founding of the Académie des Beaux-Arts before America would have an architecture school. There was no formal training of architects and engineers in the U.S. until the mid-19th century.

In the 18th century, when people in the American colonies wanted buildings, they typically hired craftsmen, not companies. The builders were the owners' employees (or their slaves). Simple buildings didn't require much architectural or engineering design.

Builders called themselves architects or engineers. For the few monumental projects, typically government buildings like capitols or courthouses, patricians with broad educations furnished the design. The architects were men like Thomas Jefferson, a politician, farmer, manufacturer and musician and William Thornton, a physician who designed our Capitol.

In 1784, Ben Franklin intended to build his new house in Philadelphia. A disputed lot line delayed the work. But Franklin had hired the workmen and was obligated for their wages, so he built an addition to his own house instead.

Jefferson was inspired by Palladio's architecture when he traveled to Italy during his residence in France. After the American Revolution, he returned home with the idea that the architecture of the first republic (ancient Greece) was appropriate for the new republic. He applied it to his home at Monticello and to the design of the University of Virginia.

Thornton's design for the Capitol was inspired by the Pantheon and the Louvre. The construction was carried out by workmen who were employed by the government. Thornton also designed the Octagon, a house for John Tayloe that later became the headquarters of the American Institute of Architects.

Despite these few and scattered monumental projects, craftsmen continued to design and construct most buildings well into the 19th century. They built houses from pattern books that provided rudimentary drawings. Sometimes groups of artisans—masons, carpenters, plasterers—would band together to make a house, barn, shop or sawmill for a price. But governments or institutions that wanted a building simply hired construction workers and built with their own employees.

Robert Mills (1781-1855) and Charles Bulfinch (1763-1844) are usually credited with being the first native-born Americans to become professional architects. Here is an interesting bit of trivia that illustrates the tiny size and cohesiveness of this collection of early 19th century American architects: Bulfinch's interest in classical architecture was influenced by Jefferson when Bulfinch toured Europe and visited Jefferson in France.

A profession forms

As the economy of the New World strengthened, owners needed multi-story buildings. Industrialization brought steel structures with central heat. By the time the century ended, buildings had elevators and electric lighting. The buildings were too complicated for apprentice-trained artisans. America needed the informed technical and creative energy of architects and engineers to build tall buildings and new cities. These men and women needed to be educated in the strength of materials, hydraulics, thermodynamics, electricity and the symbolic and aesthetic mission of design. MIT opened the first school of architecture in the U.S. in 1867. Others followed.

As the number of professional architects and engineers grew, the people who designed projects separated functionally, legally, organizationally and culturally from the craftspeople and workmen who built them. Architects and engineers left the mud and rain of on-site construction and moved indoors. They became professional agents of the owner rather than artisans selling their craft.

AEs acquired education and degrees. Following the lead of other professions, they sought professional status. They lobbied for laws that recognized them as professionals with standards similar

Dr. William Thornton's winning design for the U.S. Capitol in 1793. For his winning design, he received a prize of $500 and a city lot.

Charles Bulfinch designed Massachusetts General Hospital, completed in 1818.

The Second Leiter Building, in Chicago, was designed by William LeBaron Jenney and built in 1891. It is one of the first steel frame buildings in the United States. It's a milestone in the history of American architecture.

to those enjoyed by doctors, lawyers and accountants. They formed professional organizations like the American Institute of Architects (1857) and controlled entry into their profession with licensing.

With this rite of passage, the AE became the master of building technology. It was technology applied in an office, not in the field. The AE was the brains. The builder was the brawn.

Even then, the separation between design and construction wasn't complete. There was debate about whether masons and carpenters and other craftspeople should be allowed membership in the AIA. And it wasn't until 1926 that an amendment to the Public Buildings Act enabled the government to award design contracts to architects in private practice. It was driven by Andrew Mellon, then Secretary of the Treasury, who was committed to building the Federal Triangle in Washington, D.C. and wanted the country's best firms to design the buildings.

The last half of the 19th and the first half of the 20th centuries were the salad days of the profession. In 1950, an article in Fortune Magazine reported that architects were the most respected and best paid of the professions. But by 2000, both income and respect had diminished. By one report, only travel agents had greater reductions in average income.

The centroid of technical knowledge shifts

Ironically, in 1853, four years before architects founded the AIA, Elisha Graves Otis sold his first "safe elevator." Just as the AIA institutionalized architects as the technical experts in the construction industry, a manufacturer put a major system product in a building that the manufacturer knew more about than the architect.

Much building construction moved from the field to the factory.

At that seminal point, technical expertise began its inexorable move from AEs to manufacturers and specialty subcontractors. From then on, buildings got more complicated. And every year saw more of a building made in a factory. They were no longer masonry and iron with a little plumbing and some light bulbs. They were sophisticated assemblies of industrialized components designed by specialized manufacturers and integrated by architects and engineers. They included cooling and complex energy controls, synthetic insulations, exotic sealants, communication systems, life safety systems and security systems.

Here's one simple example. In 1950, there were only a handful of choices of glass for glazing. You could pick 3/32" crystal, 1/4" plate or do a special order of a few other products. By the end of the 20th century, a catalog of the different performance characteristics of tinted, reflective and insulated glass would be several inches thick and understanding the differences in performance would provide enough material for a five-hour college course.

The role of architects and engineers began to shift. Instead of designing all the components of a building, architects and engineers evaluated and integrated products designed and fabricated by manufacturers.

The emergence of the architecture and engineering professions and the ensuing separation of design from construction in the 19th century meant more than better design; there was a whopping big additional benefit.

The AE's job was not just to apply technical knowledge to the design of a building; the AE made the drawings that were the core of a contract. Construction drawings that showed the building's configuration, the assembly methods and the amount of materials could also be a contract document. A contractor could measure the drawings, read the specifications and agree to build the project for a price.

Now owners had someone to define the project and someone to evaluate whether they were getting what they bargained for. With a set of drawings and an AE at their side, owners could make a deal with a construction company: a building for a price. And the AE was there to make sure the construction company did their job right. So design-bid-build emerged and became the dominant project delivery method. It was good for owners, AEs and contractors.

- With design-bid-build, owners could know the cost before starting construction.
- Since owners needed AEs for both the design and the documents to facilitate the deal, the process fueled the development of the profession. Where large corporations and the government had previously staffed up with their own

Architects and engineers made it possible for owners to get a fixed price before starting a project.

Design-bid-build was not only good for owners; it benefited the professions of architecture and engineering and stimulated the growth of general contractors.

AEs, they could now hire private sector firms who could work for multiple owners and broaden their expertise.

- Owners no longer needed to hire construction labor as their own employees. Because drawings and specs defined what was required, contractors could figure the cost and submit bids. That enabled the development of general contracting.

Both the AIA and the AGC (Association of General Contractors) vigorously championed the process.

Governments passed procurement laws that mandated design-bid-build.

Governments at all levels mandated it with legislation and procurement regulations. Now that there were drawings and specifications that described the project and owners could ask several builders for a price, they could award the job to the lowest bidder.

That was particularly attractive to public owners who wanted to demonstrate an objective use of public money. Although it was far from a universal fact, it gave the appearance of buying the project for the fewest tax dollars. Conventional wisdom was that design-bid-build gave everyone an equal opportunity to do business on the public dollar and the process precluded graft.

Industrialization in the 19th century triggered a need for educated architects and engineers to design larger and more sophisticated buildings. AEs owned the intellectual capital of design. That enabled design-bid-build. Their design became the essence of a construction contract. They were the technical experts in the construction industry. The AE was the client's agent with a fiduciary responsibility to represent the client's interest. The builder was a vendor with responsibility to deliver the building as designed. The client had a fixed price for a defined product. The AE watched the builder during construction to make sure the work was done right. The AE and builder were legal adversaries.

Design-bid-build served well for a century, but now it often causes problems.

At the end of the 19th century and for the first half of the 20th century, design-bid-build served many owners well. Although there were design-build companies that tended to concentrate on particular building types, most owners used design-bid-build to procure their buildings. It was a simple, powerful idea and it dominated our industry.

This concept, rooted in the 19th century, produces agonies for clients in the 21st century. For most of today's complicated buildings, the process doesn't usually work very well at all.

PROBLEMS WITH THE PROCESS

Ironically, industrialization in the 19th century created the need and facilitated design-bid-build. Now it's killing it. The last quarter of the 20th century saw a steady decline in its use. Continuing industrialization, sophistication and the related rise of specialization are making design-bid-build inappropriate in the 21st century.

When buildings were largely masonry and wood, general contractors did most of the work with their own employees, subcontracting a little plumbing and wiring. Now a general contractor may have 50 to 70 subcontractors—each with a tier of sub-subs, suppliers and manufacturers.

Architects specialize in programming, design, construction documents and interior design. The engineers that worked on building projects divided into civil, geotechnical, testing and inspection, sanitary, structural, mechanical and electrical. And then they all began to specialize in specific building types like hospitals, airports, schools or office buildings. Soon there were consultants for roofing, window walls, kitchens, laboratories, acoustics, fire and life safety, network wiring, communications, parking, code compliance, security, audio-visual, hardware, graphics, signage and so on.

Inaccessible technical knowledge

The AE's job changed. AEs are no longer the consummate experts on construction cost and technology. The centroid of technical knowledge has shifted. Today most of the detailed knowledge of construction technology and construction cost resides in a highly fragmented form with specialty subs and manufacturers, the people who design and fabricate building systems.

The creaky old design-bid-build process deprives the project of the insight of these specialty subs and manufacturers and prevents their collaboration with the AEs during design. Unfortunately, with design-bid-build, the manufacturers have no place at the table during design. For clients of one-off, individually designed, complicated buildings, the 19th century concept of design-bid-build is a clumsy apparatus for accessing the knowledge of product manufacturers to serve 21st century building requirements.

Industrialization in the 19th century created design-bid-build. Now it's killing it.

The detailed knowledge of construction technology resides with specialty subs and manufacturers who don't participate in design.

With design-bid-build, manufacturers aren't picked until design is complete so they can't contribute to the process.

Throughout the industry, owners are struggling with endless varieties of project delivery. They are looking for ways to pull the detailed knowledge of cost and technology that is understood by subcontractors and manufacturers into design. They are trying to overlap design and construction, speed the project, increase reliability, reduce conflict and make cost more predictable. And they are looking for ways to do that and still retain competition.

The question constantly circles about the basic conundrum: "How do you get a competitive price for a product when you want the product's maker to help define it?"

Wasted effort

The Construction Documents are also the Contract Documents. These drawings attempt to show how manufactured products (from steel frames to cabinetwork) will fit into the project. With design-bid-build, the Construction Documents are done by the AE to describe what is needed so a contractor can prepare a bid and subsequently to form the core of a contract to build the project.

Since the manufacturer hasn't been picked, it can't be part of the design process. Then AE's Construction Drawings don't necessarily show the assemblies that the contractor chooses. This catch-22 means that the contractor junks about half of the construction drawings and replaces them with shop drawings that the manufacturers prepare. The amount paid to the AE for those wasted drawings amounts to roughly 1-1½% of the construction cost.

The on-site construction management team is confused with different drawings of the same building systems.

And then the construction team occupies a trailer with a set of contract documents that are not to be used for construction. Next to them is a plan rack with a large selection of shop drawings. When it's time to decide what to build, there's always a problem of finding the right set of drawings.

Long schedules

Furthermore, this design-bid-build process takes too long. Because the construction drawings are used for the core of the contract with the builder, construction work can't start until all the drawings are done. Yet there's no technical reason to delay work until all the details are settled.

Unpredictable costs

It's common to start a design a year or more before it's bid. Assuming the owner cares about the cost (who doesn't?), that means someone must estimate the construction cost a year away. Predicting construction costs may be a little easier than predicting the NASDAQ, but not much. We all know there's inflation. That's usually predictable within a percent or two. But then there are fluctuations in commodity building materials like steel, glass, concrete, plywood and lumber. It only takes a glance at Engineering News Record's annual cost roundup to see that the cost of these materials can vary 20%.

But the biggie is market conditions. Say that everybody is busy. The subs realize that they will have to scrape the bottom of the barrel at the union hall or pick up stray labor off the street. They know that productivity will be half the average. Conversely, if the same subs aren't busy they will be down to their most productive mechanics. They may call them together and say, "Guys, we are going to bid this one very tight and you fellows are going to have to break a sweat if we are going to keep this company together."

So—for an identical scope of work—bids may vary 20% below or above. That is a swing of 40% between good times and bad.

Chaotic, unbusinesslike procurement

Otto von Bismarck, the 19th century Prussian politician, said:

> *"Laws are like sausages. It is better not to see them being made."*

Otto von Bismarck should have watched a general contractor bidding a construction project. Here's a typical description: The contractor has perhaps as many as 100 subs. The subs estimate their part of the work. The contractor does a good job of defining what each sub does. But since there are multiple contractors, there are multiple definitions, and the subs have a hard time deciding what price goes with what contractor. There are mistakes. The sub's bids are collected over the phone with little legal support and frequent misunderstandings about scope.

The subs are disinclined to expose their price until bid day—they don't want their bid to leak to a competing sub. Of course, leaks occur. Since the subs know it may happen, they often float high

Design starts long before the project is priced. That makes costs unpredictable.

Subs don't usually want to expose their bids until the last minute, making the last hours of the bid process hectic.

bids early in the process. Then they drop their price at the last minute—too late, they hope, for a leak to make the rounds. (Unfortunately, that's also too late for the contractor to double-check the totals.)

The lowest price doesn't always get communicated to all the bidders. Some subs pad their bids with some contractors—anticipating bid shopping after the contract award. Competition among the subcontractors may be limited. Buddy-buddy relationships may influence who works on the project.

The last hours before the bids are due become frenzied. The longer a contractor can delay totaling up and keep email, faxes and telephones open to the flow of bids coming in, the better chance the contractor has to be the low bidder. We have seen prices drop as much as 30% in the last few hours of a bid period. The process is hectic and unbusinesslike. It's no way to spend millions of dollars.

It looks a lot better to the owner than it actually is. If there's reasonable competition, two or three bids are about the same. It looks like these fellows know what the project should cost. But if one looks under the covers, there are some surprises. The prices are tight because everyone is using a similar set of subcontractors. Yet if you examine the prices in each trade category, you will commonly see wide variations. I saw millwork bids that varied 250% and five demolition bids that varied 400%. Although those are extreme examples, a 20% variation is common.

There is a wide price variation in any trade category.

It's also common for subs to give different contractors different prices. Their favored firms get a lower price than their competitors. They may find one firm easier to work with or just like to help one another. Yet no one general contractor has the same set of buddies.

Furthermore, different contractors get different prices from different subs. If you had a chance to ferret out the low price in every contract category and assign them all to one contractor, there would be a set of prices lower than the lowest bid.

But for the most part, all the GCs are using about the same set of low subcontractor prices so the GC prices the owner sees are pretty close. Only a few crucial differences will determine the low bid.

Sometimes, a sub makes a mistake or low-balls the price. Reliable general contractors look at the number and ask themselves if they want to use that sub to try to get the job, or not use the sub and lose the job to the contractor who does.

A flawed contract

Then, after the award, the contractor is aligned with the sub-contractors, manufacturers and suppliers across the table from the AE and the owner. There's never an error-proof set of plans and specifications. There's never an owner who doesn't make changes. There's never a bid that doesn't have mistakes. So conflict is common.

There are always mistakes and changes.

The traditional process is legally frail. One of the leaders of the country's largest construction program calls it "design-bid-build-litigate."

Since the contract for construction relies on plans and specifications it assumes that AEs can prepare flawless plans and specs—a flawed assumption.

In the 19th century, when buildings were masonry and iron with a little plumbing and wiring, design-bid-build worked. Today it usually doesn't. Fifty subcontractors provide buildings systems and materials. AEs leave things out and get things wrong: they make mistakes. The world doesn't witness flawless plans and specs. So everyone suffers with claims. Legal costs add to budget overruns for clients and destroy profits for architects, engineers and contractors.

To shore up this rickety process, clients add Program Managers, CMs and other layers of consultants. The objective is to add "constructibility knowledge," have "peer reviews," schedule the work, provide management support and develop "checks and balances" to protect the owners from the biased wiles of the AEs and the constructors. Too often, this extended team just checks up on one another. Too often, the PMs try to show their worth by beating fees out of the AEs and the contractors, rolling out a new set of biased wiles. The resulting array of self-interest among PMs, AEs, GCs, CMs and subs complicates the free flow of information and the integration of knowledge. Typically disputes involve confusion over responsibility. With conflict and litigation, all parties retreat to their corners and protect their flanks instead of collaborating.

Layering multiple consultants to fix the problems of design-bid-build causes additional problems.

So when does it work?

Tradition dies slowly. Change in the construction industry moves with the speed of tectonic plates. Despite frequent failure, design-bid-build remains firmly embedded in the procurement patterns of owners and in the psyche of the industry. It's hard-wired into much of our professional training, our professional codes of conduct, our standard contracts and our laws. Some very smart industry experts insist that design-bid-build is the best option for building delivery.

About 1990, I asked a large room full of architects if they thought that design-bid-build was the right way to build anything. One lonesome hand went up. I tried to dissuade its owner from his position. Looking back, I believe he was right. Sometimes it works. Despite myriad flaws and frequent predictions of its demise, design-bid-build has a place.

It works fine when the heart of the contract—the plans and specifications—can be made nearly flawless. For instance, it works when an owner builds a prototype with drawings that are corrected after each edition is built.

The Las Vegas schools are built with a prototypical set of plans and specifications. When we visited with them, we learned that the first time they roll out a new prototype design they suffer with about 5% in change orders to correct mistakes. After that the change orders are less than a quarter of a percent.

It works for a developer who has built scores of buildings with similar systems. Hines builds a dozen office buildings a year. Just like a public client, the Hines people need to show their investors that they have bought out the building with competition. While the buildings aren't identical, they frequently use similar building systems. And they have an internal staff that does extensive peer reviews of the plans and specs. They're able to hand their contractors a complete set of well-reviewed, well-coordinated working drawings. And they have strong relationships with AEs and builders that let them work out problems that occur when the Contract Documents have mistakes.

It works when the project is simple and it works for serial builders who can get the bugs out of the Contract Documents.

In other words, it works when the project is simple, and it works pretty well for serial builders who can refine their plans and specifications over multiple projects—when a team can get the bugs out of the Contract Documents. And it sometimes works when the owner has a talented staff to check the plans and specifications or engages a third-party firm for detailed and thorough peer review.

So some owners can develop nearly error-free documents. That makes design-bid-build workable. Owners such as school districts with prototype designs, big box retailers, fast food chains, banks with multiple branches and hotel developers have an opportunity to refine a set of construction documents over multiple projects. They are using design-bid-build regularly and effectively. They will likely continue to do so. Since the number of serial builders is growing so is the use of design-bid-build.

Design-Build

Design-build in the United States flourished as the Industrial Revolution took hold. During the 20th century, it served well for building types such as factories, clinics, banks, and in recent years, for data centers. Design-builders who specialized in these kinds of facilities typically had an in-house staff of architects and engineers. They had an appealing story for clients who needed a standard building type. The design-builders could point to a project they had built and offer to build one like it for a fixed price.

Early in the 20th century, most design-builders were vertically integrated companies with both AEs and construction craftsmen as employees. Some had their own steelworks or cabinetworks. Today, design-builders are more apt to be an ad hoc assembly of specialized AEs and CMs formed for a single project, much like the movie industry assembles a unique set of artists and technicians for each movie.

In the past, most design-build contracts have been fixed-price lump-sum. However, a new form of design-build is emerging. It's essentially a cost-plus contract with a GMP but the team includes an AE.

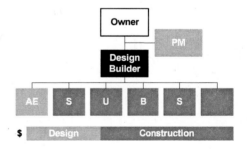

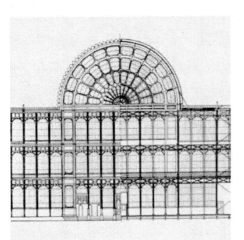

The Crystal Palace, built for the Great London Exposition of 1851, had an iron structure with glass infill.

A course in the history of modern architecture typically begins with the onset of the Industrial Revolution and the design of William Paxton's Crystal Palace. Built for the Great London Exposition of 1851, the Crystal Palace is a good choice to represent that moment in history. Queen Victoria and Prince Albert conceived the exposition to symbolize Great Britain's industrial leadership. William Paxton, the architect, gets credit for the first industrialized building. Designed in 10 days, it was built with a cast iron frame and a million square feet of glass infill. It's arguably the first use of curtain wall construction.

Samuel Austin, the founder of the Austin Company, was born in England in 1851, the same year as the London Exposition. Just as the Crystal Palace is a symbol for the beginning of industrialized construction, Austin's company epitomizes the American design-build companies that were fuelled by an extraordinary period of American industrial growth.

Neither Paxton nor Austin had a smidgeon of architectural or engineering training. Paxton was a horticulturist; Austin was a carpenter. Austin came to the U.S. in his 20s and settled in Cleveland. His company grew from a builder of homes to a builder of factories. When his son joined the company and contributed the strength of an engineering education, the Austin company grew at an astounding pace.

THE DESIGN-BUILDER AS BUILDING TYPE SPECIALIST

The early design-build companies were vertically integrated and specialized in specific building types.

The Austin Company people knew how to build factories. They designed prototypes and warehoused standard steel frames. Although they built other kinds of buildings, the explosion of industrialization and factory construction was the engine of their growth. They could quote a price before design and deliver a project faster and for less than the competition. They met a specialized need in the economic expansion of the U.S. As just one example, in the early 20th century, the Austin Company built 53 buildings for the National Lamp Company, a manufacturer of the new incandescent light bulb.

A reputation for integrity was a crucial ingredient.

The Austin Company had a critical asset—a prerequisite for a design-build company. Samuel Austin was a man of integrity. It takes a leap of faith to sign a design-build contract. There's precious little documentation describing the product that the design-builder agrees to deliver. Austin's personal reputation was as fundamental to the success of the company as the technical proficiency of his prototype designs.

Architects, of course, demonized the Austin Company and other design-builders. Architects insisted that standard building designs were bad. They argued that owners needed an architect to design a unique building (and incidentally earn a complete fee). In addition, they needed an architect to protect them from unscrupulous contractors. The AIA, 43 years old at the turn of the century (Austin Company was 49), developed a code of ethics that barred architects who built their designs from membership.

However, Austin knew his clients' needs and served them well. His company was typical of a series of 20th century design-build companies such as Marshall Erdman, Haskill or Bank Building Corporation of America that focused on building types: medical clinics, banks, food processing plants, data centers, etc. Specialization meant that the design-builder could quote a price with little or no design and show potential clients a similar building to give them an idea of what they would be getting. That's an appealing process for someone who is in a hurry—or is busy running a business and doesn't have time to deal with the design-bid-build process. So design-build grew in the private sector.

Meanwhile, for most of the 20th century, the public sector stuck to design-bid-build. They needed to demonstrate competition and provide evidence that they were not engaged in a brother-in-law deal.

THE AD HOC TEAM — A MOVIE MODEL

In the last of the 19th century and the beginning of the 20th century, it was speed and an up-front price for a standard building type that motivated most people to use design-build. As the 20th century neared its end, another reason for design-build emerged and the public sector began to participate.

The new form of design-build builds ad hoc teams for the unique requirements of specific projects.

The traditional design-bid-build process began to fail. The use of manufactured building systems and the number of specialty subs grew. AEs, previously the masters of construction technology, could no longer master all the technology or know all the costs.

Specialty subs and manufacturers held an important part of the technical knowledge of design and construction. The design-bid-build process made their participation during design awkward; subcontractors are remarkably allergic to spending much time giving advice about their costs and their knowledge of building technology when they have no assurance they will get the job. Moreover, they sure don't want to expose their prices if they must later bid against other subs.

Public clients lobbied lawmakers to enable design-build.

So many public clients lobbied their lawmakers to change procurement regulations and turned to design-build to save time and facilitate collaboration among the AEs, specialty trade contractors and manufacturers.

A new design-build model emerged. While the traditional design-builder had architects and engineers on staff and typically worked primarily on a single building type, this newer form of design-builder assembles a unique team, cherry-picked for a single project.

This new approach is similar to the movie industry. A producer, a director, some actors, a costume designer, a photographic team, scriptwriters, recording engineers, set designers and others come together in a unique team. The team works together for only one movie. Even in a sequel, there will be different players.

The traditional design-builders had in-house AEs who were building type specialists. The salespeople could show a client a similar building to make the deal. This newer form of design-builder cherry-picks an ad-hoc, best-of-class team assembled from many sources and designs a unique building. This single-performance, all-star team can produce a great building. However, there's a problem in making the deal.

The tough nut

If there were no problem in making the deal, design-build would dominate the industry.

The case for design-build is convincing. If there were no problem in making the deal, it would dominate the industry. With design-build, the people who build the building help figure out how to build it. What could make more sense? Furthermore, there's a single point of responsibility. That idea is hard to beat too.

The problem with design-build is getting to the deal. The Austin Company, and similar design-build companies that specialized in a building type, could show a client a similar building and quote a price up front. But for a unique building, there's no understanding of the product and no meeting of the minds until the design is done.

The client asks:

> *"How much will you charge to design and build my unique building?"*

The design-builder replies:

> *"I don't know yet—I don't exactly know what you want. I need to design some of it first."*

The client says:

> *"I don't want to pay you for design until I know what the whole building will cost. Who wants to buy a pig in a poke?"*

The design-builder replies:

> *"I don't want to spend a lot of money on design until I know I'm going to get the job to build it."*

It's a chicken-and-egg conundrum. However, there are a couple of band-aid patches.

The spec design
Some design-builders simply absorb the cost of the design— risking the investment until they get the contract. In essence, they are saying:

Some design builders take the risk of design. Others talk the client into taking the risk.

> *"I'll do the design for nothing because I know you'll like it and give me the job and that'll cover the cost of the design and then some."*

They may pressure an AE to do the work for little or no fee. Of course, that means that design gets short shrift. It may not be a serious problem when the project is simple or when there are similar buildings that provide the opportunity for a simple, repeatable design. However, for large or complicated projects, poor design funding produces poor designs.

The staged contract
Other design-builders say:

> *"Pay me for design. Then if you don't like the price, you can have my drawings to use with another contractor."*

That sounds OK, but we've never seen a client use drawings produced by a design-builder with another AE and GC. I guess it could be done, and probably has, but other AEs are reluctant to assume responsibility for drawings they didn't produce without review, checking and re-doing calculations.

CM-AT-RISK WITH DESIGN-BUILD

New approaches are called Integrated Services, Bridging with CMAR or GMP design-build.

As soon as we invent a new project delivery process, we tend to find ways to blend it with the beneficial attributes of other processes and morph into a third. A compelling evolution to this ad-hoc team "movie model" approach to design-build (and to Bridging) has surfaced with the wide-spread emergence of CM-at-risk and GMP (Guaranteed Maximum Price) contracts (see the chapters on CM). Although there's not a common name, sometimes it's called Integrated Services, sometimes Bridging/CMAR, sometimes just design-build.

The approach is simply to form a team that combines a CM-at-risk with design as part of the services working under a cost-plus GMP contract. Often an AE is a subcontractor to a general contractor. But sometimes an AE leads. Ellerbe, Parsons and other similar companies have provided Integrated Services. Here's how it works:

Step 1: Selection

The owner selects the AE and CM team—typically based on qualifications and a fixed fee that includes the design fee. Compensation for the CM/AE team is often a lump-sum and can be fixed from the start. (See the description of CM services, page 150.) The owner also agrees to reimburse the CM/AE for General Conditions construction and the cost of the subcontracts.

When firms are selected based on qualifications, they have an incentive to do good work so they can get the repeat work. It is a highly valuable asset—a big carrot that serial builders have.

With a fixed fee for design, overhead and profit, the team can't profit from cheapening the design or construction. And since they've been selected with qualifications as a major component, there's the classic incentive that a professional brings to the project to do a good job and get repeat work.

Some owners are worried about hiring the team and starting the project before the project cost is known and, of course, the CM/AE doesn't want to guarantee the cost of an undefined project. So a new wrinkle is added. The owner and the CM/AE team may agree to design to a Fixed Limit of Construction Cost (FLCC). This is a contractual "design-to-budget" clause.

The FLCC states that the design-builder understands the general scope of the work and believes the building can be built within the budget. The FLCC is not a Guaranteed Maximum Price; instead it stipulates that the design-builder will design to the budget. If, when the design-builder takes sub bids, the cost exceeds the budget, the design-builder must redesign without extra fees, but the owner must collaborate with the design-builder to make adjustments in scope or quality.

Sometimes the design-builder agrees that if the budget can't be met, the owner doesn't have to pay for design. At any rate, there's a bit of mutual confidence that's required from both the design-builder and owner that everyone is acting in good faith and will work together to make the project happen.

Step 2: Definition:
As described in the previous paragraphs, the owner may require the design-builder to agree to an FLCC at the start of Project Definition. Frankly, it's a good idea. It's remarkable how often there's confusion about what is in and what is out of the budget. An FLCC helps focus everybody's attention.

Then the design-builder determines the project requirements and defines them for the owner's approval. (See the chapter on Project Definition, page 39.)

The definition fee varies but it may be about 2% of construction cost. The contract may state that the owner doesn't have to pay if the price exceeds the FLCC—unless the owner has increased the scope. Of course, it's always wise for owners to stipulate that they can stop the job, pay for services to the point of termination and hire someone else anytime they want.

The difference between an FLCC and the GMP is this:

- If the cost of the project exceeds the FLCC, the design-builder must redesign and absorb the cost of the redesign—with the owner's collaboration.
- If the cost of the project exceeds the GMP, the design-builder must build it anyway and absorb the cost of the overrun.

Typically the GMP comes later—after the scope is fixed. The project starts with an FLCC and progresses through design, the CM takes bids from major subs and then provides the GMP.

Procurement is more business-like.

Step 3: Construction Documents and Procurement

Instead of a hectic bid period that commits the entire project cost over a telephone in a few hours before the bid is due (as in the design-bid-build process), the design-builder talks with the subs and then takes bids in a business-like, methodical way as the construction drawings progress.

A glaring inefficiency common to the traditional design-bid-build process is the large amount of Construction Documents discarded and replaced with shop drawings produced by manufacturers.

With the traditional design-bid-build process, the AE doesn't know what subcontractor will get the job, so the AE details steel frames, curtain wall, elevators, cabinetwork, doors and windows, ceiling lighting systems and so on.

When the AE finishes the drawings, the project is bid and subs are chosen. Then the subs do shop drawings that represent that sub's manufacturing process and products. The stuff that the AE did is put on a shelf and forgotten. The effort is wasted. That wasted effort may cost about 2% of the total construction cost.

With design-build, the design-builder can call in these subs and manufacturers for a conversation about their product. The design-builder will get focused attention from subs because they know the design-builder is the buyer. Then the design-builder can use a variety of methods to procure the system competitively. He or she can use performance specs, finish drawings and specs in phases or ask the sub to propose a system. When there's a meeting of the minds on the appropriate technology, the design-builder gets priced proposals from the subs who meet the requirements.

After the design-builder selects a particular sub, the sub or the sub's manufacturer does shop drawings and the AE can paste them into the Construction Documents. That saves a lot of time and effort and produces an integrated set of drawings that represent the way the building will actually be built. Errors are reduced: if the sub's CAD shop drawings don't fit the AE's CAD drawings, it's obvious. Meanwhile, the worm turns. Not only is the AE checking the sub's shop drawings, the sub is checking the AE's work. That reduces errors.

The design-builder can finish the construction drawings in phases, bidding and negotiating subcontracts in a competitive process that is transparent to the owner. Phased bidding allows the design-builder to bid subcontracts methodically and competitively so the client benefits from good prices and reliable subs, better technology and tighter contracts. The CM/AE can monitor the design and the cost as bidding progresses and make on-course corrections. If market conditions jeopardize the budget, there's early warning.

When the design-builder has selected most of the subs, the design-builder provides a GMP, signs the subcontracts and starts construction.

Step 4: Construction

Just think. When construction begins, most of the shop drawings have been checked and cut sheets approved. Since the designer and contractor are part of the same organization, there are no RFIs for the owner to worry about!

The project is usually fast-tracked.

Construction can start before the design is complete. Assume a 6% AE fee, a 4% CM fee and 10% for General Conditions construction and a 5% contingency. That's 25% of the cost that's known at the start. Then assume two-thirds of the subs have been selected. Two-thirds of the 75% for subcontracts is 50%. Now 75% of the cost is known. The 5% contingency is now a 20% contingency on the unawarded portion of the subcontracts (assuming everything has been bought out within the estimate). The design-builder can comfortably provide a GMP. (See discussion of a GMP on page 193.)

An owner may wish to retain an outside consultant to review the design-builder's work to make sure he or she is doing what was promised. In those circumstances, construction administration can be conducted in the traditional manner for things like payment approvals, inspection and acceptance of work and change orders.

The argument for Design-Build/CM-at-risk

Most public sector clients who work with complicated buildings have recognized the value of considering qualifications in selecting a CM and the value of having a CM on board during

The classic advantages are single responsibility, better cost control, faster delivery and better technology.

design. So the CM-at-risk process is growing. It's only a short time until the idea of integrating an AE as part of the CM-at-risk team takes hold. The value of centralizing responsibility is too great to ignore.

Here are the advantages that are frequently cited:

Single responsibility
With design-build, an owner doesn't have to watch the AE and the contractor point fingers at each other. The legal triangle of client, AE and contractor in the traditional design-bid-build process becomes a legal tangle when something goes wrong. The separate responsibility for design and construction often makes it difficult to determine who is responsible for errors. Design-build eliminates this avenue of litigation.

Better cost control
The FLCC approach to design-build provides some comfort for the owner on day one. Then a staged procurement process provides good feedback during Construction Documents.

Faster delivery
Of course, with design-build, construction can start before the AE finishes all Construction Documents. However, that does not eliminate the fundamental risks inherent in fast-track. (See the discussion of fast-track on page 45.)

Better technology
AEs and CMs understand construction technology, and many of our clients have knowledgeable construction staffs. But we all have much to learn from the people who make and install building systems. What could make more sense? Getting the people who design building products to participate in their practical application saves money and makes good buildings.

There is much to learn from the people who make and install building systems.

The Renaissance ideal was a person who understood everything—music, literature, art, architecture, engineering. Leonardo da Vinci was an artist, architect, engineer and artisan—a master builder. Today, even after narrowing the field to just construction, there's too much for one person to know. The master builder has become a big team.

The 21ˢᵗ century master builder is a team.

Imagine a perfect team—a collaborative expert for each job. AEs are there because they know design. Builders are there because they know what's practical to build and what things cost. There's close contact with subs and manufacturers who know the most about the latest building systems. The client is on the team because the client is the expert on requirements and budget.

Imagine that the contracts have been arranged to minimize the tendency of self-interest to bias attitudes. The AEs aren't trying to increase fee or escape liability. The contractor isn't plotting for claims and change orders. No one is trying to get something for nothing. What one person knows is available to all. Communications, documentation and costs are transparent. It sounds like nirvana.

We'll never get there, but we can get close.

Bridging

Bridging requires an architectural and engineering capability on the Program Management team so we will call that team the PMAE. The team may be owner employees, an outsourced Program Management company or an AE firm. Often an owner assembles the team from all three sources. The PMAE defines the project or the program requirements. The scope of the requirements will vary from project to project but will usually include schematic design, elements of Design Development and, in many cases, elements of Construction Documents. The requirements may include performance, prescription and product specifications. The objective is to define everything that concerns the owner—typically functional requirements, aesthetics, quality and performance standards.

Then the PMAE translates the requirements into bid documents, manages a selection process and receives proposals for a design-build form of contract. Selection is typically based on qualifications, a management plan and a price (a lump-sum or a GMP) for construction. The owner's PMAE will monitor and review the preparation of Construction Documents by the design-build contractor.

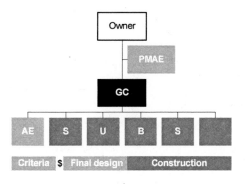

The owner has the right to terminate the contract with the design-builder at any time and pay for the services provided but, most important, may do so prior to construction if there's disagreement about the interpretation of the bid documents as Construction Documents progress. When the design-builder finishes Construction Documents, the PMAE negotiates any owner-initiated change orders and issues a notice to proceed with construction. Then the owner's PMAE administers the contract and inspects the construction.

A LITTLE HISTORY

Often, a single mind triggers a change in our industry.

We're inclined to assume that changes in technology, demographics, economics and law have a normal cause-and-effect on our industry. But our industry is so big and so dependent on traditional mechanisms to function that change is glacial. Often it's the invention of a single mind and the drive of one individual that triggers a pent-up demand for change. So it is with Bridging.

Sometime in the early 1980s, I recall sitting in George Heery's office. George T. Heery, FAIA, RIBA, FCMAA (and probably another batch of important initials) is a long-time friend and my most frequent competitor. We were talking about a joint venture—not our first.

I've always respected George's genius with project delivery. Where others methodically step through standard processes, George applies creative thought. He seems to understand the moving parts in design and construction—the people, their motivations and how to assemble them in a coherent process that serves an owner.

George explained a new idea he was working on. He'd tried it on a couple of projects and liked it. He called it the Concentrated Responsibility Contract Method and since everybody uses acronyms, he labeled it CRC. It seemed like a good idea to me but I thought the name would never last. For once, I was right on both counts. CRC was the harbinger of Bridging.

Fast forward. General Joseph A. Ahearn, then head of construction for the Air Force, hired George and me to study the DoD process for design and construction. We wrote a report and used George's new term, "Bridging." We didn't get much credit because we criticized some of the existing processes, but our report defined the procedures that eventually became common for DoD's design-build processes.

The concept

One could argue that Bridging is a form of design-build because a Bridging contractor does the Construction Documents. One can also argue that it's a form of design-bid-build because a contractor bids on a complete set of requirements and the Construction Documents are simply extensive shop drawings. Both are true.

Bridging is a hybrid of design-bid-build and design-build.

Bridging is a hybrid of design-build and design-bid-build. Properly done, it has many of the advantages of each and eliminates many of the disadvantages of each.

The concept is simple: The owner, typically with professional help from a PMAE, sets requirements with drawings and specifications that have complete contractual force. However, these drawings and specifications concentrate on defining the requirements that the owner cares about and leave many of the details of construction technology up to the design-builder, subs and manufacturers.

The drawings must set requirements for everything the owner cares about.

Architects must be planners, technologists and aestheticians. It's an ancient requirement. Marcus Vitruvius Pollio wrote De Architectura in the first century B.C.E. In this earliest surviving text on architectural theory, Vitruvius wrote that to be architecture a building must have "utilitas, firmitas and venustas." In the 17th century, those three words were translated into "commodotie, firmness and delighte." The concepts are the same but we've changed the nomenclature. We now think in terms of function (commodotie), technology (firmness) and aesthetics (delighte).

Bridging separates these three qualities. It separates the aesthetic and functional design role of AEs from the technology design role.

Aesthetics are prerequisite to architecture. Architects must work with light and shadow, transparency and opacity, color, texture, proportion and rhythm. They must understand the proper role of symbolism in architecture and know how to express ideas in form, scale, decoration and materials. Without diligence and

Texture and color
Scale
Proportion
Form
Symbolism
Rhythm
Context
Landscaping
etc.

Aesthetics   **Function**

Technology

Environment
Site planning
Affinities
Circulation
Land use
Zoning
Work flow
etc.

Cost
Labor productivity
Materials
Structure
MEP
Assembly
Systems
etc.

skill with these ephemeral qualities, the result will squander the construction effort. The building will be a blot on the environment.

Architects must also understand and configure the complex functions of hospitals, airports and factories. In the process, they must evaluate and integrate thousands of building systems designed by manufacturers. If the architects fail to fulfill all three requirements—function, technology and aesthetics—the result will also fail. It's a left-brain, right-brain responsibility.

Bridging is a different method of organizing the roles of architects, engineers and contractors. It separates the architects who deal with aesthetics and function from the architects who deal with technology.

Architects specialize in these three arenas. Some design; some are building type specialists; others are good at the technology for developing Construction Documents.

There are exceptions, but usually the country's best design architects don't do Construction Documents (even if they work in the same firm). Moreover, the country's best airport architects don't do hospitals—and so forth. The demand for specialization has led architects to excel in ever more narrow fields.

Of course, architecture is not always so neatly divided between aesthetics and function and technology. Nor should it be. It may very well be that an owner cares a lot about a technical requirement and sets that as part of the Bridging documents.

The important thing is that design is divided into two contractual components. The first focuses on the owner's requirements; the second focuses on the technology required to serve those requirements.

Who sets requirements?

The professional help on the owner's side has many titles.

There is a lot of variation and a bit of debate on who should set the requirements and what that entity should be called. George Heery calls that entity the Owner's Design Consultant (ODC). But it could be the owner's staff of construction professionals, an outsourced AE or an outsourced Program Manager. The PMAE team must not be limited to either contract management or design—it must include both management and

AE talent. Some multi-disciplinary firms (like Parsons, Jacobs or DMJM) have both AE and PM capabilities and can provide the Program Management and AE services necessary to define the requirements and manage the process.

Most serial builders have an in-house staff of Program Managers but most will still hire an AE firm to help define the requirements. In some cases, they will hire a Program Manager (like Heery's company, Brookwood Group) that is experienced with Bridging. (Check www.brookwoodpm.com for extensive resource material on Bridging.)

Many use the term "Criteria AE" or "Bridging Architect." But that can cause a problem. Some states limit the use of the word "architect" to licensed architects. Technically, the PMAE doesn't need a license because the architect of record that produces and signs the Construction Drawings will be the AE that works for the design-build contractor. There is no added value to the owner to have two licensed architects on the project (although there's no disadvantage). Nevertheless, some states and other public entities, lobbied by AEs, require a licensed architect and use the term "Criteria Architect."

We'll use the term PMAE because both management and design skills are required. But the other terms work too. Whatever it's called, that entity must define everything the owner cares about—in terms that are meaningful to the owner. The PMAE must understand Bridging and explain it in a clear management plan. Then the PMAE must create an incessant drumbeat of communication that keeps reminding the project team of the process, or members of the project team will revert to their traditional roles.

Both management and design skills are required.

How to do it

Bridging can be divided into four phases: Requirements, Selection, Construction Documents and Construction.

Requirements

The PMAE works with the owner and the users to define requirements: the aspects of the project that concern the owner. *"Everything that the owner cares about—in terms that are meaningful to the owner"* is the mantra.

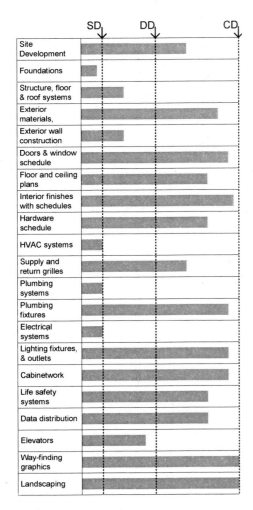

The requirements that will be part of the RFP will define what the owner cares about, but they will vary from project to project. They may include SD, elements of DD and, in some cases, nearly complete CD.

Typically owners care about functional requirements and aesthetics—things they can see and touch. They care about maintainability, energy cost, the performance of the engineering systems. They don't care about the size of the rebar in the foundations or the dimensions of the duct work—only that these things do their job.

So the terms used to describe the things the owner cares about must adapt to the characteristics of owner concerns.

The owner will care that the ducts and foundations perform—that they do their job. So they may define their requirements in terms of performance. They may also not care much about the look of the MEP equipment, but they will certainly care about its energy efficiency and maintainability. However, it's likely that they will care a lot about the look of the building, the materials and the colors that are used. So the terms that describe the requirements will change with each owner.

The details that the owner doesn't care about are left to the design-builder working with the extended construction team. If the team is good, there will be lots of collaboration with subs and manufacturers to find cost-effective systems. This is one of the powerful concepts of Bridging. As we keep saying, manufacturers and subcontractors are the experts on construction cost and technology. Getting their expertise into the design is a great benefit to the project.

The PMAE designs the project to the extent necessary and defines the functional, aesthetic, environmental, sustainability, quality and maintenance standards the owner wants to control. Typically the PMAE defines functional requirements with drawings and prescription specifications and defines engineering systems and construction technology with performance specifications.

Here's a thought to further illuminate this concept. If the PMAE fails to define something the owner cares about, there will be a change order. If the PMAE defines something the owner *doesn't* care about, it will limit the design-builder's ability to find the most cost-effective technical solution.

After defining requirements, the PMAE translates them into contractually enforceable bid documents and includes them in an RFP.

Here's a classic point in the process where newcomers to Bridging get confused. The industry usually uses the acronym "CDs" to mean both "Construction Documents" and "Contract Documents." With the traditional design-bid-build process, the Construction Documents are a vital part of the Contract Documents. But with Bridging, the RFP is the Contract Document. The Construction Documents come later. So don't use the term CDs or there will be confusion. (You may want to re-read this paragraph—it confuses many people.)

The PMAE also prepares a comprehensive management plan that defines cost, schedule, responsibilities and process.

Selection

After appropriate approvals, the PMAE manages a selection process for a design-builder. Selection usually goes like this:

The PMAE issues a request for qualifications (RFQ) and evaluates responses. The evaluating criteria are the usual: qualifications of key team members, past experience with similar projects, capabilities (construction management, architecture, engineering, etc.), financial strength, safety record and quality assurance programs. The RFQ should also ask for a description of the IT systems that will be used for documentation, reporting and communication. Then the owner and the PMAE make a short list of the best-qualified firms and issue a request for proposal (RFP) to the short-listed firms. The RFP should include the agreement between the owner and design-builder that will be used—with a paragraph that asks a proposer to list any objections.

Like the traditional design-bid-build process, the Bridging agreement includes drawings and specifications, but they are far less detailed than typical Construction Documents. Traditional Contract Documents for design-bid-build do two things: define requirements for contractual purpose and detail the technology for construction. Bridging Contract Documents concentrate on the first: the requirements for contractual purpose.

Bridging Contract Documents shift significant responsibility for the final construction technology to the design-builder. These Contract Documents describe what the owner wants to control, but leave decisions on many of the details of construction technology to the design-builder's team.

The Contract Documents are not Construction Documents.

The Bridging agreement includes drawings and specifications that are far less detailed than those used in design-bid-build.

The Contract Documents must be adequate to obtain a lump-sum bid or an enforceable GMP from the design-builder. Equally important, they must be adequate for the design-builder to obtain enforceable prices from subs with little or no additional design.

The Contract Documents define the relationship between the owner and the design-build contractor. The contractor will also use them to define the contractor's relationship with the subs. Good documents mean that the contractor can get more competition—and that means a better price for the owner.

They don't define the details of how to build the building. Instead, they should provide wide latitude for the design-builder and the subs to find ways to save time and money—and provide a better product.

The PMAE is not the architect of record. The design-builder's AE will sign and seal the drawings.

The design-build contractor's AE produces the final Construction Documents, signs the drawings and is the AE of Record. The RFP should define a schedule for reviews of the Construction Documents by the PMAE. It should also stipulate that during the development of Construction Documents, the owner can terminate the contract and pay only for the completed portion of the Construction Documents. The RFP also stipulates that the drawings belong to the owner.

A contractor will usually propose a higher fee than with a competitively bid design-bid-build contract.

George Heery believes (and I agree with him) that a contractor will usually propose a higher profit for Bridging than is typical for a simple negotiated general construction contract. However, the Bridging contractor and subs will find ways to reduce costs that will be a net savings for a better product. Furthermore, there will be far less exposure to contractor-initiated change orders, claims and post-construction corrections.

If the owner is a serial builder, the owner may select the design-builder based on previous good performance. Otherwise, the owner and PMAE will likely select the design-builder based on qualifications and cost.

"Cost" may be based on any reasonable payment terms from cost-plus to fixed price. A lump-sum is most common, but we have also used cost-plus with a GMP.

Lump-sum

The design fee should be identified.

If the bid is to be a lump-sum, "cost" will be the lump-sum. The PMAE awards a two-phase contract. The phase-one award is for preparation of Construction Documents with an option for phase two—construction.

If the bid is a lump-sum for final design and construction of the project, it should include a breakout for the fee for preparing the Construction Documents. There's a good reason to include this price in the RFP. Although a fair price for this vital phase of AE services is well known, there's no assurance the contractor will pay it to the AE. However, identifying the number in the Contract Documents will make it hard for a contractor to ask an AE to do the work on speculation. Furthermore, if the project should terminate for any reason before construction, there is a known cost for the final design.

Cost-plus with a GMP
If the bid is a GMP, "cost" will be the GMP, but the PMAE will want to evaluate fixed-fee and General Conditions costs. If one proposer has a high fee and high General Conditions cost but a low construction cost and another has the reverse, some detailed questioning is in order.

The fixed-fee and General Conditions costs should be identified.

The advantage of a cost-plus with a GMP contract over a lump-sum contract is the greater opportunity for collaboration. Collaboration can produce considerable savings that accrue to the owner.

The typical problem with a cost-plus-GMP contract is that it's signed during design with incomplete drawings to facilitate fast-track. Therefore, it's a *"defined price for an undefined product."* That's a target-rich environment for conflict and change orders. In many cases, after construction begins there's a fuss about what should be inferred from the incomplete drawings.

But an RFP for Bridging isn't based on incomplete drawings. Since the RFP is adequate to define requirements for a lump-sum, it's also adequate to enforce a GMP. (See *Arriving at a GMP*, page 193.)

The disadvantage of a GMP contract is that it's more work to administer. The owner and the PMAE must audit and approve the design-builder's costs.

Picking the AE
If an owner anticipates dealing with a design-build contractor that subcontracts the design, the owner can participate in the

The owner can participate in the AE selection.

AE selection. On the addition to the Utah State Capitol, we selected a contractor and stipulated that we would participate in the contractor's selection of the AE. If the RFP requires the design-builder to designate the AE, it's possible the best AE and the best design-builder won't be on the same team. We didn't want that to happen. If the AE is chosen after the design-builder is selected, the field has not been limited by previous competitive teaming arrangements. The PMAE and owner can offer opinions or reserve veto power. In my experience, it's always been an easy collaboration, but the owner and the owner's PMAE must be careful to not give the design-builder any indication that they assume responsibility for the performance of the design-builder's AE.

Construction Documents

The successful bidder is a design-build contractor with AEs on staff or an AE who is a subcontractor. The design-builder is the AE of record who prepares, signs and seals the Construction Documents.

In either form of contract (lump-sum or cost-plus with a GMP) the PMAE monitors the work of the design-builder while the design-builder prepares final Construction Documents and procures construction.

The design-builder must submit final Construction Drawings and specifications so the PMAE can determine if they comply with the RFP and if "the design-builder qualifies for final payment for Construction Documents." However, neither the owner nor the owner's PMAE "approves" the Construction Documents drawings or in any way assumes responsibility for the design.

The owner's PMAE may reject the Construction Documents for incompleteness or non-compliance with the RFP. In either case, the PMAE has the right to terminate the contract or allow the design-builder to correct and resubmit.

The RFP is the Contract Document. The Construction Documents augment the RFP. The RFP takes precedence over the Construction Drawings unless the RFP has been modified by an approved change order. When Construction Documents are complete, the PMAE reviews them, negotiates any remaining owner-initiated change orders and issues a notice to proceed with construction.

A Bridging project typically has two AEs. One, working as the owner's representative, typically focuses on aesthetics, function and the performance of the engineering systems. The second, part of the construction team, focuses on construction technology.

The RFP is the Contract Document.

Construction

The PMAE exercises the option for construction when satisfied that the Construction Documents meet the requirements of the RFP.

The design-builder constructs the facility and the PMAE reviews performance to ensure conformance with the Contract Documents, administers the contract between the owner and the design-builder and inspects the construction on behalf of the owner—just like an AE in the old design-bid-build process.

Incentive Clause

If the contract is a lump-sum, there can be a "shared savings clause" that provides a percent of the savings for the design-builder if the design-builder suggests changes that are approved by the owner's PMAE but are not consistent with the Contract Documents. (In a lump-sum Bridging contract, one hundred percent of the savings that are consistent with the Contract Documents belong to the design-builder.)

A shared savings clause works with a lump-sum contract, not with a cost-plus GMP contract.

With a GMP contract, the owner receives any savings obtained during procurement of subs and the resulting collaboration with the design-builder and the PMAE. For a hard-working team that can truly collaborate, that can mean a lot of money. Inevitably, the subs and manufacturers think of things to do that were not anticipated in the RFP.

It's not wise to have a "shared savings clause" if the GMP is negotiated after selection. If in a GMP contract the owner and the PMAE think it's wise for the design-builder to have an incentive, they can add a "satisfaction fee" to the contract. (See *Shared Savings*, page 196.)

THE ARGUMENTS FOR BRIDGING

Acceptance of Bridging as a project delivery system has not achieved escape velocity. Nothing happens fast in our lumbering construction industry. Yet every year, more clients are buying the idea. Some are stumbling; others are executing it with excellent results.

Bridging is a good idea. Like design-build, it provides an opportunity for subcontractors, manufacturers and AEs to collaborate effectively in setting the construction technology. That saves time and money.

Photos by Martin van Hemert

The Architect of the Utah State Capitol (David Hart), the owner's PM, the design-build contractor and the design-build contractor's AE worked with Kepco+ to develop ornate granite shop-fabricated assemblies. Some elements were thin, some up to 8" thick. The collaboration during design saved millions. Kepco+ was essentially a design-build subcontractor for the granite cladding on the additions and went on to do the terra cotta restoration on the historic Capitol. There would not have been time for this collaboration during a lump-sum bidding process, nor would the savings have been returned to the owner in a lump-sum contract.

Like traditional design-bid-build, Bridging keeps architects and engineers (the owner's PMAE) on the client's side of the table to define functional and aesthetic requirements and to represent these interests throughout the project. That retains the wonderful collaboration of AE and owner in search of creative solutions.

Bridging also provides the owner with protection by professionals throughout the project. The owner gets a bonded, complete and enforceable lump-sum or GMP contract before starting construction—in about half the time and at half the cost of the design-bid-build process.

Compared to the design-bid-build process, Bridging reduces claims and change orders because it centralizes responsibility for the result. The design-builder can't submit claims for errors or omissions in the Construction Documents since the design-builder produced them. During and after construction, there's no argument over whether the AE or contractor is responsible for a problem.

Bridging reduces design cost. In the design-bid-build process about half the Construction Documents are replaced by shop drawings. And the Construction Documents are the largest component (about 40 percent) of the design cost.

With Bridging, generic drawings for many systems can be replaced by shop drawings done by manufacturers after they are selected. Since the design-builder can work with these manufacturers while preparing Construction Documents, the shop drawings can be pasted directly into the Construction Documents—producing a final integrated set.

That reduces mistakes. When the design-builder's AE pastes CAD shop drawings into a final set of Construction Documents, they must fit or the dimensional problems are obvious. It also provides multiple plan checking. Profit motives drive the contractors, subcontractors and manufacturers to review the AE's drawings.

Bridging reduces the liability of owners, contractors and AEs and reduces the cost of errors and omissions (E&O) insurance. The owner's PMAE will qualify for a low rate. The design-builder is in a position similar to a design function in manufacturing. In those situations, product liability replaces professional liability.

PROBLEMS WITH BRIDGING

So why isn't there more Bridging? Certainly one reason is that an AE selected by an owner will get less fee if he or she convinces the owner to use Bridging. That doesn't encourage AEs to recommend Bridging.

How much less? There's considerable variation in the amount of design appropriate for the requirements. Traditionally, Design Development is considered to be 35% of the AE's fee. The part of the total fee allocated to design is 75%, which means Design Development is 46.5% of an architect's design services. That would be the total if the owner or a Program Manager handled bidding and construction. If the AE handled all the phases, the AE might have 35% of a complete normal fee for setting the requirements and 25% for Bidding and Construction Administration.

So a Bridging AE might get about 60% of the fee for a design-bid-build project. Although our experience is that the profit is better and the risks are lower, not many AEs, inexperienced with the process, are inclined to see it that way.

Like all alternative project delivery methods, misunderstanding is a common problem.

On our first Bridging project, our government owner thought they didn't need our services after we finished the bid documents. They had their own in-house PM and despite the fact that they hadn't done a Bridging project, they decided to manage the work themselves. After they picked the construction team, the design-build contractor's AE design team forgot who they were working for. They assumed the traditional role of representing the owner. They made design changes with user groups and incorporated them into the Construction Documents without telling the contractor. That increased the cost. It caused lots of pain and consternation before it all got straightened out.

There's an unfortunate misconception that a set of Bridging Contract Documents are about 35% of a typical AE fee (approximately design development). That's wrong. Although the total scope of work for the Contract Documents may be approximately the same or slightly more than design development, some aspects of the work will be far more, others

An owner's AE gets less fee with Bridging than with the traditional design-bid-build process. That doesn't encourage AEs to recommend Bridging.

far less. Using DD as a set of Bridging documents will lead to problems similar to those that occur with a GMP on a partially complete set of documents. The Contract Documents might be roughly equivalent to design development, but it will likely go farther than standard design development documents for some building systems and not as far for others.

BRIDGING AND PROGRAM MANAGEMENT

The U.S. General Services Administration, perhaps one of the world's largest Program Managers and one of the largest serial builders, uses Bridging for many of their projects. One of the largest is the $400 million headquarters consolidation for the U.S. Census Agency. SOM worked for GSA and did the Contract Documents. Their fee was about a third of a traditional full service fee. They took the shell and core design to concept design, the interiors well beyond Design Development, the parking structures to 50% Construction Documents and used performance specs for the civil, MEP and structure—a well-conceived approach to defining the owner's concerns.

A joint venture of DMJM and Heery provided CM services. Skanska was the low bidder with HKS as the production architect.

Jag Bhargava, Executive Director of the Capital Development Division for the General Services Administration, likes Bridging, and he gives SOM high marks. Nevertheless, he points out that Bridging is no guarantee of a trouble-free project. The Census project was awarded to Skanska in September 2003. A sharp rise in steel prices followed, painfully increasing Skanska's costs after their bid.

Skanska started construction on the parking garage before HKS finished the Construction Documents on the main building. That meant GSA and Skanska were pretty firmly married to one another as the drawings unfolded and as steel prices increased. Had GSA waited for complete documentation to start construction, they may have avoided some of the problem. But GSA didn't have the luxury of waiting and suffered one of the inevitable problems of fast-track.

One of the points Jag makes is that the RFP needs to state that there should be a hierarchy of precedence in the Contract

Documents and the RFP should take precedence over the drawings. In particular, since the civil work is bid with a performance spec, it's important to state that the Bridging contractor must verify existing conditions in the RFP.

Bridging is a great strategy for a serial builder that has similar requirements but needs facilities that may be unique to their communities—or respond to regional technologies.

For instance, many urban school districts want to build schools that have uniform functional requirements but respond to community aesthetics and different site requirements. The PMAE could easily set functional and technical requirements for all schools and still create unique designs for each project.

Another instance—an international company that builds similar facilities in different countries or different regions will find it far more cost effective to use a construction technology that is appropriate for the country where the project is to be built.

That makes Bridging a natural. The functional requirements might be similar but the building technology should change to be cost-effective with local practice.

Valeo Climate Control, an international company headquartered in France, produces heaters and air conditioners for automobiles. After the elimination of trade barriers by NAFTA, Mexico was favored as the location of a new facility. Valeo built a 7,000 square meter production plant in Toluca, near Mexico City. We were the PMAE for this project.

We used international standards for the requirements and selected a local design-build contractor for construction technology. The total planning, design, construction and start-up time was 12 months. The Valeo story became one of the projects featured by Harvard in a publication for a colloquium on international construction.

Bridging is a splendid approach for a serial builder that has similar project requirements but needs unique facilities in different physical, cultural or technical environments.

CM: Agency and at-risk

In the United States design separated from construction and became a profession in the mid-19th century. In the mid-20th century, management separated from construction and became a profession. Specialization that stimulated the proliferation of subcontractors enabled the change and inflation triggered it.

At first, private sector owners increasingly selected general contractors based on managerial skills and negotiated cost-reimbursable contracts with a guaranteed maximum price (GMP). However, most public agencies were required by law to take competitive bids. To obtain benefits similar to the private sector, public owners hired construction managers as professionals (CM as agent) and took competitive bids for multiple trade contracts that the owner would hold.

But many of these owners were uncomfortable with multiple contracts and no price guarantee for the total project. They observed the private sector's use of negotiated GMP contracts and lobbied their lawmakers to pass enabling legislation for alternative project delivery processes that would give them the same opportunities.

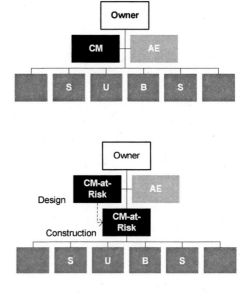

The result was CM-at-risk, similar to the private sector approach to a negotiated contract. It's gaining wide popularity in the public sector. It allows an owner to select a CM based on qualifications, make the CM a member of a collaborative project team and obtain a bonded, guaranteed maximum price. CM-at-risk is taking its place along with the more traditional process of design-bid-build as an established method of project delivery.

Knowledgeable construction professionals who deal with CM concepts will disagree on the definitions.

Now I tread on thin ice. As I type each sentence, I hear the voice of some respected colleague offering a different view or disagreeing outright. CM is only a few decades old and the concepts are less defined than design-bid-build and design-build. Any conversation with knowledgeable construction professionals who deal with CM concepts will be contentious. The more expert people become, the more they disagree on definitions. Try to get three architects to agree on the definition of architecture.

Many general contractors who have bid a job under a design-bid-build process call themselves CMs. Many clients hire a company or an individual to help them watch over an architect and a general contractor and name that service CM. Some call their internal staff of construction professionals CMs. That brings up another point: CM is a term used to describe both people and processes. A firm is retained to be the CM and provide construction management.

That's the confusing nature of vocabulary in our industry. But for the purpose of this discussion, I am going to use two terms: CM-agent (or CM-agency if referring to the process) and CM-at-risk. Here is what I mean when I use the terms.

A LITTLE HISTORY

In 1971, I gave a lecture on construction management at the national AGC convention in Houston. For some in the audience, it was the first introduction to the idea that a client could hire an organization to drive the construction process as a professional representative of the owner. The room was packed. About half the contractors in the audience seemed positive about the idea—they knew they had insights into the construction process and felt that it sounded like a good way to get involved in a more collaborative relationship.

The other half acted as if it were a seditious plot. It was too much change from the hard-bid, lump-sum traditions of general contracting. But there was also a well-founded concern that with no barriers to entry (like bonding capacity), incompetent people would call themselves construction managers and be hired by naive clients.

Change it was—and an abrupt one at that. CM arose spontaneously around the country and spread quickly. For two centuries, the construction industry had become increasingly specialized and technical— each year demanding more and more knowledge from the people who designed and built. Industrialization and specialization continued.

By the mid 20th century, most of a building was built by subcontractors who combined field construction tasks with building systems manufactured in factories far from the site. Hundreds of organizations were involved in a construction project. To succeed, a construction contractor needed management skills—brain rather than muscle power.

Construction companies created a tier of people within their organizations who managed these many subcontractors. It was a small step to separate those people and sell the service as a profession. However, the construction industry has enormous inertia. It took economic force to trigger the change. The late 1960s provided that force: the construction industry began to suffer with double-digit inflation. The need for speed—to get things built before the price increased—was the trigger. By hiring the management of construction as a professional service, owners could fast-track projects.

I first heard of the CM idea from Bob Marshall, a senior vice president at Turner Construction Company. It made all kinds of sense to me. It was taking far too long to build. So I talked Frank Matske at the New York State University Construction Fund into hiring us to do a study on accelerating design and construction. We named it "Fast-Track." That was the event that coined the term. Then we talked some clients into trying it.

Just as design separated from construction in the mid-19th century, managers began to separate from construction in the mid-20th century. Some organizations formed that did nothing but construction management. They started institutions such

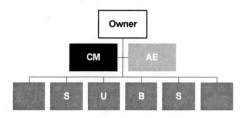

A CM agent represents a client's interests for a fee and takes bids from multiple trade contractors. The contracts will be between the owner and the trade contractor. The CM does not guarantee the schedule or the cost. Some people call it CM, some call it CM-agent or CMa.

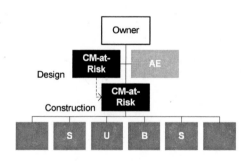

A CM-at-risk advises the team during design as a consultant, but as the project is bid, the CM holds the subcontracts, provides a GMP and becomes a vendor of the construction. Some people call this CM-at-risk or CMAR. Some government agents call a CM who holds contracts a CMc, and then shorten it to CM.

The separation of management from construction is reminiscent of the separation of design from construction a century ago.

as the Construction Management Association of America (CMAA). The march to licensing has started with the Certified Construction Manager (CCM) certificate. The whole chain of events looked much like the separation of design and the formation of the AIA a century earlier.

THE PROFESSIONALIZATION OF CONTRACTORS

Most organizations, particularly public ones, have traditionally selected architects and engineers (AEs) based on their qualifications and general contractors (GCs) based on competitive bid.

AEs have been thought of as professionals selling intellectual content while contractors have been vendors of products. That's changed.

The rationale for this difference in selection procedure is that it's difficult to specify and measure the experience, wisdom or creativity of AEs. Moreover, AEs typically represent their owner's interests with a fiduciary responsibility. So selection is based on qualifications. But constructors deliver a product that can be specified and measured, not a professional service. So selection is based on price.

Competitive bidding gives everybody an equal chance to do business on the public dollar, prevents favoritism and gives the appearance of least cost. But the increasing specialization and technical complexity of construction complicate this simple idea for most projects and most owners. Many owners want to start construction before design is complete. And many private sector owners select GCs based on relationships and qualifications so they can get their advice during design and start construction before design is complete.

NEGOTIATED GENERAL CONSTRUCTION CONTRACTS

CM-at-risk began with the private sector and negotiated general construction contracts.

During the quarter century roughly from 1950 to 1975, half of America's workforce moved from farms and factories into office buildings. Developers built them. These private sector owners, unfettered by public procurement regulations, recognized that contractors have experience, wisdom and creativity too. They wanted cost reliability on their side of the table during design. They wanted a more manageable and predictable procurement process for construction. They needed a firm price for construction to get a lending commitment early in the design process.

So they selected a GC during design to provide technical advice. As design progressed, the AE produced a "mortgage package," the GC provided a price, and the developer obtained a financing commitment. As Contract Documents progressed, the contractor negotiated or took bids from subcontractors and proceeded to build the project under a cost-plus-a-fee contract, usually with a GMP. The projects benefited from the insight into construction technology and cost provided by the GCs, specialty trade contractors and manufacturers during design.

Since the developer typically chose the GC based on relationships or qualifications, and since the developer was a serial builder and could do so again, the GC was motivated to serve the owner's interest in anticipation of repeat business. The GC began to look and feel like a professional service provider.

Agency CM

In an attempt to gain similar benefits, but restricted by procurement regulations, public owners figured they could extract the management function of GCs and hire them under a professional service contract—often using AE procurement regulations. However, it was important to change the name to reflect the fact that a service, not the building, was being bought. These public owners gravitated to the title of "construction manager." A manager clearly provided a service and was not a vendor of a product.

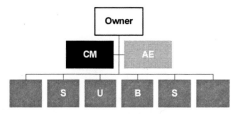

An Agency CM does not hold the contracts for construction.

The CM was often a GC. Many general contractors like Turner, McCarthy, Kitchell and Gilbane quickly grasped the opportunity. And some AEs were heavily involved in managing complicated construction processes and could fill the role as well. CRS, The Smith Group, 3D/International and others formed CM groups.

The CM could provide advice during design, take bids for construction from multiple prime trade contractors and then manage the prime trade contractors, assuming the functional role of a GC. The owner held the contracts to keep the CM in a professional position and avoid the appearance that the CM was a vendor of bricks and mortar. These owners and CMs often used fast-track procedures to save time. Originally, CM agency was simply called CM. The "agency" suffix only appeared when CM-at-risk emerged.

How to do it

Selection

The process for selecting a CM-agent and a CM-at-risk is similar because it focuses on qualifications.

Of course, the objective is to select the best CM for the project for a reasonable fee. Most owners issue an RFP, receive proposals, ask for fees and interview a short list of the most qualified firms. Some of the more careful owners visit the CM's office, check references and examine their control systems in detail.

Typically the information requested by the RFP for either CM agency or at-risk will include questions about:

- Qualifications of key people
- Experience with the owner and with similar projects
- Capabilities (construction management, architecture, engineering, etc.) and experience with other forms of design and construction
- Approach to the work (pre-construction services and field services)
- Financial strength
- Safety record
- Quality control/assurance program
- Management systems for documentation, reporting and communication
- Fees and reimbursable expenses
- An estimate of General Conditions construction

Ideally, selection is at the start of a project (before or just after selection of an architect).

Services

The CM becomes a collaborative member of the project team.

Preconstruction services include budgeting, cost estimating, scheduling, constructibility reviews and value engineering studies. As construction drawings progress or near completion, the CM may prequalify firms, take bids (usually in an open forum) and deliver the bids to the owner.

The CM, architect and owner review bids for compliance with the Contract Documents and determine which bids to accept. If they have short-listed firms, there's a moral reason to select the lowest bidder—or, if they do not select the lowest, provide a clear explanation of why not.

The CM then prepares cost estimates for the unbid portion of the project, adds a contingency, establishes a budget for the General Conditions construction items and, if "at-risk," provides a guaranteed maximum price and a bond and manages construction as a general contractor would.

The CM keeps the costs in accounts available for the owner's review. In some states, a general contractor's license is required to provide CM services.

TERMS OF PAYMENT

The payment for a CM-agent is typically like any other professional service agreement. It's either cost-reimbursable or a lump-sum.

CMs are paid like most professionals.

Either way, the estimate of the total fee is typically calculated by assessing the level of effort (the number of man hours required and the rate for those), applying a multiple to the labor cost for overhead and profit and then adding in the direct job costs for printing, travel, communications and perhaps a trailer for a site office.

The payment structure commonly used for CM-at-risk is usually cost-reimbursable with a GMP. It's the same as with any form of project delivery that uses a GMP contract. (See *Typical Payment Terms in a GMP Contract*, page 190.)

PERCEIVED PROBLEMS WITH CM-AGENCY

Despite frequent good results, many owners were troubled by:

- The administrative burden of managing many contracts for a single project
- A concern that third-party liability might accrue to them if one prime trade contractor damaged another
- The lack of a single, guaranteed, bonded price for the total project (Often only the larger trade contractors were bonded.)

Most disturbing, the opaque veil of the general contractor was stripped away and the messy process of procuring and coordinating subcontractors was painfully exposed to the light of day. It made owners nervous. They thought the construction industry ought to be run in a business-like manner.

The messy process was painfully exposed.

Theoretically, a CM as the agent of the owner implied that the owners didn't need their own construction management organization. But in many cases, since they held the contracts, owners were drawn into the process. The owners felt the need to oversee the CM's oversight. That increased the owner's cost and confused the CM's role in the eyes of the prime trade contractors.

There are few barriers to entry for CM-agency services.

Furthermore, just as the GCs at the AGC convention in 1971 had worried, there are few barriers to entry for CM-agency services. There are no licensing requirements as there are for architects and engineers, and there are no bonding requirements as there are for general contractors. Professional liability insurance is often required, but it's not hard to obtain. Unqualified firms produced poor results for owners who didn't have the sophistication necessary to pick a qualified firm. However, in recent years, the Construction Management Association of America (CMAA) has developed a certification process for CMs that is gaining widespread acceptance.

CM-at-Risk

As CM-agency became common, many general contractors began to provide the service. Those that had experience with negotiated contracts argued that they were essentially the same as a CM-agency contract except they held the contracts and provided a guarantee of price. Both owners and contractors began to refer to a private sector negotiated contract as a CM contract. To distinguish it from CM, they named it CM-at-risk. When that happened, the old CM became CM-agency to distinguish it from CM-at-risk.

As the field became competitive, the contractors harped on their ability to hold the contracts, bond the job and guarantee price. Many owners bought the argument and soon public owners were lobbying their legislatures to allow CM-at-risk for public work. Many states did so and the process has become common.

The arguments about the processes

The owner can select the CM based on qualifications.

Both CM-agency and CM-at-risk have many attributes that appeal to owners. The owner may select the CM based on qualifications so owners get better firms working for them. And since CMs are selected based on qualifications, CMs are inclined to maximize their service and their allegiance to the owner in order to obtain repeat work.

CMs provide advice on construction cost and construction technology during design to keep the project in the budget and reduce design errors. And during design, CMs and AEs provide checks and balances on one another. The CMs can also use their relationships with trade contractors to get design input during the design process.

CMs can provide advice on construction matters during design.

CM minimizes risk for everyone. The CM's construction experience is combined with the wisdom, creativity or engineering skills of AEs and with the owner's understanding of requirements. That tripod has more complete control. Together they command the classic territories of construction, design and functional requirements. Properly structured and rigorously managed, they are non-adversarial and collaborative. They make better decisions.

The owner, AE and CM are a tripod with control over most of the project issues.

The CM can review the AE's drawings and often catch errors, reducing the AE's and owner's risk. The AE can review the CM's approach to the work, making helpful recommendations. The CM is allowed to take bids from subcontractors during completion of Contract Documents, which reduces the risk and provides useful input to design. The procedure is methodical, manageable and predictable. It's far less risky for all than the process of trying to take all bids on a single day.

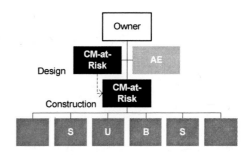

A CM-at-Risk holds the contracts for construction and typically provides a guaranteed maximum price.

Public procurement of trade contracts increases competition—no cronyism or bid shopping in contract awards. Competition is wider and fairer: all subcontractors have a chance at the work. It sends powerful messages of fairness and tends to get the best prices. Each trade contractor has a fair shot at being the low bidder, so the owner winds up with the low sub-set of prices.

Procurement is more business-like. By bidding contracts methodically over a period of time, the CM can find the lowest price in each category. By taking bids as the Construction Drawings progress, the project team can get hard money feedback and make on-course corrections to meet a budget.

The CM can bid a portion of the work before Construction Drawings are complete and fast-track the project. The CM process is transparent. Clients know more about what is going on behind the scenes.

There is early feedback on cost.

CM AGENCY VS. CM-AT-RISK

If you sit in a room with some people who provide CM-agency and some others who provide CM-at-risk, you will hear considerable debate over which works best.

The CM-at-risk will quickly point to the fact that they guarantee the price and bond the job and that provides security to the owner. The CM-agent will argue that it's typically a defined price for an undefined product and add that if the job goes bad, the CM will put the owner's interests behind its own. Furthermore, if that happens, the CM-at-risk quickly assumes the character of hard-bid general contractor.

Then the CM-at-risk will point to a long list of successful projects and say that it just doesn't happen.

The CM-at-risk will explain that there's a potential for multiple trade contractor claims if the CM fails in its duty to coordinate contractors and the owner takes no corrective action.

Then the CM-agent will point to a long list of successful projects and say that it just doesn't happen.

The CM-agent will argue that since the CM-at-risk often is allowed to take bids on most of the work before the GMP is issued, there is no risk and therefore they don't deserve a larger fee for the risk.

Then the CM-at-risk will often, ever so politely, suggest that if the CM-agent thinks the fees are excessive for the risk, they should come on in, the water's fine. Few CM-agents do.

The CM-agent will argue that the CM-at-risk requires more oversight by the owner, the AE or a third party, resulting in added costs.

But the CM-at-risk will point to the administrative cost the owner will have in holding multiple contracts. The CM-agent will claim that they will administer all the contracts.

The CM-at-risk claims that the CM-agent has no real liability for cost and schedule overruns or quality failures. The CM-agent claims that it remains in a fiduciary relationship with the owner throughout the project. If things start to go bad, the CM-agent has a contractual duty to serve the owner's interests first, and that's better for the owner.

The CM-agent will contend that the CM-at-risk controls job-site documentation, which can be used against the owner or AE should claims arise.

The construction industry is infinitely variable. All those arguments bear weight and hold elements of truth. But none may apply to the next job. However, the CM-at-risk argument of holding the contracts and providing a GMP trumps the CM-agency argument in the minds of most owners. In those states that allow CM-at-risk for public work, there are few CM-agency projects.

DOES CM-AT-RISK COST MORE THAN DESIGN-BID-BUILD?

Nobody will ever prove it either way because we are never able to have identical comparisons. However, there are some cases where CM-at-risk may cost more.

- If an owner asks for a GMP before the Construction Documents are well along, the CM-at-risk will make conservative estimates and may make non-competitive handshake agreements with subs to shed risk.
- A CM-at-risk can influence the list of subcontractors who bid the work and can wave off flaky companies that might be low bidders in a design-bid-build scenario. (See page 125.) That gets the owner better work and a less troubling process, but it may cost more.
- Some general contractors who provide CM-at risk do work with their own forces, discourage competition and make a good profit on their labor and equipment.

Against these arguments is the undisputable fact that done properly, either a CM-agent or a CM-at-risk can add much insight during design. That will save money and reduce the potential for conflict.

CMS AND PROGRAM MANAGEMENT

CM—either agency or at-risk—provides a powerful vehicle for implementing the opportunities that present themselves to Program Managers. Because a CM is selected on qualifications, a Program Manager can choose a team to work on multiple projects. Continuity of people, processes and products is possible—with all the benefits that entails. (See *Rotation, Repetition and Refinement*, page 22.)

Alliancing

Alliancing is an innovative project delivery process that theoretically maximizes collaboration by removing contractual partitions between the key project companies. There are multiple variations.

Since it's new, there is a tendency to adjust the approach with each new implementation. But in general, it works like this: Selection procedures are rigorous. When the owner selects a firm, that firm is added to the selection committee to participate in the selection of the next firm. All the firms are selected for a core project team. They sign a single, multi-party contract with the owner and form a management committee. The owner establishes a set of project goals—cost, time and quality—plus other conditions such as the use of minority firms, community relations and safety. The owner's auditor audits the companies and the owner reimburses the prime firms at their cost. They receive a predetermined profit if they meet the goals. The profit is reduced if the project falls short of the goals and increased if it exceeds them.

Alliancing makes most sense when a high degree of collaboration is crucial and the project's importance will capture the attention of the prime firms' leaders.

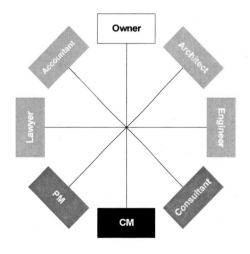

One day, I was discussing project delivery with Phil Bernstein. Bernstein was teaching professional practice to aspiring young architects at Yale and working as a vice president of the AEC Solutions Division at Autodesk. He ponders the future of project delivery. He is knowledgeable about innovation in project delivery and is at the front edges of the subject. He said:

> *"I have no idea how to explain project delivery strategy clearly to my students anymore. Every day seems to bring a new process."*

If he's challenged, he should be. The options are infinite. As we researched the methods used by serial builders, it became clear as a mountain creek that each of these builders invented a new deal; they developed unique processes to fit their own mission and their own constraints.

The construction industry is increasing its attention to processes that enhance collaboration.

But there are directions. One of the most evident is that our industry is giving increasing attention to processes that enhance collaboration. Alliancing is an example.

SOME HISTORY

In the middle of the 20th century, the conventional wisdom was that contract language, tight controls and the punitive consequences of non-performance would produce the right results with contractors. But guess what? Legal action inevitably ricochets. When a client sues a contractor for a mistake, the contractor's retaliatory defense is to identify the mistakes of the client and the AE. And by the time a project is finished, everyone has made plenty of mistakes. So a lawsuit initiated by one party clones itself and migrates through the extended project team like a computer virus.

Punitive contractual requirements increase everybody's liability.

So the focus on punitive contractual requirements usually delivered the unintended consequences of increasing everybody's liability. Claims grew. By the 1980s, professional liability insurance cost was half of the average AE's profit. Few large projects finished without claims—often morphing into lawsuits. This state of affairs gave more validity to the frequently heard quip: "design-bid-build-litigate."

Furthermore, the pain of enforcement in federal or state courts was usually greater than the pleasure of winning a settlement. Legal processes are long, complex and expensive. So warring parties settle most conflicts by mediation, arbitration or on the courthouse steps. Inevitably, the compromise satisfies no one.

Some implacable owners added more pages to their contracts and more consultants for checks and balances to their project teams. But other more creative industry pundits began to look for ways to avoid conflict. Rather than concentrating on retribution, they argued that aligned self-interest and shared project goals would produce collaborative personal relationships and a project culture that inspires mutual support. And that would improve results.

This shift in attitude took many forms. Some owners began to treat contractors as professionals and made them a part of the project team from the start. Construction management, in its many forms, sprouted and blossomed almost overnight. Best-value and qualification-based selection procedures began to replace low-bid selection.

Some owners began to treat contractors as professionals.

Many owners recognized the importance of processes that focus on interpersonal relationships and the human aspects of design and construction. They looked for ways to enhance performance through collaboration. Partnering and Total Quality Management (TQM) contributed collaboration processes. Although non-contractual, they helped. However, with traditional adversarial contracts, commitments often waned soon after the Partnering session. The lack of contractual mechanisms to support the Partnering goals often left them ineffectual in the face of a serious conflict. Each ship rode on its own bottom, and many project players held the belief that there could be some winners and some losers.

Alliancing adds contract concepts to collaboration and Partnering and holds promise. Its roots, as far as our investigations would take us, are in the energy industry. In 1990, British Petroleum was struggling with the high cost of building an offshore drilling platform in the Andrew field—a relatively small reservoir in the North Sea lying some 230 km northeast of Aberdeen. It appeared commercially unattractive. The development initiative had been started and stopped for 16 years.[1]

Alliancing adds contract concepts to collaboration.

1 The project is described in *No business as usual: An extraordinary North Sea result*, copyright 1996, Terry Knott. Published by British Petroleum Company P.L.C. Britannic House, 1 Finsbury Circus London EC2M 7BA United Kingdom.

A BP in-house team became intent on building a collaborative organization from disciplines and contractors that were traditionally adversarial. They formed an integrated group that combined engineering, subsurface and commercial interests and produced striking results.

They were spectacularly successful. The team drove down the cost from the initial estimate of £450 million to £290 million and finished six months ahead of schedule. In 1997, the UK construction industry presented the project with two awards: "Major Project of the Year" in the Quality in Construction category and "Project of the Year" as the overall winner across all industry sectors.

Alliancing migrated from the North Sea to Australia. Understandably, the first projects were in the oil and gas industry. The Wandoo Oil Field Project, a Western Australia offshore oil field, began in 1994. It was delivered $13 million under the target budget of $377 million, and in 26.5 months against an industry norm of 34 months.

Then Alliancing migrated to public infrastructure projects and public buildings. The first building project we found that used Alliancing was the National Museum of Australia. Parliament allocated $155 million for the project. Perhaps, with the agonizing memory of the Sidney Opera House cost overruns still lingering in their psyche, they said:

> *"Don't come back. Spend it all if you need to, but don't ask for more."*

Alliancing produced results on the National Museum of Australia.

The Alliancing team delivered a high-quality building on time and in budget. Andy Anway (president of Amaze Design, Inc. in Boston, Massachusetts) was the exhibit designer on the museum project. When we talked to him, his comment was in the form of a question:

> *"Have you ever worked on a project where everything seemed to click?"*

The National Museum of Australia was funded by the Australian Commonwealth Government "as a 'flagship' project opening the Centenary of Australian Federation celebrations." It was finished within the budget and completed a day before the opening. As of this writing, the project has won at least 13 awards for the quality of the building and the quality of the process. You can see photos and read more at http://www.nma.gov.au/about_us/the_building/.

How to do it

Before we describe the process, let's make something clear. As we write this document, there is little track record for Alliancing in the U.S. So Alliancing requires an owner who wants to think outside the box, is willing to take the risks and has the authority and managerial competence to take those risks.

Remember, although pioneers take the arrows they also get the most fertile ground. Although there are variations on the themes (and there will clearly be more), following are the salient components of the process:

Pioneers take the arrows. They also get the best ground.

Selection

In most of the examples we studied, Alliancing starts with a radically improved team selection process. The steps aren't unusual but the intensity is.

Alliancing starts with an improved team selection process.

It begins traditionally. The owner invites organizations to present their qualifications, shortlists a small group and then holds interviews.

Tradition ends there. The interviews are not the typical, wooden, one-hour PowerPoint show-and-tell followed by superficial Q&A. It's a workshop. The firm under consideration may spend the first hour on a presentation, but the rest of the time is spent without props. Discussion turns to the project and how to do it. Among other items of discussion, the interviewees are asked to evaluate the program and the initial plans—a reverse interview.

The objective is to use the selection process to evaluate collaborative and innovative skills. The interview process continues through dinner and late into the night. (We were told that occasionally the Australian tradition was to lubricate communication at dinner with a bit of alcohol.) So another objective is simply seeing how the people like each other.

When the owner selects the first firm, that firm joins the selection team. Then the expanded selection team picks the next firm, and it too joins the selection team—and so on.

Team selection is sequential—with each selected team joining the selection committee.

The core project team signs one contract. Each member is paid at cost. They all share in profits if the goals are met.

CONTRACT AND COMPENSATION

There's one contract. The owner and all the prime firms sign. The result is an organization of principal participants—AEs, consultants, PMs, CMs and builders—that covers the primary bases necessary to deliver the project. The firms participate in a multi-party contract.

The owner provides a lawyer who counsels with all the prime firms (the signatories) in drafting the contract (although there's nothing to prevent the prime firms from consulting their own lawyers as well). Everybody agrees to the same terms and conditions.

The owner has an accountant who audits each of the prime firm's books to determine the firm's normal overhead and profit rates. The auditor develops a formula for each of the prime firm's basic compensation and then for the upside and downside participation in bonuses or losses.

A management committee made up of members from the core team members guides the project.

A management committee guides the project. (The management committee was called the Alliance Leadership Team on the Australian National Museum.) The management committee includes the owner and top executives from each of the prime firms. In some cases we heard that decisions must be unanimous—a tough hurdle.

Normally the contract states clear project goals and defines ways to measure achievement. The goals may include the classic cost, schedule and quality, but other goals of safety, small business or minority participation or community relations may be included. The owner may evaluate some of the performance subjectively.

Some of the Alliancing contracts stated that the mission of the core team firms is to deliver performance at the highest level that anyone on the team has experienced in the best project of their lives—not business as usual. That statement, like much of the Alliancing language, is contractually difficult to interpret.

Alliancing is not a concept that most owner lawyers would invent. The scope of work for the prime firms who are members of the management committee is general—not highly detailed. The management committee may adjust it as the project progresses.

The parties to the contract agree to avoid disputes and litigation. They commit to notify each other openly of differences of opinion or conflicts of interest. They promise to strive to a resolution in open discussion. And they agree to do it quickly.

Each of the contract signatories (the prime firms) agrees not to sue any of the others unless there's fraud or willful default.

Christopher Noble of Noble & Wickersham LLP in Cambridge, England, is a knowledgeable and nationally respected construction attorney. He helped negotiate the Alliancing contract for the National Museum of Australia and participated in conferences on the subject. When I asked him if this clause was enforceable, he responded:

> *"Who the hell knows? But it sure encourages people to work out problems."*

The owner reimburses each firm at cost. "Cost" is determined by the owner's accountant and depending on the project, or the stage of the project, each firm may work within a guaranteed maximum. The management committee may adjust the distribution of work and the guaranteed maximum. However, the management committee can't change the sum of the GMPs without agreement from the owner.

Everybody's feet are held to one fire. A single pool of money finances the entire project and is divided into categories for costs, profits and bonuses for the prime firms.

If the team meets the project goals, the participants share in the profit pool based on their normal profit rates. If the team exceeds the goals, the profit is enhanced from the bonus pool. The British and the Australians name this bonus pool Gainshare. It's a risk/reward payment made to or paid by the Alliance participants in addition to direct costs, overheads and normal profit. It's calculated on the basis of performance.

There are variations on compensation terms. In some cases, each of the prime firms provides a GMP for its services so the project cannot (theoretically) exceed the budget. In other cases, a benchmark budget is set. If the project costs less than this budget, the owner pays less and each of the prime firms (in addition to normal profit and bonus) shares some of the savings, according to a formula.

The core team members agree not to sue one another.

In other cases, the budget is set and there's a "pain/gain" formula. Everybody shares in the reward if there are savings, but if the project overruns the budget, everybody's toes get singed and the team pays into the pool to cover the loss.

The contract stipulates the goals and the metrics for measuring and exceeding the goals. The management committee may adjust the goals or the metrics by unanimous decision, which includes the owner, as the project progresses. (My guess is that most owners would want veto power on any adjustment.)

The management committee prorates the profit and bonus pools based on level of effort, performance and risk.

All the firms must collaborate to meet the budget, but the owner must collaborate as well to adjust scope so the budget is achievable. An Alliancing project could conceivably fix scope or schedule and leave cost as a variable—or keep all three variables adjustable.

There are lots of workshops.

The prime firms recognize that the result will come from collaboration, and collaboration is enhanced by simply working together in the same location. So there are many workshops. Often the team is housed on the same site.

Some problems with Alliancing

First, it's not well understood. Tradition provides the primary set of operating rules, the functional structure that people in the construction industry understand, albeit imperfectly. Tradition fits the myriad organizations into place and provides guidelines for their relationships.

When an owner abandons tradition, there must be enormous emphasis on communication or everyone will simply revert to traditional roles. Then the gears of tradition will strip, grinding against the parties that are implementing the new processes.

It is impossible to completely align everybody's complete interest.

There's no way to arrange contractual mechanisms to produce the same goals and interests. There will never be a perfect alignment. It's an imperfect world. For instance:

- Some designers will still be inclined to study the project more and delay the delivery of drawings. Some constructors will still be production minded and will want to get the drawings early.

- The owner reimburses everyone at break-even. That minimizes the inclination to load people on a job to increase profits. Minimizing helps, but an organization that has surplus labor may want to park it on the job, while one that is short of labor may short the job.

- If a budget isn't set at the start of the project, and if the project team has the responsibility to define the scope, cost and schedule, the participants are setting the yardstick that will be used to measure their performance. That's a conflict of interest. If they set the budget and then share in budget overruns, the tendency will be to set a high budget.

- If the project management committees don't include the company leaders who are empowered to make decisions Alliancing won't work. So unless there's a very large project or very prestigious project involved, the brass from a large company won't be interested.

- Despite the success of the BP Andrew Field project, Alliancing didn't become common in the energy industry. Many contractors wanted lump-sum contracts that had a chance for windfall profits and didn't require all that top management attention. Many owners wanted fixed prices. Many groups that financed projects wanted fixed budgets.

WHEN TO USE ALLIANCING

Alliancing appears to make consummate sense for a unique, prestige project where the need for collaboration is high, the danger of cost overruns is prevalent and where participation of top leadership from the core project teams is likely.

Alliancing is right for prestigious projects that will attract the core team leaders.

Unique, prestige projects are characterized by great ambition from the designers to make a unique, prestige design. That inevitably threatens the budget. There's a looming danger of runaway costs. (The Sydney Opera House blew its budget into the ionosphere. The Australian Commonwealth Government didn't want an encore so they made clear that their appropriation for the National Museum of Australia would not be augmented.)

Prestige projects get the attention of the top brass from the participating companies—a necessary ingredient for the management committee, the Alliance Leadership Team.

Alliancing is a transparent, collaborative form of design-build.

In our research, we've discussed many serial builders. It's hard to see Hines, Target and the Post Office using Alliancing. It's easy to see GSA using Alliancing on a courthouse or Rice using it on a major departmental building or The Methodist Hospital using it for an innovative, cutting-edge lab building.

A PHILOSOPHICAL VIEW OF ALLIANCING

Alliancing is a form of design-build with special contract conditions. These special conditions are designed to increase transparency among all parties, align everyone's goals, enhance collaboration and minimize conflict. What in the world could possibly make more sense?

A century ago, a company like the Austin Company could deliver a building with an integrated team under a single contract. The team goals were aligned because everybody worked for the same company. Now the industry is specialized and fragmented. A project is an ad hoc assembly of specialized organizations, each operating with its own prejudices and self-interest. Each views the world from its own corner. Each works on its own turf.

The team members must engage one another to produce the result the owner needs. So organizations are collected into groups and managed by a handful of traditional players: AEs, CMs, PMs, GCs, etc. Flanging them all together in a unified project contract is a simple and logical next step.

In my career, I have participated in many joint ventures with other companies to design and/or construct a project. We have found that the best form of contract is one where each JV partner bills the JV at break-even cost. A JV management committee allocates the resources of the JV partners. Then, if there's profit, the JV partners split it according to a fixed agreement.

That's the core concept of Alliancing. It's only a short hop to include all the members of the project team in such a joint-venture contract.

Alliancing is simply a design-build contract, with a Fixed Limit of Construction Cost (FLCC). (See a discussion of a FLCC on page 122.) The new wrinkle is that the owner participates on the management committee.

Think about that. What a great idea! The owner we've been hired to serve, the people who will either praise or pan us as a reference for future projects, is on the team. We are, finally, willing to acknowledge the need and the value of their active participation in the planning and management of the delivery process. The simplicity of the concept is astounding.

It's a process and a set of agreements based on incentives rather than punitive consequences, morality rather than legalities. And when you think about it, common sense over the alternative. There's a powerful and positive message: everybody must sink or swim together. Of course, that's the way we always said it was in the construction industry, but traditional contract arrangements don't really reflect that reality.

Alliancing is based on incentives instead of punitive consequences.

Alliancing sounds great to inspire collaboration, mutual support, shared goals, pooling of intellectual capital and sharing risk and rewards. Alan Fleishacker, who was 3D/I's general counsel and has degrees in both architecture and law, said:

> *"It's great to prevent things from going wrong. However, what happens when they do?"*

That's an insightful and penetrating question. The answer is perplexing. But it can't be worse than the alternatives.

Job Order Contracting

Job Order Contracting (JOC) is by definition a program tool. JOC is designed for organizations that have multiple projects.

JOC was invented to get small projects done fast. It provides owners, particularly public owners, with a competitively selected, on-call organization that can jump on a small job with short notice, bypassing the typically sticky wickets of procurement.

I'm not sure there's any statistical evidence, but if there were, I'd bet it would show that the U.S. has the world's most ethical procurement processes. The procurement officers in our large corporations, institutions and government organizations deserve much credit.

However, the safeguards that serve our industry so well hinder an owner with a modest project that needs immediate attention.

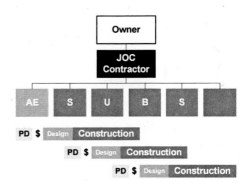

Invented for small projects, JOC is essentially a cost-reimbursable, multi-project contract with reimbursement usually based on predetermined unit costs .

Many organizations must design, bid and award to the lowest bidder for all projects—an unreasonable amount of hassle for small jobs.

When the roof is leaking, there's a need for a selection and contracting vehicle to get it fixed quickly.

Before JOC, many organizations, particularly public organizations, required every project to be designed, bid and awarded to the lowest bidder—no matter how small the project. It was an unreasonable amount of hassle. It took too long and carried too much administrative attention for small projects.

So JOC was invented. It started in the Air Force in the 1980s. The process caught on and spread rapidly. In the last few years, many states have authorized the use of JOC.

JOC provides quick response for small jobs with minimal design requirements. It's inappropriate for major projects. It's typically used for maintenance, renovations, alterations, additions and minor new construction. Some states prohibit the use of JOC for projects over a stipulated dollar amount, typically in the range of a million dollars.

The JOC concept is not intended to avoid careful and fair procurement processes. The idea is to do one selection process, pick one or a small group of qualified contractors and establish cost and contract terms that can be applied to undefined future projects.

How to do It

Establishing cost parameters and contract conditions for unknown future work presents some challenges, so naturally there are variations in the approach. Following is a discussion of the most common.

The RFQ

A JOC contract is for multiple small projects.

Typically a JOC contract is initiated by an owner who has a continuing need for small design and construction projects. The selection process looks pretty much like a standard public selection. The owner provides a broad description of the scope, issues an RFQ (request for qualifications) and evaluates the respondents.

The scope might be very narrow, limited to repetitive work like traffic light signalization or street repair. More often, the scope is quite broad and includes architectural, civil and MEP design and construction services. Consequently, those kinds of JOC contracts attract providers with broad capabilities in several design services as well as construction activities.

The owner should explain the potential scope to the bidder, including the maximum and minimum project size that will be let under the contract. And the owner should explain the volume of work that can be expected. It's a good idea for the owner to include the form of contract in the RFP and ask the bidders to identify any clause they object to and suggest alternate language they would accept. The evaluating criteria are the usual:

The owner stipulates the maximum and minimum project size and the expected work volume.

- Qualifications of key people and firm capabilities (construction management, architecture, engineering, etc.)
- Experience with design and construction, experience with JOC, experience with the owner and experience with similar projects
- Resources available for the work and the ability to handle multiple jobs simultaneously
- Management systems for documentation, reporting and communication
- Financial strength
- Quality assurance program, safety program and safety record
- Current client references

Many owners will assign numerical values to these items, weight them and then score the contractors for a short list accordingly. I've never liked that approach. It's putting precise values on imprecise judgments. It can produce the wrong result. For instance, if I had great experience with a firm, confidence in their integrity and had a track record of solving sticky problems with their leadership, I would want to shortlist them even if they were outscored in other categories.

The RFP

After the owner, or the owner's PM, makes a short list, the owner issues an RFP (request for proposal) to the short-listed firms. The firms are asked to bid a coefficient. The coefficient is to be applied to a price book that the owner names.

Firms bid a coefficient. Projects are priced by multiplying the coefficient times the unit prices from the price book.

A price book is a list of unit prices for all the conceivable labor and materials that could possibly be included in a normal construction project. The most widely used is published by RSMeans and has factors to adjust prices for different geographic locations. The price book is adjusted periodically for inflation.

Projects done by the JOC contractor are priced by multiplying the coefficient times the unit prices from the price book. So if the owner wants a new sidewalk and the price book says it's $10 a square foot, and the JOC contractor has bid a coefficient of .92, the cost of the sidewalk to the owner is $9.20 a square foot.

The RFP usually stipulates a maximum dollar amount that may be assigned and a minimum total that is promised. This vision of steady work creates an incentive that attracts competition among a wider range of contractors. Then the owner may select the firm with the lowest coefficient. Or the owner may hold interviews and make a "Best Value" selection, considering qualifications and interview scores as well as the coefficient.

PROJECT EXECUTION

The owner defines the scope; the JOC contractor designs the project, does a quantity take off with unit price book and the coefficient and establishes a lump-sum price for the project.

Implementing an individual JOC project is comparatively easy. The owner identifies a need and contacts the JOC contractor. Together they review the requirements, review the location of the work, define the scope and perhaps consider different approaches. Then the JOC contractor designs the project (if necessary), does a detailed quantity take off of the required labor and materials and, using the chosen unit price book and the coefficient, establishes a lump-sum price for the project. The owner reviews the design and the price and either makes changes or issues an authorization to proceed.

Most JOC contractors use an in-house design staff or an architect already under contract to design the work as the need arises, saving substantial time.

Usually the master JOC contract will include a guaranteed minimum dollar amount of work to be done during the initial term of the contract and during subsequent option years, providing an incentive for the contractor to perform well. Typical JOC contracts also set a maximum at a few million dollars, but there's no reason this maximum couldn't be much higher.

Typically JOC contracts have a base year and several option years. There may be options for extension of the contract. The longer the relationship between the owner and the contracting firm, the more benefit is gained, so it's in the best interest of both owner and contractor to make the partnership work and extend the contract beyond the initial term.

Although JOC contracts are usually made with a single institution, related entities sometimes come together and combine their purchasing power to form a cooperative for economies of scale. For instance, the MOHAVE Educational Cooperative in Arizona allows all public agencies to use their procurement vehicle with a pre-selected JOC contractor.

VARIATIONS
Nobody does it the same. Each JOC selection procedure seems to have some variation.

Variation 1: Skip the RFP
Sometimes the best-qualified contractor is selected after the RFQ—before the RFP and before bidding the coefficient. Then the terms of the contract and the coefficient are negotiated with the selected firm. If there's a sticking point, the next firm on the list is considered, and so on down the line until an agreement is reached with one of the companies on the short list.

The JOC contractor can be selected on the basis of qualifications only.

When negotiating a proposed price coefficient, it's useful for the owner to test the coefficient by selecting a recently completed project, not done under a JOC contract, that is characteristic of the upcoming work program.

The owner, or the owner's PM, estimates the test project using the coefficient and the price book and compares the result to the project's actual cost. The estimate should be less than the actual because having many jobs covered by the JOC contract should produce economies of scale.

Variation 2: Pick multiple firms to bid
Another approach—a greater deviation from the standard—is to pre-qualify a small cadre of firms, perhaps three, eliminate the price book and simply ask for bids from each of the three firms. Most contractors don't like this approach. The cost of collecting subcontractor bids creates overhead for the general contractor, and there's competition between general contractors for the best subs. And it takes more time so the owner isn't much better off.

There can be multiple firms that are selected to bid each job—skipping the need for an RFQ.

Variation 3: Use a CM approach with a satisfaction fee
This is my favorite. The owner goes through the typical selection processes. In the RFP, the owner does not ask for a coefficient.

The JOC contractor can be picked on qualifications and fee. Then the JOC contractor can bid and be reimbursed for subs in a transparent process—like a lot of mini CM-as-risk contracts..

Instead, the owner asks the contractor to bid a fee for overhead and profit that would be applied to the construction cost. The fee might vary depending on the size of the job. The JOC contractor manages the design, procurement and construction and is reimbursed for these contracts at cost. Perhaps there's a GMP on each project.

If the fee is a percentage of construction cost, the owner may feel that the JOC contractor has a reverse incentive and will not try to save money. That's unlikely. The JOC contractor will be far more interested in gaining the owner's confidence and extending the contract through the option years.

Furthermore, a satisfaction fee will allow the owner to reward the JOC contractor for cost savings. And all the other benefits of the satisfaction fee will benefit the job. (See page 198.)

PROBLEMS WITH JOC CONTRACTS

Although there's a unit price book and a fixed coefficient, there's always room for disagreement and misunderstanding.

The price books have costs for different levels of assembly. There may be prices for total systems and separate prices for the components that make up the systems. Because there are differences in the assembly methods for combining components into a system, the price for the system may be more or less than the sum of the components. So a project estimate that uses systems might have a different price than the same project estimate that uses components.   The choice of pricing approach affects the price.

An estimate that includes both systems and components can be confusing. We've seen estimates that had prices for the total system and then some more prices for components that were integral to the system—a cost duplication.

Of course, a smart owner can review the estimate to ensure that line items are correct and not duplicated or that there are not costs for unnecessary General Conditions items. But it takes time and attention.

Also, there's always some judgment involved in the rules for a quantity take off. For instance, if you are pricing drywall and painting and there's a small window in the wall, that window is not subtracted from the wall area—it will just produce waste and more trouble. But if it's a large window, say from floor to ceiling and 10 feet wide, it will be subtracted. How big does a window have to get before you subtract its area?

Some line items in the price book are a little high and some are a little low. The coefficient from the contractor is based on an average of the entire price book. If the owner "cherry-picks" the low items the JOC contractor will sooner or later start declining projects and the program will fail. (Most, but not all JOC contracts allow the JOC contractor to decline a particular job.)

There's judgment involved in a quantity take off. It's not pure engineering.

An owner who asks for a lot of estimates but does not do many projects causes another problem. It's wise for the JOC contractor to help the owner develop a preliminary budget with a parametric estimate to check commitment to the project before a complete, line-item estimate is performed. This exercise is euphemistically known as an ROM (Rough Order of Magnitude). The ROM typically takes just a couple of hours and prevents a lot of wasted time for both parties.

There is fairness in the laws of large numbers, but specific items can be off.

THE ARGUMENT FOR JOC

Simplicity
Public organizations aren't the only ones with layers of procurement regulations. Many institutions and many large corporations have developed complex acquisition regulations. We've heard frustrated managers in large organizations complain that it costs more to hire a contractor than it costs to do the job.

The appeal of JOC is the administrative simplicity.

With JOC, it isn't necessary to pass through all the procurement wickets to select contractors and negotiate contracts for each little job. That's done once. Then the contractor and the terms of the contract are in place. All that's needed for a specific job is to fix the scope of work and set the price.

Speed
The work typically starts within a few weeks after the owner identifies a project. Sometimes a project can start within days. On one project, we began work only hours after an emergency phone call.

The obvious benefit of JOC is speed.

Organizations with sticky wickets in their selection processes love JOC—particularly on a Wednesday afternoon when the roof starts to leak.

The process stands the test of public scrutiny.

Objectivity

Since the coefficient is set competitively and prices are related to an objective price book, the process meets the fairness-in-contracting test for public procurement.

JOC reduces the owner's overhead.

Procurement efficiency

Since procurement procedures create significant overhead cost and require staff resources for both owner and contractor, going through the process only once amortizes the cost over many jobs.

Competition

If an organization buys small projects one at a time, it may have trouble attracting competition among the best contractors. If the same organization promises to buy a large collection of projects from a contractor, more contractors will be interested and the field of bidders will increase.

Culture

JOC is a method of contracting that is rotated from the project workflow to the program. The greatest benefit is subtle and hard to measure. In the best of worlds, the owner and JOC contractor develop a long-term, trusting relationship. Since collaboration improves as the JOC contractor gains understanding of the owner's culture, procedures and expectations, long relationships are good for both owner and contractor. Everybody wins. The owner gets better value and the JOC contractor has a happy client and steady work.

A PHILOSOPHICAL VIEW OF JOC

Unit price contracting is an old and wide-spread practice in the construction industry.

The use of unit prices to set the total cost of construction is a pretty old idea. For more than two centuries and throughout the British Empire, the common process has been for a licensed Quantity Surveyor to estimate the amount of the building materials in a job and for the contractor to bid unit prices to purchase and install those materials. Much U.S. highway work is done with unit prices for cut and fill. Developers usually price interior fit-out for new tenants with unit prices.

The philosophical underpinnings of the traditional "coefficient-based" JOC contract are sound and endowed with ample rationale and precedent. There's clear competition and the process stands up under public scrutiny. It's a good way to get things done.

But, like all the other processes for contracting for design and construction, there are flaws. No cost book reflects the true reality of construction costs at any place or any time. There are always—repeat, always—current market conditions that influence costs. A JOC contractor knows that and provides a contingency for unknown and unmanageable risk in the coefficient.

A JOC approach that uses a coefficient with a price book is not as good as a JOC approach that simply selects a design-build contractor on the basis of qualifications and stipulated fee that can be scaled for different volumes of work. Following the selection, the JOC contractor can take competitive bids from trade contractors on a project-by-project basis—essentially implementing a series of mini CM-at-risk with Design contracts.

MORE INFORMATION ON JOC

Information on Job Order Contracting is available at The Alliance for Construction Excellence (ACE), part of the Del E. Webb School of Construction at Arizona State University, through its Center for Job Order Contracting Excellence at http://construction.asu.edu/ace/.

Concepts of Project Delivery

Project delivery strategies change through time. Technology, economics, culture, tradition, the structure of design professions, the specialization of contractors and, most important, the character of owner organizations influence these changes.

In the last two centuries, industrialization and specialization marched forward. The building design function separated from construction and, now, because of the wealth of specialized subcontractors, management is separating from construction.

So Program Managers must envision an assembly of companies to design and construct the buildings in a program. Then the Program Manager must decide how to select them, what the relationship should be and what terms of payment are appropriate.

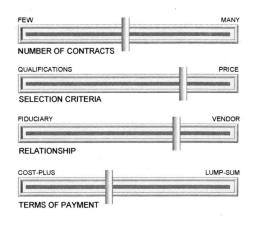

Although there seem to be infinite choices for project delivery, the points between opposite ends of four interrelated spectrum decisions are crucial. How are firms selected: price or qualification? What is their contractual relationship to the owner: agent or vendor? How many contracts should be used to do the project: one or many? How are they paid: lump-sum or cost plus? Then, at the program level, the crucial decision is to determine the project-oriented contracts and the program-oriented contracts.

Perhaps at the dawn of civilization, some cave dweller, watched by a mate anxious to move out of a dank cave, scratched a drawing in the sand and traded a mammoth tusk to get some help with building a hut. The cave dweller and the tusk-getter made a deal. It's likely that after work started, the cave dweller had some new thoughts about the design. The requirements changed, irritating the tusk-getter who thought he had a clear understanding of what he was supposed to build.

Around 1100, the Ancestral Pueblo People, often referred to as the Anasazi, built additions to their cliff dwellings in New Mexico by gouging holes in the stone face of the canyon wall and inserting pine logs for roof beams. Then they added rooms in front. The work must have been done by groups. One can't help but wonder what kind of agreement was used to assemble the construction teams. Surely there were agreements, albeit unwritten, and surely there were disagreements as well.

The Anasazi built additions to their cliff dwellings by gouging holes in the stone to support beam ends. Then they built rooms in front. There is no history to tell us what kind of barter was used to organize the construction crews.

Since then, in the pursuit of clear, enforceable agreements, we've invented infinite ways to structure the deal—to assemble and contract with the hundreds of specialized companies for the extraordinarily complex tasks of making a single building.

A building is the world's largest common product, built by the world's largest industry, custom-designed in many offices, fabricated in shops around the world and assembled outdoors in the mud and the rain. In a program, the process is further complicated by the need to purchase multiple buildings. If making and maintaining an agreement was tough for the cave dweller and the Anasazi, think of today's deal-making challenge.

The best project delivery process (the sequence of selecting and bundling organizations, defining scope, relationships, responsibility and compensation) is a source of constant debate throughout the industry. In the search for better approaches to solve the problems of the last project, the world's construction industry has invented a cornucopia of choices to deliver the next project.

So project delivery strategies change—constantly. Technology, economics, culture, tradition and, most important, the character of organizations shape these choices. However, in a global sense, they are influenced by the technical abilities of the people and the structure of the professions.

Design-bid-build didn't become predominant until there were an adequate number of architects and engineers. Similarly, CM agency and CM-at-risk depend on trained CMs who advocate the process and sell it to owners.

PROFESSIONS EMERGE AND PROJECT DELIVERY CONCEPTS FOLLOW

Industrialization in the 19th century created prosperity, the need for larger buildings and the need for trained architects and engineers. AE firms flourished and founded the AIA. Licensing of architects and engineers followed. Design separated from construction organizationally—and culturally. That enabled design-bid-build.

History is repeating itself. Continuing industrialization has steadily increased the number of subcontractors on a building project. Procuring and managing these subs is increasingly demanding. Now management is separating from construction. CM agency, CM-at-risk and Program Management are becoming common. CMAA was founded in 1982 and certification began in 1995.

INFINITE CHOICES FOR BUILDING DELIVERY

As the 21st century begins, the U.S. construction industry exceeds a trillion dollars, over a quarter of the world market.

Project delivery has been sophisticated by the industrial revolution, hindered by traditions, influenced by different organizational missions, constrained by regulations, changed by evolving technologies, complicated by the proliferation of specialized subcontractors, bent by the particular convictions of

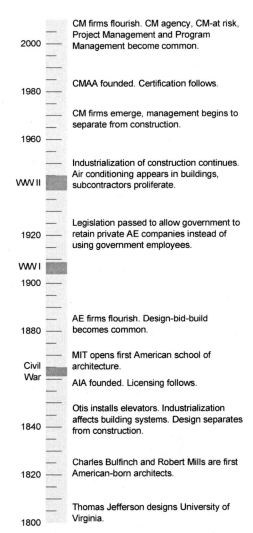

AE firms that emerged in the latter half of the 19th century enabled design-bid-build, just as CM firms enabled CM-agency and CM-at-risk at the end of the 20th century.

Industrialization has fostered specialization. Specialization has fostered the proliferation of subcontractors. More subcontractors demand more management.

individuals running large programs and set by corporate policies and public legislation. Today owners and their Program Managers have infinite choices to organize the design and construction of their projects.

And many owners and PMs are adding to the choices—being as creative with the process as the product. So as I describe these project delivery strategies, forgive me. Each process I describe has multiple variations. As I type each paragraph, trying to outline one of these basic approaches, I imagine my colleagues continuously arguing the flaws and fine points. All of us ponder the choices. All of us would like to use the best available processes. And all of us would like to anticipate how it will change next time.

FOUR KEY PROJECT DECISIONS

Many years ago we worked on a mega-project in a country with little construction infrastructure. Our job was to devise the project delivery strategy. We talked to everyone we could and heard deep convictions for an endless variety of approaches. Everybody had a core belief about the right way to do things.

Amid the confusion, we asked ourselves if there were some basic principles we could understand that would encompass all the choices. And if so, how should they guide us? The challenge started a life-long pursuit to understand the principles of making a deal for design and construction.

The institutions that represent the various sectors of the construction industry tend to see the best project delivery choices from their own point of view.

GCs, CMs and AEs have formed associations to advance their approach to business. You can obtain plenty of material on project delivery by contacting the American Institute of Architects (AIA), the Association of General Contractors (AGC), the Design-Build Institute of America (DBIA), the Construction Management Association of America (CMAA) and so on. Don't assume you'll get the same message. As you might imagine, these organizations see the world from their corner of the industry and their self-interest and professional bias is natural and to be expected.

Begin with the owner's natural desire to know what a project will cost and how long it will take. Add the fact that a design and construction operation involves hundreds, sometimes thousands of organizations and millions of parts. Consider that many of the people will be working together for the first time, and most of the systems will be assembled in ways they haven't been assembled before. Then think about the benefit of having subcontractors and manufacturers collaborate in the design process and the contractual barriers to making that happen. Add in an unreasonably long delivery time, weather uncertainty, price fluctuations, political pressures, changing regulations and diverse contracting procedures. Then stir in the archaic traditions of the construction industry.

Finding the best project delivery strategy becomes at least as challenging as the technical demands of design and construction. Conflicting motivations shape the process. We want to provide our clients with a contractually supportable definition so the sheets of drawings and specifications grow, but at the same time, we look for ways to save time and start construction before the drawings are complete. We want to choose specific products, but we want competition. We want to be professionals at our clients' side, representing their interests, but our clients understandably want responsibility and accountability.

The design of the best project delivery strategy takes as much creativity as the design of a building.

Our clients staff their own organizations with architects and engineers to manage the AEs, CMs and GCs they hire. They wisely define the process and cherry-pick companies and cherry-pick the people within the companies to work with. Meanwhile, they want to minimize the number of contracts they must deal with.

There are nearly infinite ways we assemble the nearly infinite number of interlocking parts required for a building program. All the processes exist because they satisfy different motivations to varying degrees. With good people, any of the common processes can work.

Many volumes written by project delivery pundits treat the subject as an exercise in assigning risk. The basic concept is that there is a fixed amount of risk in a project and it should be doled out to the organization best equipped to manage that risk. That's only partially true. A better thought is to bundle up a team, pick talent, build a collaborative culture and create a process that minimizes risk for all.

The objective is not to assign risk as much as to minimize it.

And there is another compelling school of thought that an owner can never fully shed risk. There are countless ways to

FIDUCIARY   **VENDOR**

service   product with service   product

RELATIONSHIP

An organization may have a fiduciary responsibility and represent the client's interest. Or, at the other end of the spectrum, an organization may be a vendor who delivers a specified product for a price.

contest any agreement in the world of design and construction. So the trick is to design the project delivery process that balances collaboration and accountability, minimizes risk for everyone and enables a project team to perform at their best.

So, with infinite choices, how does one go about choosing? We worked out the following parameters for decision making—and have been polishing and thinking about it ever since.

Relationship

A fiduciary is an agent: a person or an organization entrusted with the power to act on behalf of and for the benefit of another. A vendor is the opposite: a vendor sells something. In areas where we lack knowledge or skills, we are inclined to devise a relationship at the fiduciary end of the spectrum. For instance, we choose doctors and lawyers to represent our interest with this implied fiduciary relationship.

But if we know what we want to buy or exactly what we want done and the way we want it done, we tend to form a vendor relationship.

Traditionally AEs represented a client who was inexperienced in the labyrinthine practices of design and construction. So the AE was at the agency end of the spectrum. AEs defined requirements and then put the contractor at the vendor end. But inexperienced clients are disappearing and attitudes about agents and vendors are changing. As clients become serial builders, they hire construction professionals as in-house managers to run their projects.

These in-house construction professionals recognize that the professionals they hire can't provide flawless guidance and—like everyone else—are biased by self-interest. And these in-house construction professionals usually know what they want and how to get it. They bundle packages of responsibility and treat AEs more like vendors of designs, plans and specifications. And then many of them nudge the builders toward the agent end of the spectrum when they ask them for advice during the design phase and for help procuring and managing construction.

Furthermore, throughout our economy, vendors that sell products for a fixed price have recognized that a pervasive commitment to customer service is crucial. Like all consumers, clients want quality products with service *and* guarantees. They want the creative, collaborative relationship that is characteristic of professional traditions. They want a reliable product and a price they can count on. The sophisticated serial builder wants both.

Terms of payment

Contractors may be reimbursed based on their costs or they may be paid a fixed-price. There are many variations in between these extremes, such as:

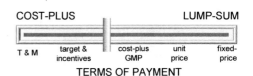

TERMS OF PAYMENT

Contractors may be paid in a lump-sum for a defined body of work or reimbursed for their costs as the job requirements unfold. There are many choices in between these extremes.

- *Target price with incentives* The contractor is paid actual costs plus a fee. However, a target price is set, and the contractor shares in the savings or the overrun.
- *Cost-plus with a GMP* The contractor is paid costs plus a fee. But a maximum price is set. If there's an overrun, the contractor eats it.
- *Unit-price* The contractor is paid a predetermined amount for each unit of material put in place (or removed).

Different payment terms may be combined in a single contract. For instance, many contracts are fixed-price with unit-price provisions for tenant work during lease-up. The terms of payment gravitate to the fixed-price end of the spectrum when the requirements can be clearly defined and to the cost-plus end when the scope is unknown.

The number of contracts

The first tier of contracts in a project can be awarded to one company, as in the case with design-build; to two companies, as with the traditional design-bid-build process; to many companies, an AE, perhaps 40 prime trade contractors and a CM when the agency approach to a CM contract is used; or perhaps hundreds in the case of direct purchase of building materials, equipment and labor.

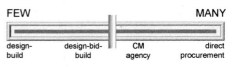

NUMBER OF CONTRACTS

As the number of contracts increases, so does the ability to save money, save time and increase quality. But risk increases too.

Multiple contracts facilitate fast-track. Unbundling design and construction eliminates overhead markups and allows selection of specialists and pinpoint selection of specific manufacturers and trade contractors. The opportunity to save time and money and improve quality increases as the number of contracts increases. So do risk and the burden of management. Clients who work with multiple contracts must manage them well or take responsibility for management failures. Consequently, most clients without strong construction management staffs look for ways to package contracts under a contractor or a CM to manage the risk.

Selection criteria

QUALIFICATIONS   PRICE

Brooks Bill   priced proposal   bid

SELECTION CRITERIA

If the product or service is commonly available, easily defined and straightforward to evaluate, selection can be based on price. Otherwise, qualifications must be considered.

The selection criteria should be governed by what is to be bought. If it's a common product, easily defined and easily evaluated, there's little reason not to choose based on price. But if it's a proprietary product or if value received is hard to measure (such as intellectual qualities of creativity, wisdom, judgment or experience), the selection will be based on qualifications.

Traditionally, AEs were selected with an emphasis on qualifications, and construction contractors were selected based on a price for their product—the building.

For the first 70 years of the 20th century, the AIA had a code of ethics that prevented members from quoting a price prior to selection. There was a fee schedule that the members agreed to. But in the late 1960s, the Justice Department decided that professional ethics can't intrude on anti-competitive prohibitions. The AIA was made to sign a "consent decree" that said, in effect, architects could be asked to quote a fee before they were hired. The obvious implication—the AIA's code of ethics was unethical. The fee schedule was price fixing.

Builders have been selected based on price, AEs on qualifications. That's changing.

About the same time, Congress passed the Brooks Bill that stipulated our government would select AEs based on qualifications and negotiate a fee after selection.

Meanwhile, specialization was marching on with more and more subcontractors for a single project. Smart owners recognized that the management skills of a construction contractor were crucial to project success, and qualification-based selection of contractors became more common.

Most owners now consider both price and qualifications for both AEs and builders.

Although the U.S. Government is still required to select architects and engineers based on qualifications, most private sector organizations consider price too. Selection of architects, engineers and contractors typically includes both price and qualification. Often, a sophisticated client requires a management plan as well.

So much depends on the experience and technical skill of the owner. For instance, a large developer with an in-house team of architects and engineers may well have more experience with the design and construction of the kind of buildings they build than the AEs and GCs who work for them. So they will likely short-list good organizations and ask for fixed prices. They know what they want and can tell whether they are getting it or not. They may also be pressured to demonstrate competition to their investment partners.

ROTATION

A Program Manager must make a new set of decisions that project managers didn't need to worry about. The Program Manager must consider what contracts should be awarded for the entire program and what contracts should be project specific. (See chapter on *Rotation, Repetition and Refinement, page 17*.)

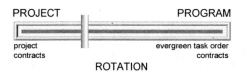

project contracts — evergreen task order contracts

ROTATION

FAST-TRACK AND GMP

Fast-track is construction industry jargon for overlapping design and construction. Fast-track saves time. It's also risky.

Clearly, the prudent course is to develop a fully coordinated set of construction drawings, precisely define the scope of work for all the subcontracts and price them methodically before committing to construction. But for many owners, in many situations, the value of time may be greater than the risks and headaches of fast-track. Maybe it's pressure on time-to-market for a new product, high interim financing costs or just a pressing need for new facilities. Furthermore, some projects are so big that they must be built in smaller bites.

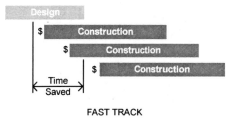

FAST TRACK

Fast-track will work with any process: CM-at-risk, CM-agency, design-build or Bridging. Even with design-bid-build, it's possible to award a few contracts to initiate a project and then assign them to a GC bid later when all the Contract Documents are complete.

Bridging is a good choice for a fast-track project. A project team can get Project Definition done faster than a complete set of working drawings. And the Contract Documents are fully enforceable. However, even with Bridging, there's a disadvantage. If the owner fast-tracks the project, the owner will forfeit the right to approve the complete set of Construction Documents to ensure a complete meeting of the minds before authorizing construction.

Fast-track is also straightforward with a CM-agency contract. The CM simply awards contracts based on complete Contract Documents for the items of work on the critical path and starts construction. The owner holds the contracts. But if the owner must build to a fixed budget, the owner must rely on the CM's estimate of the downstream contracts. That's proven to be a thin reed to lean on.

Two fast-track risks

The owner must take one of two risks.

Fast-track is technically easy. Obviously, you can begin clearing the site before working out the cabinet details. The problem is that once construction starts the owner is committed and there's no assurance of the final cost. So owners suffer with uncertainty about the total cost of their project.

Owners who fast-track their projects must take one of two risks.

1. They must depend on an estimate of the cost of unbid construction and hope it's right.
2. Or they must accept a defined price for an undefined product.

It's a poor choice. But despite frequent failures, good people make both approaches work—and do so every day.

Risk 1

If the CM makes a mistake, or if the market changes and the downstream contracts come in over the CM's estimate, the owner has to come up with the additional funds. Or the owner must cut scope—and that may be a tough thing to do after construction starts. Driven by unpredictable market conditions that might be global or local, double-digit annual variation is common for basic building products such as glass, steel, concrete, copper, PVC and lumber. And labor productivity can vary by 20% or more. If subcontractors are busy, they will hire inexperienced workers and plan for low productivity. Furthermore, there is just old-fashioned cost growth. Just stop and reflect on the disconcerting tendency for owners and their AEs to think of things to add to a project as it progresses through design.

Of course, good CMs can consider these matters and plan for them. Many fast-track projects succeed with good estimates and fat contingencies. But some don't. We all know of many situations where owners, after they have begun construction on a fast-track project, have been shocked by bids for downstream contracts that were painfully above the estimate. The construction industry is replete with projects that provided nasty cost surprises

Risk 2

Consequently, many owners have asked their contractor for a promise that the project can be built within their budget—a guaranteed maximum price (GMP). Sounds wonderful, doesn't it? But like Risk #2, a GMP, has problems too. It's a defined price for an undefined product.

A GMP is typically a defined price for an undefined product.

A GMP contract is shorthand for a cost-reimbursable contract with a guaranteed maximum price. It's typically given by a CMAR, a GC or a design-builder[1] in connection with a fast-track project. The owner wants to start construction before Construction Documents are complete but wants assurance that the project won't exceed the maximum.

The underlying message from the builder is:

> *"Not all the details are worked out so I don't know exactly what it will cost, but I know enough to know the maximum. Pay me for my costs as they become evident, and I promise the total will not exceed a maximum."*

It's an example of Risk 2. It's a defined price for an undefined product. Stop and think about it. If the documents were complete, the owner could bid the work or negotiate a lump-sum contract. But they aren't. It must be a cost-reimbursable contract.

The builder provides a GMP for comfort. But since the documents aren't complete, there can be (and frequently are) disputes about details that emerge as construction and the final drawings progress.

---

1 For simplicity, we will avoid endlessly repeating "CMAR, GC or design-builder" and just refer to this group as the "builder." If we refer specifically to a general contractor, we will use both words.

All the project delivery processes are flawed. Despite the problems in a GMP, the industry usually makes it work.

Nevertheless, although a GMP that is given on partially complete documents is legally inelegant, good people make it work every day. Much of the project is defined and the room for argument and dispute is narrowed. Following is a description of the common approach to making a GMP contract work.

TYPICAL PAYMENT TERMS IN A GMP

With CM-at-risk, design-build or a negotiated general construction contract that is based on a cost-reimbursable contract with a GMP, construction can start before the AE finishes working drawings. That saves time.

However, most owners want a GMP before starting construction. A cost-plus-a-GMP contract typically contains the following terms:

Fixed Fee for Overhead and Profit

Despite the fact that it's a cost-reimbursable contract, this part of the compensation structure is typically a lump-sum, not a percentage markup on construction cost or a cost-reimbursement item for a level of effort.

Reimbursable General Conditions

General Conditions Construction is the non-permanent construction work necessary to support the project. The builder is reimbursed, typically at cost without markup, for such items as bonds, insurance, security, the on-site trailer and office equipment, communications, printing and the necessary work to support the construction activity (temporary utilities, fencing, signs, cleanup, barricades, site toilets or perhaps gravel for a workers parking area).

The on-site management team is usually part of the General Conditions. It is also reimbursed at cost to give the contractor flexibility in adjusting the size of the team as the project progresses. The contractor can downsize the team to save the client money. Or the contractor can add to the team to improve results. Since reimbursement is at cost, the client doesn't suspect the contractor of trying to increase profits.

Some owners want a separate GMP on the General Conditions although most builders will argue that it should be a flexible number constrained only by the total GMP.

A CM can put these items of work into a subcontract or procure them directly. For instance, the gravel, barricades or site toilets could be put in the package of work done by a site-work contractor. However, the site-work contractor would likely add overhead and profit to those costs.

If the CM procures that work directly, the CM takes on more work and is reimbursed at the cost of the purchase without markup. That saves money for the owner and makes more work for the CM. So a CM that proposes a large budget for General Conditions construction items may be saving money for the owner and assuming extra work without extra fee.

Therefore, the cost of General Conditions construction should not be considered part of the CM's compensation when comparing one CM's fee to another. It should be reviewed in detail to compare the competing CMs' understanding of the project.

If the owner requires the CM to provide a performance and payment bond, the cost of the bond is included in the General Conditions. The CM may also require bonds from major subcontractors that will be included in their costs.

Subcontracts

The builder is reimbursed the total cost of all the subcontracts at cost without markup. Typically the builder doesn't pay the subcontractors until the builder is paid. The builder agrees to a payment schedule with the subcontractors based on a schedule of values that will consider retainage, percent complete, material on site, or a labor-loaded CPM schedule. The builder calculates the amount due, approves the invoice and submits it to the owner for reimbursement.

Contingency

Typically the GMP is given after some, but not all, subcontracts have been bid. The builder knows the estimates of the unbid subcontracts are fallible. And, of course, everybody knows there are bound to be unpredictable events.

Estimates for unbid work are fallible.

Therefore, there's a contingency. It's a line item within the builder's GMP. It reflects the builder's inability to predict the cost of unbid work with absolute accuracy. It may also cover ambiguity in the plans and specifications or those unpredictable, unanticipated costs that may arise during construction. Most contracts stipulate that the contingency can cover the builder's mistakes.

The earlier the GMP, the greater the contingency.

If an owner wants a GMP early in the project, the contingency will be larger than if the owner can wait until most or all of the subcontracts are bid. If an owner insists on negotiating a modest contingency, the builder will estimate unbid contracts conservatively, effectively increasing the contingency.

The builder's contingency belongs to the builder to pay for variations between estimates and bids, unpredictable events and mistakes.

The contingency is within the GMP and belongs to the builder if it's needed. But any unused contingency should be returned to the owner. (See *Shared Savings*, page 196.)

The owner should also have a contingency. It should belong to the owner and be controlled by the owner. The owner's contingency is for changes the owner will inevitably want to make during construction.

The builder's contingency is inside the GMP, the owner's contingency is outside the GMP— usually.

So the builder's contingency is within the GMP and usually the owner's contingency is outside the GMP. However, in some cases, perhaps for financing or appropriation accounting, owners have asked a builder to include a line item for an owner's contingency within the GMP that is controlled by the owner for owner changes.

If the builder gives a GMP prior to the completion of Construction Documents, and if items "not logically implied" by the GMP documents are added to the Construction Documents, or if the owner or the architect make changes, that nasty term "change order" will be loud and clear.

As long as the subcontracts are within the GMP and they are reimbursed to the builder, the builder is inclined to represent the owner's interest in negotiating changes with subcontractors. This is particularly true if the owner is a serial builder. The carrot of repeat work is attractive to the builder. However, all builders, particularly those who bid work competitively, also rely on good relationships with the subcontractors.

So there are plenty of allegiances among the construction community that might dilute a builder's allegiance to an owner. And if the builder feels the costs may exceed the GMP, the builder's allegiance will quickly turn to self-interest in negotiating changes.

Self-performed construction

There are regions of the country where it's still common for a general contractor to do the concrete work and perhaps the carpentry or the masonry. In those areas, the general contractors will argue vigorously to do that part of the work. In private sector work, it may be the best of bad choices, but it's seldom good practice. It leads to a perceived (or real) conflict of interest and it confuses project accounting.

Self-performed construction by a builder working under a GMP is a bad practice.

It's always a bad practice for public work and should be avoided. Perceptions are important in the public sector. A builder working under a GMP should take bids for all of the permanent construction work to give everyone a fair chance at the work and demonstrate fair pricing. Then the builder should see to it that each of the subs delivers what is specified. A builder cannot perform that role convincingly on work done by the builder's own employees.

Some owners have been persuaded that it's an acceptable practice if the builder bids their work against other subs. That usually doesn't work well. The other subs don't want to work for the builder if they just beat that builder out of some work. Furthermore, they feel that the contractor has an advantage.

Builder-furnished equipment

Furthermore, it's bad practice for a builder working under a cost-reimbursable GMP contract to furnish builder-owned construction equipment to the project. Even though the CM-at-risk might refer to some national authority for fair rental rates, such rates are notoriously overstated, and there have been situations where builders "parked" equipment on site when it was not needed elsewhere. Again, even if the CM-at-risk is scrupulously fair, the perceptions are wrong.

It's also bad practice for a builder working under a GMP to furnish construction equipment for the project.

ARRIVING AT A GMP

There's a right way and a wrong way to set a GMP.

The wrong way

We've seen many owners operate under the assumption that a builder can estimate the cost of construction and provide a properly priced GMP based on partially completed construction drawings and specifications. In several cases, we've watched

Asking for a GMP too early in the process will produce fat estimates, brother-in-law deals and conflicts over scope.

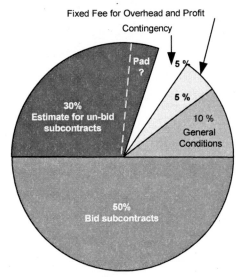

Fee Components in a GMP

owners insist on a GMP at the end of Design Development so they could go to a board or a legislature with a price for approval of the project.

That approach will work but it will invariably cost the owner money, scope, unhappy users or all of the above.

Since the drawings and specs are incomplete, they are inadequate for Contract Documents that the builder can use with subs. The builder can't competitively bid contracts with the subs. Nor can the builder negotiate from strength. So an early GMP will cause one or all of the following problems.

Fat estimates

The builder estimators don't want their company to lose money on the downstream contracts so they will estimate conservatively—to pad the estimate and include contingencies to avoid risk.

We've seen a number of projects where the builder provided estimates during design. Then, when pressured to provide an early GMP, the builder added a large pad and increased the price to cover the risk. The consequence is a gnashing of teeth, an unpleasant "value elimination" session and painful down-scoping. Then on bid day, lo and behold, a low price, well under the budget.

But the users were still mightily unhappy because they gave up some of the facilities they wanted, and after the low bid it was clear that they could have afforded what they had sacrificed. So the owner loses scope, the architect may lose fee and the builder loses face.

Good-old-boy deals

To shed risk, the builder chooses trusted subs for estimates and extracts agreements that the subs will bid the work within their estimate—essentially asking for the same kind of "defined price for an undefined product" that the builder has agreed to.

Consequently, the subs pad their estimates to cover risk and since they don't have competition, they usually include a better-than-good profit. Because the viability of builders is rooted in a trusting relationship with their subs, they do their best to get the work to the firms that did the estimate—limiting competition and increasing cost.

Conflict over scope

Finally, as drawings are completed after the GMP, there are potential disputes over what was "logically implied" but not included in the incomplete plans and specifications. We've heard many owners tell us they believe they are paying a premium for CM-at-risk and other negotiated GMP contracts over design-bid-build. In most cases, after a little questioning, we've learned that the owner was asking for an early GMP.

Here's the point. If an owner asks a builder to take an unpredictable or unmanageable risk, a reliable builder will include a contingency to cover the maximum risk. The builder can break even if the risk hits maximum or the builder can make a windfall profit if the risk fades away. The owner will break even or lose. So there are few situations where an owner should ask a builder to take an unpredictable or unmanageable risk.

The right way

A process that allows the builder to take bids for subcontracts in a methodical way lowers the builder's risk and will reduce cost for the owner. So a better approach to getting a GMP in a fast-track project is to bring portions of the Contract Documents to *100%* completion in stages. Here's the right idea: *instead of setting the GMP with 100% of the drawings 75% complete, set the GMP with 75% of the drawings 100% complete.*

The way to do that is to choose subcontracts of the project that are:

1. Easy to document and specify with little work (that might be roofing, carpeting, curtain wall)
2. On the critical path (site clearing, foundations, structural frames, basic core and shell

With 100% complete documentation for those subcontracts, the builder can award enforceable contracts in a competitive process. The builder can estimate the unbid work, add an appropriate contingency and give a sound GMP. The process is transparent. The contingency is exposed, as are all the subcontractor bids. The contingency, if unused, is returned to the owner. In either case, the size of the contingency will invariably be proportionate

The right way is to take bids in a methodical way and provide a GMP when the project is substantially procured.

When the subcontractors are selected, the AE can design around their specific products.

to the degree of completion of the Contract Documents. A GMP based on completed Construction Documents minimizes risk and the contingency.

This deliberate phased development of Construction Documents and procurement of subcontractors benefits the design. During the completion of Construction Drawings, a builder will bid or negotiate prices for alternate building systems (such as elevators, curtain walls or mechanical equipment). When the most cost-effective system is selected, the AE can design around it (not every elevator will go in every shaft). Furthermore, the AE can include the manufacturers' shop drawings in the final Construction Documents.

There's another benefit. The builder can get the subs to check the AE's drawings and submit shop drawings while the AE is finishing the construction drawings. That eliminates the redundancy of replacing Construction Documents with shop drawings and provides an integrated set of Construction Documents. The final Construction Documents actually represent what is to be built. That saves money and reduces error during construction.

SHARED SAVINGS

Some owners worry that if, in a cost-reimbursable contract, during the course of the procurement, it becomes clear that the cost is less than the GMP, the builder will have little incentive to save money. To create an incentive to the builder to continue to reduce the cost below the GMP, some clients agree to "share the savings." The "shared savings" are defined as the difference between the final cost of the project to the builder and the GMP. In essence, the clause says the builder can keep some of that difference. The percentage is stipulated in the shared savings clause and might range from a few percent to considerably higher.

If the contract is a lump-sum and the builder is a low bidder, a shared saving clause makes sense. Essentially, you say to the builder:

> *"Go to work and see if you can't see something that isn't consistent with the plans and specs but that will be acceptable and save us money. If we accept it, you get a reward for your effort."*

But a shared savings clause with a cost-reimbursable GMP contract usually has unintended consequences. Assume the owner selected a builder based on qualifications to participate in the design phase. The builder estimates the cost of the work as the drawings progress. Then the builder will bid most of the subcontracts, estimate the cost of the unbid contracts, add a contingency and set a GMP. Under this arrangement, a shared savings clause is a problem. Here's why:

A cost-reimbursable GMP contract with a shared savings clause sounds good but usually has unintended consequences.

The builder estimates the cost of the unbid subcontracts. Knowing that prices always have an unpredictable element, the estimate of the unbid contracts is typically conservative—there's a pad. Then the builder negotiates a contingency. The GMP is the sum of the:

1. Fee for overhead and profit
2. General Conditions
3. Bid contracts
4. Conservative estimate of unbid contracts
5. Contingency

With a shared saving clause, the builder gets a percentage of the difference between the final cost and the GMP. In most cases the "savings" are most likely to come from the builder's ability to negotiate a large contingency and from the "conservative pad" built into the estimate for the unbid subcontracts.

The savings may come from padded estimates and an inflated contingency.

That's a great deal for the builder. Say that the builder is paid a 5% fee for overhead and profit. Say that half of that is profit. Say that there is a 10% pad in the unbid work that is 25% of the total contract value. That's 2.5% of the total contract value. Then say the contingency is 5%. That's a total of 7.5%. If the shared savings clause is 50%, the builder stands to increase profits from 2.5% to 6%—from the pad and the contingency.

So with a shared savings clause, the builder will be influenced to make the contingency as high as possible. The savings don't come from hard work or increased productivity. The savings will come from conservative estimating and from the unused portion of the contingency.

That produces a conflict. If the builder gets to keep part of the contingency, an owner is reluctant to let it be very large. A difficult negotiation ensues. And to stay safe, the builder is likely to make the pad fat and inflate other line items in the General Conditions construction. That will cause the architect and the owner to reduce the project scope needlessly. It's not in the owner's interest for the builder to feel risk. If that happens, candor is driven underground. The transparency in the relationships on the project team becomes cloudy.

There are two other undesirable consequences of a shared savings clause:

First, unshared, unbalanced goals

Project goals invariably include schedule and quality as well as cost. If the owner pays the builder a special reward for cost savings only, it will unbalance the builder's goals and will produce conflict with others on the team who support all the project goals.

Second, an erosion of trust

Shared savings will produce a perception of bias in the builder's advice. When the builder suggests something that will save money, others will suspect the builder of cheapening the project for profit.

The best arrangement is to give the builder time to take bids on most of the work, provide an adequate contingency and require that the entire unused contingency be returned to the owner.

The real incentive

The most important issue for any company is survival. An opportunity for repeat work is far more important than a killing on a change order.

If a builder is selected based on qualifications, the motivation is the same as the AE's. The most important issue for any company is survival. For many companies, good references and repeat work at a fair profit are more valuable than a killing on a change order. By far the most important incentive that an owner has is the promise of repeat work. But there must be a perception that repeat work will follow good performance.

A Satisfaction Fee

A satisfaction fee may apply to all the project goals, not just cost.

Other incentives are worth considering. While a shared savings clause often has bad side effects, a satisfaction fee may work wonders. Everybody's job is to produce a satisfied owner and the owner usually has many goals—cost, schedule, quality, community relationships, relationship with users, environmental concerns and on and on. Some of the success factors, such as cost and schedule, are quantifiable. Others are subjective, such as collaboration and the builder's initiative when the unexpected event occurs. Indeed, the builder (or other team members) must accept that many crucial matters are subjective.

One good approach is for the builder to set aside a portion of the fee and for the owner to match it.

The satisfaction fee should be parceled out and awarded to the builder periodically, perhaps quarterly, based on the owner's satisfaction with the builder's performance. The owner grades the builder and distributes the fee for that period. Holding periodic reviews during the project is important. It's smart to have feedback when the team can respond. When the project is completed, people can't correct the past.

It doesn't make sense to award the satisfaction fee at the end of the job. Nobody can change what's already happened.

The meetings should include the project managers from the owner and the builder, along with the principal executive management of each organization. In addition to the owner (or the owner's Program Manager) reviewing the builder, the builder should be invited to offer suggestions and criticisms as well. A two-way street helps.

The builder owes the owner superb performance. The owner owes the builder a clear description of the owner's expectations and an opinion of the builder's performance. And the owner owes the builder the time and attention to discuss those matters.

Systems to
Manage the Detail

PMIS

We develop Program Management Information Systems (PMIS) because our design and construction programs produce such enormous detail. Our brains can't host it all, not even all the data that is generated in a typical day. Yet we need to know promptly when things go off track. And all the members of the extended program team need frequent access to program information.

A good PMIS not only provides information to improve project results, it improves people. It's a simple thought: in a design and construction program, accurate information presents knowledge. It tells true stories about the program, informs management and engenders improvement—in the products, processes and, most important, the people.

The system must be tailored to a unique set of requirements and change as the organization's other systems change. Installing a PMIS is a journey, not a destination.

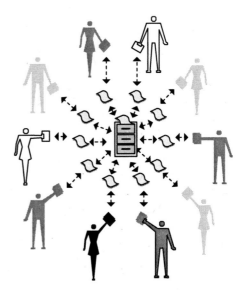

Information is the input and the output of Program Management. We gather information; integrate and validate it; record and distribute it. We add wisdom, experience and good judgment, and then we report. Finally, we provide directions. The directions are in the form of information too.

So obviously, information technology is enormously helpful—a necessary tool for effective Program Management.

PROJECT VS. PROGRAM INFORMATION

Program Management Information Systems (PMIS) are not the same as project management information systems.

Let me start this chapter with a crucial and much misunderstood fact: too many multi-project design and construction programs struggle forward with only *project* information systems— continuing the flawed management strategy of looking at a program only as a series of projects. Just as there is an important difference between running a project and a program, there's an important difference between project information systems and Program Management Information Systems.

Project management software, such as Prolog from Meridian or Expedition from Primavera, provides good tools for a general contractor to manage a tier of trade contractors.

These products typically provide detailed project accounting and reporting capabilities. The software also helps manage such information as owner and subcontractor changes, claims, RFIs (requests for information), submittals, payments, daily reports, weather logs, labor on-site, schedules and correspondence. The programs have matured and been accepted by many contractors who are using them skillfully.

Although many versions of project management software were developed during the 90s and died with the dot-com bust, several vendors with good products and staying power continued to refine their products and now have stable organizations. Meanwhile, to their benefit, young computer-literate men and women who received their higher education after the emergence of the PC have matured and taken positions of leadership among GCs and CMs. Few contractors limp along today without these effective tools.

Typically project-oriented products don't roll up information from multiple projects into program information or provide robust capability for collaboration across an extended program team. And, typically the products aren't easy to customize for unique owner requirements and procedures in large organizations: the vendors are interested in selling a product, not a service.

While project management software manages the details of a single project, Program Management software (a PMIS) must add new functionality. Some of the traditional vendors that provide project management software and some new companies have developed products aimed at owners and managers with capital programs rather than project-oriented general contractors and CMs. Meridian (now a subsidiary of Trimble) has developed Proliance and ProjectTalk, Autodesk has purchased Constructware, and Skire has produced effective software that is being used by many institutions of higher education.

PMIS software must report on the status of the entire program as well as individual projects.

Let me describe the characteristics of a good PMIS. I've broken the characteristics down into three categories.

1. Reporting: A good PMIS will record the capital plan, measure progress and report status to inform us and our management about the program status. Then we make on-course corrections. Most important, it will tell true stories and the program team will learn from one another's experience.
2. Documentation and Communication: The system should document project information, roll it up into program information and provide ready but controlled access to all the program stakeholders.
3. Control: A PMIS is not passive. It is a tool that managers use to instruct and control the extended project teams. We create formats and procedures to help manage and control these teams.

REPORTING

A Program Management Information System (PMIS) is first and foremost a tool to inform the program leadership about the current degree of success or failure in achieving a plan so they can operate the levers of control and make on-course corrections. Additionally, good reporting is probably crucial to keep clients happy. I remember a project that was in the ditch. Our client was cross at us and felt we weren't performing. We thought we were. Our joint-venture partner was complaining to me that

The first function of a PMIS is to keep leaders informed so they can apply their judgment.

the client simply didn't know what was going on and that we were doing a good job. He gave me a distressed look and asked: :

> *"How do you explain to a client that you are doing a good job when they think you aren't?"*

I asked to think about it over the weekend and then call him back. When I did I told him that I couldn't think of any way that didn't sound defensive. It was clear that the client didn't know what we were doing and that was our fault. Our job is to open a window into the program for the client to see. There's that transparency idea again.

The plan

The foundation of a PMIS is the plan that includes the scope of projects and an estimate of cost and time. Then, with regular accurate and disciplined input, the PMIS can measure progress and compare it to the plan so managers can manage.

"If you don't know where you're going, any path will do."

...The Cheshire Cat in Lewis Carroll's Alice's Adventures in Wonderland

Like most terms in the construction industry, "The Plan" has different names in different organizations. It's often called a capital improvement plan, frequently abbreviated to CIP. However, a school district may call its construction program a bond program, since it's typically financed by municipal bonds, and a retail chain may call it a roll-out plan. Other owners may call their plan a building program or a master development plan.

The capital plan is one of several plans that organizations make. Here's a brief lexicon:

Strategic plan
A strategic plan describes an organization's goals and the operations it will undertake to achieve them. It's typically an alphanumeric document that may be largely qualitative and not have much detail.

Master plan
A master plan illustrates how a strategic plan will be translated into bricks and mortar over time—perhaps an undefined long time. The master plan might be a vision of many years of development while a capital plan typically encompasses only a few predictable years. A master plan is usually presented as a rendering (maybe a physical or a virtual model) of the anticipated result, but there is substantial alphanumeric data to back it up.

Business plan

A business plan includes the depreciation and amortization costs of the capital plan plus the income and operating costs associated with the strategic plan. The business plan produces the organization's bottom line.

Cash flow plan

The cash flow is the actual cash-in, cash-out projection. It's different than income and expense. The projection of income and expense will not include the initial cash cost of capital expenditures. Buildings, real estate and equipment will be capitalized and depreciated at some rate over time. A cash flow will recognize those outflows.

For non-taxpaying public institutions, the cash flow is crucial. Typically tax-supported organizations don't bother much with balance sheets that capitalize and depreciate capital expenditures. They simply view capital expenses as cash events.

Scenario plan

A scenario plan presents a "what if" variation of the master plan. Recognizing that capital plans are rarely executed in their original form, owners and their Program Managers develop scenario plans based on speculations about the future.

For instance, if population increases and enrollment increases by 10%, how much more facility space will a school district need and what will it cost? If an experimental cancer treatment becomes successful, how much space will be required to implement it in the community?

Capital plan

A capital plan is to a program what a budget and schedule are to a project. It is a list of *capitalized* items rather than *expensed* items.[1] It schedules the capital costs necessary to implement the master plan—or perhaps a phase of the master plan if constrained by the available resources. The capital plan includes budgets for new facilities, renovation, major items of equipment and the capital renewal of existing facilities.

---

1. The cost of a capitalized item remains an asset on a balance sheet. In essence, one asset (money) is replaced by another asset (a building). Expensed items do not remain on a balance sheet. An asset (money) may be spent for items such as labor or utilities. After the expense, no asset remains.

Program Managers use the engineering tools of estimating and scheduling and apply insights into procurement and project delivery strategy to develop the plan details.

A PMIS will have a capital planning module to help the planning team develop budgets over multiple years, track project requests and authorize funds, report on deficiencies and deferred maintenance, prioritize projects through objective scoring, perform budget transfers, manage bonds, project cash needs, allocate funds to individual projects and capture funding sources.

Plans change

A capital plan is based on assumptions about cost, schedule and requirements: all three will change during the program.

Capital plans, the foundation for a PMIS, always change. I've never seen one executed as intended. Cost and schedule assumptions erode with the vicissitudes of time. Users change requirements.

Costs and schedules change

The plan is based on assumptions about the future: what construction will cost and how long it will take to design and build. Those assumptions often prove embarrassingly wrong. It's not that planners are inept. No one can predict the future and it's unrealistic to expect otherwise. Unexpected prosperity in Bombay may drive up the price of steel and bust a budget in Kansas City.

As the future becomes the present, assumptions are replaced with reality, conditions change and the Program Managers must be able to make on-course corrections.

Those of us who are AEs and CMs are eager to sell our services in a competitive environment. We tell potential clients how good we are at estimating cost and managing schedules. This marketing rhetoric leads many owners to believe we can forecast the future accurately and that the conditions that affect project delivery are predictable. They're not. Costs and schedules are determined by extrapolating experience and the unpredictable future will inevitably skew extrapolations one way or another. The result is an unhappy client. (See discussion of cost unpredictability on page 232 and schedule unpredictability on page 249.)

Requirements change

Plans fail because the future changes the assumptions.

It's not only the unpredictable construction industry that assails the plan. Technology, demographics, competition and the economy affect our clients. Programs with complicated buildings and long implementation schedules suffer many changes. And so the plan must change.

The need to adjust

These eddies and currents of change mean we have to know where we are as we are executing the plan. There must be information systems to inform Program Managers of drift from the plan or a change in the location of the target so they know to adjust.

We need the ability to make adjustments—to stay in control as the future unfolds. That ability includes:

- Convincing the owner's governance to expect change and realize that adjustment will be necessary so change will not cause confrontations and delay

- Having significant contingencies at both the program and the project level

- Developing flexible contracts with service providers and builders so change is not hampered by extended negotiations and legal review. Inevitably, that will mean having detailed cost information from the service provider so negotiations can be straightforward

Conventional wisdom holds that a good manager makes a plan and then executes it—as planned. When applied to our messy industry, that wisdom is misleading and inevitably brings disappointment.

The classic management steps are to plan, organize, monitor and control. But to manage a capital plan, stretched over years, we have to add adjust, compensate and modify.

It takes years to execute a building program. Inevitably, the three assumptions of requirements, cost and schedule change. And guess what—the entire plan is founded on those three assumptions. Bad things happen when a manager doggedly continues to execute a plan after these conditions change.

In a book on making musical instruments I read that the reason Antonio Stradivari's violins were superlative was that he could correct errors in craftsmanship and materials better than any other luthier. The ability to make corrections is equally valuable to a Program Manager.

The ability to evaluate and adjust is a critical asset for a Program Manager.

The ability to adjust, to make on-course corrections, requires information from several additional modules in the PMIS.

A PMIS presents both program and project information.

Project status

For the Program Manager to understand the program status and to know if adjustment is necessary, the PMIS must provide information at the project level. (See the example at the right.)

Project-level information typically resides in hierarchical levels within the PMIS. For example, owners might group projects by locations that contain a subset of projects, which in turn contain sub-subsets of contracts (e.g., designers, consultants and contractors) or some other variation. The system then must summarize these multiple projects into a program-level, "executive friendly" view.

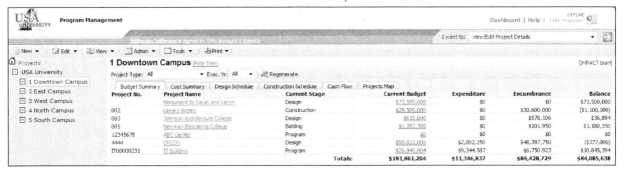

Above is a collection of projects at the Downtown Campus of a fictional USA University. A user could click on the top element in the project tree to the left to see all of the projects in the Capital Building Program or could drill down further to see individual projects.

The Program Level view should include the ability to select projects to review by user, location, fiscal year or range of years, or by any other user-defined project grouping criteria. A user should be able to drill down to review contract facts, planned and actual project expenditures (budgets, contract amounts, contract changes, contract forecast amounts, payments and other information), milestone schedules and more.

Contract status

The PMIS should also have a "Project View" and a "Contract View." Obviously, projects have multiple contracts. But many contractors and consultants work on multiple projects. So the program needs to organize financial or milestone schedule information by both horizontal contracts (that may apply to many projects) and vertical contracts (that collect costs for a single project) without the chore of multiple entries and without accidentally doubling the information in reports.

The information for both project views and contract views will include planned and actual cost (budgets, contract amounts, contract changes, proposed changes, forecasts, payments,

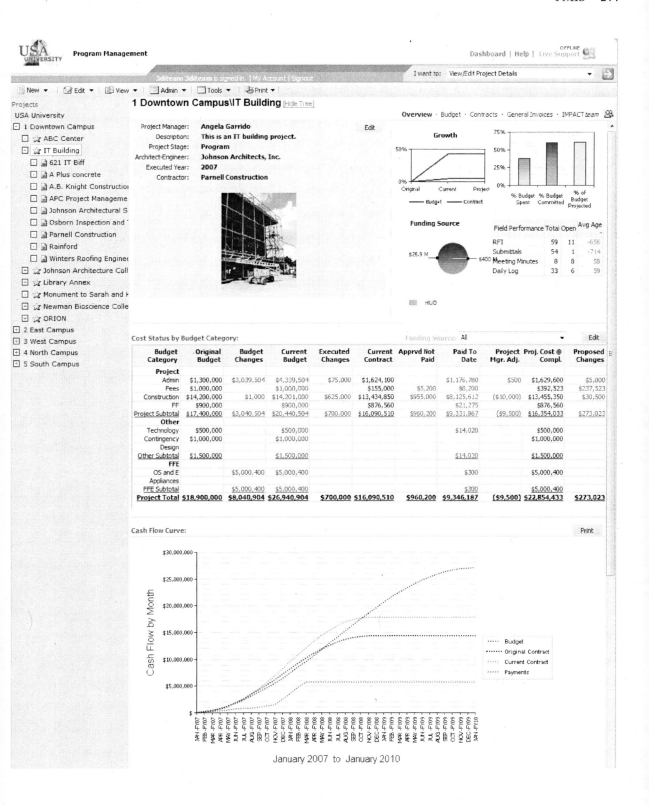

milestone schedules and more). The user should be able to drill down from summary detail into levels of raw data.

Consolidated information from multiple projects
A good PMIS will not only report project status, it will roll up project data into higher summaries. The USA University screen shot lists all the projects and their current status for the fictitious Downtown Campus for USA University.

And then the program information can move even further up the tree to see similar information for the entire program.

A good PMIS will have an executive dashboard to review the vital signs of the projects at the summary level. But the user should be able to drill down to individual projects for more information. Managers will be better able to manage risk by reviewing job costs, tracking and managing pending change orders, viewing contract histories and tracking late or missing information.

Trends and critical metrics
Software that stores historical data can establish and track trends and critical metrics by monthly or yearly intervals. The metrics should normally involve reporting cost and schedule growth in user-defined groups or provide aging summaries for items such as requests for information, requests for proposals, submittal reviews, change order resolution or other project-level detail.

Reports should output green, yellow and red traffic signals that immediately alert busy executives to program problems.

Tailored to the owner's organization
No two clients we have ever worked with have had the same approach to project workflow. Not only are organizations different—they also change. So the system must be tailored to a unique set of requirements and change as the organization's other systems change. Installing a PMIS should be viewed as a journey, not a destination.

If an owner uses an outsourced software vendor for its Program Management software, there must be a form of agreement that will allow the owner to make changes. Furthermore, the agreement must make it clear that the owner owns the data and, if the owner chooses, can retrieve and archive that data on the owner's servers using the owner's software.

Many software companies price the use of their software by the number of users. That kind of deal hinders the purpose—to get as many users on the platform as possible. So the nature of the deal should provide the owner with the ability to add users (particularly outside users such as AEs and constructors) without the hassle of having to purchase and register subscriptions.

Custom reports

No matter how many standard reports are built into the software, there will be need for custom analysis. And our clients will want something we haven't anticipated. So the software needs a simple and intuitive custom reports feature to provide insight into special issues. Users should be able to pick data items to include in a report and filter them by various criteria. (See example at right.) It should allow non-technical users to extract, sort and arrange data and then download it for custom reports and/or presentations using common programs such as Microsoft Word, Excel and PowerPoint.

Executive level information and interface

Traditionally, a technical staff that requires comprehensive detail and uses their software every day develops the requirements for Program Management systems. Then enhancements accumulate. Soon the program is robust, but the user interface is too complex for an executive to understand easily. Vital signs may be buried in detail.

The software needs to communicate clearly. How many times have you looked at mysterious commands in a program or cryptic column headings on a spreadsheet and wondered what they meant?

Few executives are facile in using their organization's information systems. Moreover, few executives have time to be trained, and if they're trained, their use is so infrequent they forget and fumble with the interface. Yet there are few things that will help an executive understand what's going on more than punching a few keys to get either global or detailed program information.

So we need to correct that problem for the program's executives. A Program Management system needs to have a simple user interface that uses common navigation tools. It must present the big picture and have a summary level that's intuitive. If the system does that, the boss will like it and support it. If it doesn't,

Pricing software by the number of users hinders its purpose.

A good PMIS will provide the ability to select specific items of data for a custom report—perhaps exported to spreadsheet or presentation software.

A PMIS needs to be executive friendly—that means Peter Rabbit simple.

the boss will ignore it, the system team won't get the support it needs, people will not be disciplined to provide timely input, the information will not be current, people will distrust it, and the PMIS will fail.

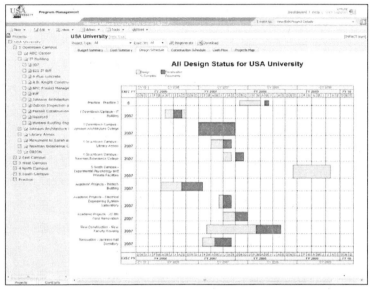

Program Management software needs to present executives with a global, conceptual view of the capital plan's vital signs and then provide the ability to drill down to grass roots detail.

Measurement: true stories

A human pyramid reporting system is often inaccurate, inconsistent and biased.

Anyone who has managed an organization understands the leader's frustrating problem of getting good information about the organization's performance. If the boss asks for a report and there's no standard for reporting, there will be a couple of problems.

1.   The boss may receive carefully selected information that presents a biased or limited point of view.
2.   Each report will come in a new, author-invented format that may take some time to understand.

Over the last two centuries, accountants have developed Generally Accepted Accounting Principles (GAAP) that measure an organization's financial performance. They tell a reasonably accurate story about an organization's economics. The format conventions of Assets and Liabilities (with the Liabilities listed in the order they're due) are consistent so a financially educated person can quickly grasp a company's financial condition.

We don't have an industry standard for measuring the performance of a design and construction program. That leaves us with a problem. Without consistent, factual reporting, there's an abundance of events that can be selected to support many different positions.

So a good Program Manager will install standard formats in the reporting system to present the important facts—not apocryphal, fictitious, self-serving or political stories. The reports will reveal honest insight that both managers and executives will learn from.

Without this systematic factual presentation, formatted consistently over time, there is a danger that people will act (or fail to act) on the wrong information or learn the wrong lessons.

Yet this crucial task is the most neglected of all the important tasks in the field of Program Management.

Since there is too much information in a building program for one person to know, managers have traditionally formed a pyramid reporting structure. The executive layer delegates responsibility to middle management, who in turn delegate to project managers and field engineers to gather project information. The field engineers and project managers periodically pass it up to middle management who summarize and repackage it for top management. Along the way, it may be delayed, filtered, confused or spun. Top managers deal with concepts, avoid micro-management and leave the detail to the project managers and field engineers.

And meanwhile, everyone spends a lot of time with the reporting—often re-inventing it for each new edition.

Web-based information systems have changed that reporting structure. Twenty-first century managers who insist on disciplined input from the field can turn around in their chair to the computer on their credenza and get un-spun, un-filtered, near real-time project status reports with a few mouse clicks.

Now executives can review the facts for themselves, relieving the project managers of chores and improving the collaboration between the Program Managers and the project managers.

GAAP principles have created standard formats for accounting, but standard formats don't exist for reporting on design and construction programs. That means we have to puzzle out each new report that someone invents.

Standard formats are essential.

It's stunning to realize how few managers take advantage of this technology.

Many Program Management systems have been cobbled together from project management systems that bury the vital signs with detail. Managing a large program by looking at detailed data from a series of individual projects is like trying to tell time by looking at the second hand.

The systems that provide project detail must be designed to roll up data and summarize the status of projects for executives. These systems should present a conceptual, comprehensive, panoramic view of the entire program. If there's a problem, top management can drill down to the project details, uncover the problem and cause action.

Here's an example. Say the system tracks and records RFIs. It will report the content, status, event dates and comments for each RFI for each project. If a senior executive tries to understand all that detail, he or she will quickly lose the overview. So he or she simply reviews the RFI aging report. On the other hand, if the report red-flags an aging problem, the top manager drills down into the details of a single project and sees that an MEP consultant is a bottleneck. So he or she arranges a quick conference call and learns that the MEP engineer is ill. With focus on the problem from top management, the team develops a work-around solution.

A little micro-management when crucial deadlines or millions of dollars are involved is a good thing.

Good control systems make better projects. They also make better managers. They increase collaboration and the program benefits from collective judgment. How many times have you watched arguments that were triggered by the simple fact that the arguers had conflicting information? Good information systems provide everyone with the same set of facts so the extended project team can keep one another from a crash and burn.

Owners want Program Managers—either in-house our outsourced—for a universal reason. They want people to represent their interest who understand design and construction and can cause the right action. In a perfect world, the Program Managers would have the best understanding of what's going on and the best judgment about what to do. Therefore, a crucial

Managing a large program by looking at detailed data from a series of individual projects is like trying to tell time by looking at the second hand.

A good PMIS will make good Program Managers. A crucial function of good control systems is that they teach the team.

function of a control system is to enhance judgment by a clear presentation of reality.

Given the choice between good people and good process, the smart choice is always good people. But here's the point. Good controls make good people better because they're educational.

Control systems that present accurate facts accelerate experience and improve judgment. There's an old saw:

Question: *"How do you get good judgment?"*
Answer: *"Experience."*
Question: *"How do you get experience?"*
Answer: *"Bad judgment."*

True. But it's better if we can figure out a way to get good judgment without going through the bad experience. The idea is to find ways to improve everybody's experience—to make sure that all the managers know what's going on with accurate facts. The right control systems deliver history—true stories. That's on-the-job training. That widens the experience of the team. Managers learn the right lessons.

Furthermore, these systems are windows into the program's true events. It doesn't do much good to have smart, experienced people with good judgment who understand the process if they don't know what's going on.

Too often, the big picture is buried in detail. A user wants to know the status of a project and gets lost in a delayed RFI. So good Program Management software should be designed to present executives with a global, conceptual view of the capital plan's vital signs and then provide the ability to drill down to grass roots detail.

A good PMIS will present global and detailed program, project and contract status and will forecast trends.

The system needs a capital planning module to assist the planning team to develop budgets over multiple years, track project requests and authorize funds, report on deficiencies and deferred maintenance, prioritize projects through objective scoring, perform budget transfers, manage bonds, allocate funds to individual projects and capture funding sources.

Project-level information typically resides in hierarchical levels within the Program Management software. For example, owners might group projects by locations that contain a subset of projects, which in turn contain sub-subsets of contracts (for instance, designers, consultants and contractors) or some other variation. The system then must summarize these multiple projects into a program-level view.

Of course, the software has to provide project accounting. The software needs to anticipate situations where clients contract with a supplier or a contractor to provide materials or services across multiple projects (horizontal procurement). It needs to organize contractual, financial or milestone schedule information by both horizontal contracts (that may apply to many projects) and vertical contracts (that collect costs for an individual project) without the chore of multiple entries and without accidentally doubling the information in reports.

DOCUMENTATION AND COMMUNICATION

Most meetings and most individual work efforts require information. Having the right information at the right time is sure a big help. Think of the times confusion ensues in a meeting that could easily be settled if the right facts were available. Think of the time you spend digging for the information you need.

Traditionally, programs have been staffed with people and companies who store information on their own computers or in their own filing cabinets. Then information passes through a chain of command. That presents classic problems:

- Everyone invents their own formats that are confusing to others.
- Information is inadequately shared. Some people thoughtlessly neglect to share information; others hoard it deliberately, knowing that information is power.
- Information is corrupted. As data passes through layers in the organization, it gets distorted. When middle management wants a report, the people on the line may shade the facts. When top management wants understanding, middle management may also shade the facts, or simply not know.
- It takes too long. By the time a piece of paper makes the rounds (and waits for someone who is on vacation or ill) it's usually stale.
- The records disagree. Inevitably, if the same information is stored in different places, it will not be exactly the same. My name in one person's contact file is Chuck Thomsen.

Traditionally, everybody keeps their own file cabinet and has their own formats. Frequently, the same data is in multiple file cabinets and doesn't agree.

In another it's Charles B. Thomsen. If the files are merged, there are two people. Sometimes the differences are trivial, other times significant.

A central filing system that's web based is more accessible, timely and correct. Conflicting duplications are eliminated. Erroneous information is reduced because more people will scrutinize items of information, providing more opportunity for corrections.

To truly enable the project team, the system should be accessible with an Internet browser from any computer anywhere. Of course, it needs levels of password protection for different categories of users. For instance, some people will have access to information on their project only, others will have input and read-only privileges, others may modify documents, etc.

Productivity increases because it's easy to access online documents. A PMIS will facilitate creating, time-stamping, tracking and storing design and construction information exchange such as transmittals, submittals, meeting minutes, change orders and RFIs. Correspondence is streamlined since it can be saved once and sent to multiple companies.

Folders (or other data locations) in the system can be made "smart" with rules for information distribution. For instance, if an RFI is posted in a project folder, the folder can "know" who should receive the RFI and distribute automatically. The folder can also have a blog site for discussion of the RFI. (Some owner's have had trouble with this functionality—the routing must be restructured every time there is a change in the organization. And if someone is sick or on vacation, the RFI is held up without the sender knowing it.)

A central database will reduce the staff costs of copying, filing and faxing. And because reports can be made automatic, it will reduce the cost of executives who spend nights and weekends generating reports for management.

The central documentation increases accountability for the extended project team and the legal implications are significant. Unfortunately, design and construction programs have disputes. Consistently managed, current centralized documents will lower discovery costs. And when there is a dispute, those with the best documentation have a strong advantage.

The Internet allows everyone to use the same web-based filing cabinet. So good Program Management software needs to be web based, provide a central repository of information and documentation and be a resource to the entire extended program team.

Lessons learned databases

Organizations with multi-building programs have an opportunity to avoid repeating mistakes. A "lessons learned" database captures and shares issues, events or circumstances where the outcome either exceeded or failed to meet expectations.

The challenge in creating a lessons learned database is in getting everybody to agree on what the right lesson is. When something is done wrong, there is often disagreement about what "right" should have been.

We thought that would be an easy assignment to implement. It's not. The difficulty centers around agreement on what the real lesson is. Here is an example: say there is a problem in a program with vinyl tile coming loose from a concrete slab. The person inputting the problem thinks the problem is moisture and the solution is a specific set of measures to ensure moisture protection. Another thinks it's the wrong adhesive. Someone else thinks vinyl tile is simply the wrong material for the job.

A Program Manager must exercise some control to have reliable data. A lessons learned database requires a standard form of input. Then there may be a review committee to accept or edit the "lesson" to make sure that the solution to the problem is indeed the right solution.

Another less labor-intensive approach is simply to blog the issue. If there is a problem anyone can post it and everyone can throw in their two-bits on what a good solution should be. Everyone can say how to keep the slab dry or what adhesive works. Eventually, the Program Manager can pick a solution and make it a standard.

Here's an amusing but sad story about a lessons learned database. The Los Angeles Unified School District is running the largest building program in the U.S. They kept a lessons learned database. The Los Angeles Times loved taking shots at the building program because they were spending so much money. A reporter at the Times learned of the database and figured that since it was a list of things that went wrong, it would be rich with facts that could be used to embarrass the district. So the Times subpoenaed LAUSD for the database. They went to court and LAUSD won, but not without a fight. It's sad that political agendas can get in the way of managing a good program.

Baseline documents and design guidelines

Organizations with multi-building programs develop standards. Their management software should store and access electronic files for standard items, such as contracts, memoranda of agreement, design guidelines, building systems and components, specifications and photographs. The program should link to standards already web-accessible (such as federal and state regulations) and store, access and view prototype documents and drawings from document or CAD files.

I've never liked the term standards. Baseline sounds better—it sounds more like a standard that is only sitting there waiting to be improved upon.

Collaboration among the extended program team

A PMIS should be accessible with a web browser, 24 hours a day, 365 days a year, not tied down to a local area network. The system should provide program information from a single database to the extended program team—from the owner's executives to the field engineers.

Access is typically secure and controlled, providing a client-defined structure with independent permissions (a CM on a single project may be limited to accessing data on that project). However, the PMIS can help a Program Manger increase program transparency—a benefit to all.

As a Program Manager begins to implement software, everyone—owner groups and outsourced companies—will have useful information to supply to the program. They will also want to receive information from the program without duplicating the labor of key stroking data. So these surrounding organizations will all want to influence the interfaces. They will fervently hope to exchange data without a new round of data entry. If the Program Manager can arrange that, life will be happier.

But everybody is probably using some brand of software of their own choice that is appropriate for their activities. And, guess what—the software packages don't talk to one another.

So the issue of data transfer with other programs used by the extended program team (AEs, CMs, constructors) and with the owner's groups (accounting, legal, administration, O&M, users and stakeholders) will rear its exceedingly ugly head.

Let's look at the design and construction side first. Many GCs and CMs use project management software written by one of several vendors mentioned earlier. But the programs are not interoperable. They don't share data seamlessly with other project

A web-based PMIS increases accessibility and transparency.

management software and hence with other GCs. So there's a problem. The Program Manager wants to collect data from each of the GCs or CMs and roll it up into program reports. But everyone hates duplicating data entry. It's bad enough the first time and errors always occur in the duplication process.

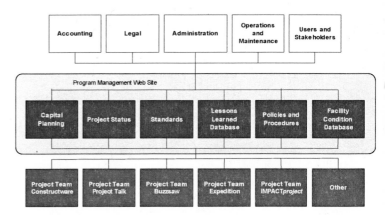

Everyone—owner groups and outsourced companies—will have useful information and will also want to exchange data without duplicating the labor of key stroking the data entry.

One solution is for owners to have their own software or pick one vendor and decree that the extended program team will use it. We have done that on some programs. Sometimes it works but it usually meets considerable resistance.

Most firms have commitments to one of several good brands of software. So on a program there are likely to be multiple systems that are not interoperable.

The GCs and CMs working on individual projects don't like that approach. They argue that they have company-wide corporate agreements with a software vendor. The fees for the licenses have already been spent. Furthermore, they've trained their staff to be skilled with their chosen applications and all their people have brand loyalty to the tools they know how to use. If they use the owner's software, it will require new training and perhaps the cost of new seat licenses. They argue, correctly, that it will add to the project's cost if they can't use the tools that are paid for and they're familiar with. However, if they continue to use their own software, they will also complain about having to enter data into their own systems and then re-enter it into a client's program-wide system.

If the owner has only one contractor, it might make sense for the owner to adopt the contractor's software—if there is only one contractor and if the contractor's software will serve the program adequately. But those "ifs" are rare. If the owner adopts one contractor's software, it won't be operable with any other.

The owner's organization has the same problem. The Program Manager wants to stay on top of the program costs: payments and total obligations, pending claims and change orders, etc. The owner's accounting department wants that same information too. The Program Manager will want to budget work for capital repair and renovation and will want to share data with the operations and maintenance department. There is useful data exchange with the legal department on pending claims. And the administrative groups, the users and stakeholders will provide information to the Program Managers and will want to know what's going on.

So the program information scene is like Babel. None of the programs used by these many groups talk to one another.

The problem of data exchange is further complicated by turf issues. As information moves from one company to another or from one part of an organization to another, people who are responsible for the information that comes from their group must scrutinize it, approve it and perhaps act on it. A Program Manager will not allow a contractor to push information into a program-wide system without review and approval. Accountants will not let Program Managers within the same organization push information into their accounting system without review and approval—and vice versa. The same is true for all the components of the extended program team. So these groups form barriers, indeed very reasonable barriers, to information flow.

The bureaucracy is more difficult to deal with than the technical problems of data transfer.

Furthermore, some of these groups feel that their data is proprietary. The GCs don't want the owner looking into their databases, and the owner's accounting department doesn't want outsiders having any form of access either.

There's no technical problem in writing data bridges between programs. All it takes is a simple translation table that maps data fields from one program to another—assuming the data has the same meaning and same format structure in each program—which it seldom does.

We have made data bridges and some have worked for a long time. However, different parts of an organization and different AEs, GCs and CMs upgrade their software periodically. When they do, the new versions often change the data structure. The result: a carefully structured data bridge collapses.

Microsoft Office often provides a simple, near universal exchange format—a system Rosetta Stone.[2] In our experience, almost all programs used by the extended program team can input and output data in Excel. So Excel can work as a translation table interface within the owner's organization and between the owner and the outsourced companies. It's on everybody's personal computer and is well understood.

An owner working with multiple contractors may simply specify a precise set of data fields for each contractor to provide on a periodic basis and provide an Excel template. They may then review the spreadsheets and approve the data before they pull it into their system. The whole thing can be done without additional key stroking. The same approach can be used for data distribution within the owner's organization.

Handheld connectivity

The proliferation of wireless handheld telephone computers creates a new window of accessibility. Reports should be accessible to handheld wireless devices such as a BlackBerry, iPhone or Treo.

The development of the Internet has been a windfall benefit to our needs for information at our fingertips. Web-based computer systems provide us with a great tool for developing a PMIS.

CONTROL

We're all familiar with IT as a productivity tool. Computers help us type, calculate and draw faster. With the Internet, we benefit from a wide-ranging network that improves communication. With databases, we can store and retrieve information faster and in different arrangements.

But for 21st century managers, it's also a management tool. Leaders distribute procedures and assignments faster and

2. The discovery of the Rosetta Stone was the key to translating hieroglyphics. It has writing in hieroglyphic, demotic and Greek. Jean-François Champollion deciphered hieroglyphs in 1822 because he could read both Greek and Coptic. He was able to figure out the demotic signs in Coptic and then could compare them to hieroglyphic signs.

systematically. Control systems for building programs define how people work together, how teams are structured and how information is passed person-to-person and organization-to-organization. The input/output routine will set a cadence for communication, meetings and progress reports. IT and management processes become symbiotic. They're mutually supportive.

Winston Churchill, in a famous speech before Parliament in 1945, said:

> *"We shape our buildings and then our buildings shape us."*

In the 21st century, we shape our information systems and then our systems shape us.

These systems provide guidance for common procedures for the extended project team. They generate checklists for action; record and communicate detail; analyze data; track progress; document decisions and agreements; record history and predict cost and project schedules; produce reports and so on. They have a profound effect on the structure, behavior and effectiveness of the extended program team.

Control systems define the management procedures the leaders want to implement for their building program. So the systems must reflect the intentions of the leaders or the behavior of the organization and direction of the leadership will eventually suffer conflict.

Control systems

All control systems require feedback. With all the computers at NASA and all the fixed laws of the physical universe, we can't hit the moon without tracking the rocket's trajectory and making on-course adjustments.

Some control systems are automatic. To maintain the temperature of a room, a thermostat measures the current temperature, compares it to the planned temperature and feeds signals back to the HVAC system for adjustment.

That's pretty hands-free. A user sets the target—the temperature. Then the system does the rest. Other systems need humans at the controls. To steer a car on its path to a destination, you look at the road, the traffic lights, street signs and vehicles around

A PMIS is a tool for leaders to increase their span of control.

All control systems require feedback to stay on course. Crucial components of a capital plan are the policies that provide the necessary control to make on-course adjustments.

you. Then you make adjustments to the wheel, accelerator and brake. The destination is your target; your eyes are the information feedback mechanism; your hands the control. Think how impossible it would be to drive through the unpredictable behavior of traffic without this visual feedback and on-course correction.

Program Management requires managerial adjustment as well as engineering precision.

Design and construction programs are not like the temperature controls, they are more like steering a car in traffic. They require human, not automatic, control. The thermometer uses temperature for feedback. In design and construction, we use information. With the thermostat, the system stays on track automatically. With design and construction, the system relies on informed human intelligence and action. And just like driving a car, the system often needs quick reactions.

So it's probably a misnomer to call a PMIS a control system. It's an information system. People do the controlling. The mechanisms for information feedback and the routine for information gathering should be as automatic as possible, but it will always rely on human input. So our PMIS is the feedback mechanism that informs us as we execute a plan. We make decisions to adjust and stay on track.

But unlike trying to hit the moon that is on a predictable track, determined by the predictable physics of the universe, our target may change, determined by the unpredictable vicissitudes of human behavior.

When it comes to navigating a design and construction program, we need to rely on managerial adjustment as well as engineering precision. We can't plot a course, go on autopilot and expect to arrive at the destination. We stray from the course and the destination changes during the journey. We have to stay in control. That requires a plan with flexibility: no flexibility, no control.

Procedures manuals

A small team working on a single building project can communicate informally, innovate their own processes based on their experience, design their own filing system, do reports in Excel and get the job done just fine.

Programs are different. Some people work at the program level, on many projects. Others do specific tasks on individual projects. Many will never have worked together before. Each brings a different body of experience. Each has learned different procedures. It sure helps to get everyone on the same page. Clear documentation of procedures enhances collaboration, brings consistency, efficiency and a common direction to a program. Everyone's performance improves by knowing what to do and how to work together.

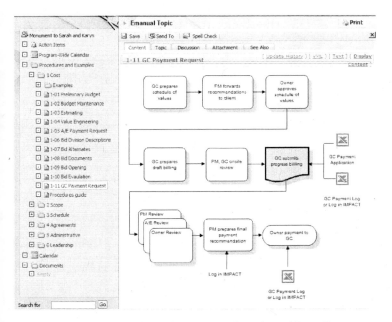

A web-based policy and procedures manual can have interactive diagrams that help people quickly grasp the right procedure or download the correct form.

So most organizations have policy and procedures manuals to guide their building program. Unfortunately, most of these manuals are paper documents that are hard to find in the first place, and when they surface it's hard to find the topic at hand. And then it's hard to update. The next step is to put those manuals online as Adobe PDF files. But that is still user-unfriendly documentation that requires concentrated reading.

A web-based manual provides clear directions to the extended project team—at their fingertips and with all the benefits of electronic navigation. It can be enormously useful to the project team by providing company directories, calendars, FTP sites for drawings, documentation and correspondence files.

| Accounting | Legal | Administration | Operations and Maintenance | Users and Stakeholders |

Program Management Web Site

| Capital Planning | Project Status | Standards | Lessons Learned Database | Policies and Procedures | Facility Condition Database |

| Project Team Constructware | Project Team Project Talk | Project Team Buzzsaw | Project Team Expedition | Project Team IMPACTproject | Other |

Not only is it useful for the project teams to be able to exchange information with the Program Manager's systems, various owner groups will also want to access or share the same data.

Even the best processes are of little value if they're buried in some dust-covered, inaccessible notebook. The Web is the medium enlightened leaders use to put procedures under the fingertips of their organization. Updating policies and procedures is easy since it happens in only one place—on the web server. There is no need to retrieve and reissue written documents.

IMPLEMENTING A PMIS

Managing the implementation of a PMIS is harder than developing the technology.

Most organizations go through technology purgatory when they decide to implement software to manage their program. They put together a large study group to decide on the desirable functionality. The study group thinks of a lot of nice things the software could do. They attempt to design a full-blown, comprehensive system. Then years are spent trying to get the program operational in the face of many different groups of people who don't want to change and with a requirement to input and vet hordes of detail.

Implementing a PMIS is always a cultural shift that requires new discipline. It will not happen without pressure from the top. The start-up phase of these systems is typically accompanied by substantial grousing. The grumbles are inevitably given credibility by the simple inescapable fact that there are always glitches and false starts as the system begins to function. And just as it begins to work, it's enhanced with new capabilities and breaks again.

Consequently, a wise Program Manager will start small and implement only the part of the system that provides the most crucial information as a first step. The best strategy is to implement something useful that will be easy, get everybody in the habit of maintaining data and then expand, viewing the process as a continuous journey, not a final destination.

The program's leaders will need to maintain a regular and persistent drumbeat of insistence for the discipline to develop and the system to function properly.

Three Controls

The classic trio of controls are Cost, Schedule and Quality. They require control because the future is unpredictable and will change the assumptions that the capital plan is based on. The assumptions include such basics as construction cost and the owner's requirements. They inevitably change. So we have to constantly make on-course adjustments to deliver the proper outcome.

COST CONTROL

The classic view of cost control is that one makes estimates, establishes a budget, estimates design as it progresses, works diligently to prevent scope creep and hits the budget at the end of the job. The problem is that prices, part of the budgeting assumptions, change and present us with unpleasant surprises. And owners change their requirements. Since we can't control those price events, we need to have adjustment mechanisms.

Unpredictability

Budgeting and estimating are predictions of future costs
and are rational processes. But bidding can be irrational and
unpredictable. Eventually, on every program there'll be a budget
bust, grievous embarrassment and a big problem to solve. Our
ability to predict future costs exceeds our ability to predict the
stock market—but not by much. Here's why:

Material costs

Double-digit annual variation is common for basic building commodities.

A glance at the Engineering News Record price reports makes
it clear that a double-digit annual variation is common for basic
building commodities such as glass, steel, concrete, copper, PVC
and lumber. Sometimes it's more.

A boom in construction can produce shortages; a hurricane in
Florida can double the price of plywood; a foreign war can make
heavy equipment expensive; economic growth in Asia or Latin
America can affect the price of steel.

Labor costs

While material costs are part of a national and world economy,
labor is more affected by local conditions. It's easier to transport
steel than to uproot families and move workers.

Assume that several major projects are starting in a community.
Inflation is tepid, but everybody in the community is busy so
subcontractors must hire inexperienced labor. They will figure
low productivity. And as long as they have to miss their fishing
trips, they might as well include high profits.

A variation in labor supply can affect labor costs plus or minus 20%.

Now, assume the reverse is true: projects are scarce. The subs
need work to keep their most productive craftspeople on their
payroll. They will bid high production rates and minimum profits
to keep their core team. That can easily produce a 20% decrease
on bid day.

Competition

Estimating is logical. Bidding is emotional.

Bidding gets emotional. Some contractors chase a job as if it
were a blood sport—particularly true if they need work. The
passion of the hunt leaves rationality in the dust. Bidding on one
of our science building projects at Texas A&M took place in a
hungry market. In the 24 hours before the bids were due, the sub
prices leaked around (as usual). The price of the project dropped
from $34 million (the official estimate) to $26 million.

Avarice

Sometimes, it almost seems as though everyone conspires to blow the budget. Of course that's not true, but what is true is that the extended project team has "attitudinal inclinations" that tend to increase, not decrease, the program cost. The companies working on the program would like to have more money. Users want more facility. Architects and engineers want to design better buildings. Contractors will have change-orders—with premiums. Left unattended, program costs will rise like a hot air balloon that dropped its sandbags. Given this near-universal pressure, a Program Manager must provide constant push back to keep the lid on. It's not a job that wins friends.

Most of the extended project team will have tendencies to increase project and program costs.

Rules for budgeting projects

Somewhere in the world there must be projects with unlimited funding. But in half a century, we've never seen an owner who didn't care about a budget or want some control of the bottom line. Moreover, we've never seen a project that somewhere along the line didn't have some confusion about what the budget was.

One of the reasons there are so many busted budgets is an unfortunate "attitudinal inclination" at the start to set a tight budget. Owners want to spend as little as possible and want to stretch the project team. The user wants as much facility as possible. The AEs want to be supportive and agreeable. And at the start, it doesn't hurt to have a tight budget. It's like jumping out of an airplane without a chute. It doesn't hurt until the end.

There are five cardinal rules for establishing a budget:

Five cardinal rules for a budget.

1. Maintain flexibility with line-item budgeting and include a program contingency.
2. Make achievable budgets and design to them, estimating soon and often.
3. Establish cost categories that can be verified against future contracts.
4. Define project costs and program costs, and make sure everybody understands all the budget components.
5. Keep the budgets updated as conditions change—in increasing levels of detail—and manage them with insufferable attention.

Let's elaborate on these rules.

1. Maintain flexibility with line item budgeting and include a program contingency.

One of the great pleasures of our profession is forming a trusting relationship with a client you like and admire. Dr. Dennis Smith, as superintendent of Placentia-Yorba Linda Unified School District, fit that description for many of us who worked for him. So one day I asked him what he worried about most in his building program. We thought he might say something like "collaborative teaching layouts." He didn't. He said:

> *"I want to make sure we build the last building in the stream of projects that we promised our taxpayers when they approved our bond election."*

Of course, Dennis felt an obligation to his community who provided the money for schools. And he knew that if delivering a project within budget is hard, delivering a program is harder. If it's good to define a project, it's great to define a program. It's a lingering death not to. In a program of many projects, as Dennis knows, it's possible to get to a point where you are out of money and you aren't through. It's too late to correct. You're dead.

Most capital building programs are an assembly of independent line items.

Many, indeed most, programs are budgeted as a series of independent line items. A board, legislature, city council, congress or some other governing body vested with the responsibility to allocate financial resources to the perceived value of building the facilities approves a list of projects with independent budgets for each.

The project budgets are based on estimates of construction cost. These budgets will likely anticipate inflation. And each project budget will likely include a contingency to cover the unknown and provide some ability to react to surprises. We're smart enough to know that unpredictability is predictable.

> *But if the program is viewed as a series of independent projects, each with its own contingency, it's highly likely that the program will exceed the original budget.*

Here is what will happen:

As the program unfolds and time passes, there will be cost swings, above and below a core inflation rate, driven by temporal market conditions.

When the subs aren't busy and material prices drop, the users get a good bid. They feel that the appropriated budget (with its project-specific contingency) is theirs to spend. They increase the scope and spend the contingency. Then, when the subs get busy and material prices are up, projects overrun their budgets. The Program Manager must cut scope or return to the governing body, hat in hand, and plead for additional funding to cover the cost increases—or maybe the last building in the program doesn't get built.

So in a program with many projects, there's a tendency for price valleys to get filled with scope increases, and the peaks are climbed with embarrassing supplemental appropriations. The inevitable price fluctuations cause inevitable program overruns.

Here's another way to say it. Over a period of several years, price fluctuations above and below a rate of inflation are a sure thing. If Program Managers live with contingencies on a project-by-project basis, without the ability to move contingency funds from one project to another and with users having the right to use their line item funding plus their contingency, the likelihood of a program cost overrun is pretty high.

Of course, there are situations where project budgets will be inflexible. A developer may have different sets of investors for each project. If a budget overrun makes the project a bad investment, the developer will wisely abandon it. If a budget runs under, the developer and the investors happily pocket the profits.

However, a school board must provide equal facilities for each community. The same school will carry different price tags as market conditions vary. If the scope is allowed to increase in the price valleys, the next set of users will want the increased scope. Adding the scope increase on the next project that hits a price peak produces a double whammy. The bond program will overrun the budget and embarrass the superintendent, the board and the Program Manager. Heads may roll.

In these kinds of programs, a smart Program Manager eliminates project contingencies and develops a program contingency. Then the Program Manager sets firm scopes, and when market conditions are good, he or she keeps the savings for a rainy day. Given the fact that there can easily be a 15% swing in market conditions, a 7.5% program contingency isn't too much.

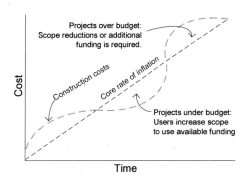

Construction costs vary more widely than the core rate of inflation. If there is line item budgeting with no program contingency, users will use their budget for scope increases when the construction market is slow and costs are low. Then when the market is busy and construction costs are high, scope must be cut from projects or they must receive additional funding.

Some owners must provide similar facilities for each project.

Program Managers have the law of large numbers to help with total program capital costs.

Program Managers have opportunities for on-course corrections that project managers don't have. The law of large numbers helps average extremes—over and under, shorter and longer. There are more events and more places to adjust. So with the ability to make on-course adjustments, it's easier to deliver a program than a project within the budget

2. Make achievable budgets and design to them, estimating soon and often. A good way to run a program over the budget is to develop designs for the projects, estimate them and then live with a delay while Congress or some Legislature deliberates funding. As the cost of labor and materials changes, the design may not match the budget when the bids come in.

A good approach is to start with an achievable budget and design to it.

It's far better to start with an achievable budget and design to it when the time comes. Then make frequent estimates and adjust the design as the construction costs vary. But that requires good historical information and good parametric estimating to make the budget achievable. (See *Budgeting*, pages 239 and 240.)

Organizations that replicate prototypes adjust budgets for each project.

Organizations that replicate a prototype simply need to adjust their budget for a specific project. The common approach is to guess about the inflation and use a coefficient to adjust labor and materials costs to a specific location. If the schedule is short, some managers will add another coefficient for temporal market conditions.

Other organizations build unique facilities. If they have a limited budget (an appropriation, a donation, a corporate authorization) setting the budget is crucial. It must be achievable. If not, downstream work will need to be redone, managers are embarrassed—and sometimes individuals and companies get fired.

Designing a building and then delaying for an extended period for funding deliberations is risky.

A number of years ago, it was common for the U. S Air Force to obtain funding for the design and construction of a new project in stages. The first stage was design. After design was complete, they would estimate the design and return to Congress for construction funding. The project might be on the shelf for up to a year while Congress deliberated. The theory was that there should be a design before there could be a reliable estimate for Congressional approval. It didn't work very well. When the project was bid, after a year's delay, inflation and market conditions often produced a nasty surprise. The Air Force decided to develop a parametric estimating system that would establish an achievable budget without design. In essence they said, "This is a reasonable amount of money to spend for this facility. Give us the money and we will design to budget." The results were a lot better.

3. Establish cost categories that can be verified against future contracts. How many times have you seen this? A budget was set with categories that didn't match the eventual contracts. When bids came in there was a cost overrun. But the team didn't know where the problem was because the budget categories didn't match the bid categories.

If you want to track a budget through the phases of cost control, you must establish budget categories (a work breakdown structure) that can be compared to the final costs. To do that, the budget categories must be the same as the eventual contract structure.

Budgets must be verifiable against future contracts.

Additionally, you will need systems to slice and dice the budget to provide useful information for other team members.

For instance, program budgets should monitor the costs of both projects and contracts. Obviously, the projects have multiple contracts. But what's not so obvious is that some contracts may apply to multiple projects. For instance, on a university capital renewal program, we awarded a multi-year roofing contract. The roofing contractor mobilized forces and simply went from one building to another. We needed to manage the roofing contract. We also needed to monitor the cost attributed to each building because there were budgets for the buildings that included other building-specific contracts. You need to be able to report on costs both ways. (See *Program Management Information Systems*, page 210.)

You will also want to re-categorize eventual contract costs into cost information for the building, for the building systems and for functional areas. During design, the owner wants to know what the functional areas cost; the designers want to compare the cost of one system to another; the Program Manager wants to track the trade contracts. The trade costs will be the real costs, the hard numbers of reality that will eventually come from the marketplace. But the owners and designers need their information too.

Most project teams have confusion about the budget.

4. Define project costs and program costs, and make sure everybody understands all the budget components.

Construction is only a portion of a program's total cost. Every owner seems to want to include and exclude different costs. Project costs may include feasibility studies, AE fees, owner management overhead, cost of money, legal fees, testing, furnishings, permits, contingencies, etc. The construction cost may be only two-thirds of the project cost and even less of the program cost. I will always remember announcing to a client on bid day that a project was bid within the budget, only to hear the bone-chilling reply:

> *"But the low bid is our whole budget. How are we going to pay your fee?"*

At the beginning, there is a tendency for everyone to be optimistic about the budget.

There will be costs that are hard to allocate to a project. We've scratched our heads bloody trying to find a rational way to distribute our Program Manager costs to a collection of projects. Should they be prorated based on building cost, on building area, on schedule? Should everybody charge time to projects instead of the program? The topic of assigning overhead costs can always start a good argument.

A program presents more challenges in cost categorization than a project. Many owners budget projects and have strong attitudes about keeping overhead down. However, the great advantage of managing a program as a program rather than a collection of individual projects is the opportunity for economies of scale, continuous improvement and all the other things we talk about in this book. Some owners will want to assign those costs to projects. Do you assign on the basis of cost? Square feet? Function? The decision will be arbitrary. Pick a policy and stick with it.

5. Keep the budgets updated as conditions change—in increasing levels of detail—and manage them with insufferable attention.

Probably every key meeting should begin with a review of the budget.

As the project progresses, the level of detail will continue to expand. Somewhere along the line, someone will want to change all the categories. Don't do it. Keep adding detail and keep reviewing the bottom line with the project team.

Budgeting new projects

Look out for the attitudinal bias at the start of a program to budget optimistically. The owner is inclined to want to stretch the team to deliver as much as possible. New members of the project team may have made optimistic promises in the marketing and want to please their new client. But the best way to be a skunk at the end of the project is to be a bunny at the beginning. If the budget isn't achievable, it will be a lousy program. Downstream work will need to be redone, producing losses and delays.

There are three classic ways managers establish achievable budgets:

Historical examples

Program Managers have access to solid cost feedback from similar projects for the same owner. Of course, in order to have the luxury of historical examples, you have to have a database with the historical facts in a useful form. You want to be able to collect the cost experience from projects and compare the results. So there must be a rigorously enforced format—and the definitions for the categories must be precise or they will make no sense when you budget the next project.

Program Managers have an opportunity to access historical costs that's unavailable to single-project managers.

The database should categorize the cost of previous projects into both Uniformat and CSI categories. There should be unit cost breakouts for functional areas. There should be coefficients to normalize building costs for location and time so the cost of individual buildings, built at different times in different locations, can be compared.

When there is a new project, the Program Manager can adjust the normalized cost with a location and escalation factor, consider anticipated market conditions and make adjustments for special conditions.

Systems estimates

A detailed estimate of hypothesized building systems and materials is a big job and it takes time. Furthermore, it takes a very good estimator to include everything that isn't on a set of Construction Documents, add in the soft costs and produce a bottom line. However, many estimators default to this approach because they're used to estimating buildings that are already designed. It's a useful exercise because putting price tags on building systems before design is helpful to the design team. But to repeat a mantra of this book:

> *"The precision of the process is greater than the accuracy of the assumptions."*

A blunt approach is for an estimator to simply hypothesize a set of building systems and materials and make a detailed estimate as if the building were designed.

The parameter that interests an owner is the unit of value that the building provides.

Parametric estimates

A Program Manager can build a detailed model of a given building type and then enter parameters to vary cost based on specific project requirements. Typically parametric estimating has a primary parameter that may be adjusted with secondary and tertiary parameters. Some methods also allow users to tweak space allocations, building system and material selections. Of course, there must be a way to include soft costs.

Owners are not interested in tons of steel or yards of concrete. The primary parameter that interests an owner is usually the unit of value that the building provides. For instance, the primary parameter might be:

- number of beds in a hospital
- number of seats in a theater
- number of net rentable square feet in an office building
- number of students in a school

Here's an example: The Defense Commissary Agency (DeCA) builds similar grocery stores at military installations. However, because each base is a market, the commissary size changes with the size of the base. The exterior varies because each military base has a unique set of design guidelines. Furthermore, the requirements change as DeCA continues to improve its stores.

We developed a simple computer program that used a commissary that DeCA liked as a base model. The size and cost of the commissary is the anticipated volume of sales, determined by the base size. Therefore, the anticipated dollar volume of sales is the primary parameter. It drives the computation of areas that vary by sales volume (checkout lanes, shelf space, freezers, etc.). It keeps fixed those areas that don't change with sales volume (janitor closet, manager's office, loading dock, etc.). It generates secondary parameters of area and tertiary parameters of volume. The user can then go into detail and tweak building systems, materials, configurations, areas and so on. There is a way to insert location factors, anticipated escalation and soft cost. The output is both CSI and Uniformat.

Piece of pie

A budget can be built from a detailed estimate of a representative part of the project.

A Program Manager can make a detailed estimate of various building systems that are likely to be used for various functional areas. This will produce a collection of unit costs that may be applied to entire projects within the programs.

You can use all three of these methods. It's wise to do so. However, the historical method is the easiest and it's usually the best. Construction professionals have all been burned by projects that overran a budget, and they have an instinctive desire to be conservative. They put a little contingency into each component of the estimate and voilà! The project is over the budget before it starts.

Budgeting repair work

Most owners have existing facilities, so most building programs include the capital renewal of these facilities. (Capital renewal is the fancy name for repair, renovation and remodeling that's a capital expense—not an operations and maintenance (O&M) expense.)

That means that we need to know what it will cost to fix things that are presently broken and worn out. We also need to predict future failures so we can forecast that cost as well. Nobody wants an unexpected boiler replacement to derail the strategic plan.

Because the inventory of buildings in the U.S. is aging, many owners have budgets for renewal that exceed the budget for new buildings.

The work required to budget capital renewal and forecast the cost of repairing future failures is called Facility Condition Assessment (FCA). The tools and processes are different than those used for budgeting new construction. FCA has become a specialized service. Like all services that suddenly begin to grow rapidly, it's changing and each year our industry understands how to do it better.

Our company had always evaluated buildings when a client asked us to do so. During the 80s we measured all the teaching spaces in all the Texas public schools. Before that, we had evaluated the U.S. embassies behind the iron curtain.

However, in the 90s, the schools and universities built for the baby boomers in the 50s and 60s began to age and fall into disrepair. Most of these educational clients had lived through an age of new construction only. But by 1990, the need for capital renewal exceeded the need for new facilities. A boom market for condition assessment services for educational facilities developed and the services became specialized. It became a core business for us. By the end of 2006, we had assessed over 2 billion square feet of buildings.

Initially, we took a classic engineering approach. We would walk through all the spaces, look at things that were broken or worn out and estimate the repair cost. We examined everything: basic building systems like structure, MEP (mechanical, electrical and plumbing), roofing, or simply torn carpet or smudged walls. We developed good software that let us collect data in the field on tablet computers and upload it over the Internet to a database. The software allowed us to slice and dice deficiencies based on more than a dozen criteria such as CSI category, building system, life safety or one of many "user defined" categories set by our clients or our field team. The program could use any cost database (such as RSMeans). We could forecast life-cycle renewal costs and produce lots of pretty graphs.

But once again, the precision of the process exceeded the accuracy of the assumptions. There is no way the cost projections could be accurate at a detailed level. Here's an example of why it's so hard. At one university project, we had categories of renewal mapped to a 5-year program. If we thought a repair was necessary to prevent further damage or for life safety, it was priority one and needed to be fixed immediately—in the first year. Environmental remediation, like asbestos removal, was priority three, slated for the third year. Cosmetic repair was priority five, scheduled for the fifth year.

Repair work rarely follows the assumptions of a facility assessment.

That made sense to the facility staff and to us. But after a year of work, the board looked around and said that after all the money they had spent, they didn't see any change. We explained that the cosmetic repair would come in year 5. They said we were wrong. They were trying to attract students. Cosmetic repair should come right away.

The assumptions

That was the first change. The second change came with packaging strategy. In setting up the unit costs for the database, we had assumed that the asbestos removal would all be done under a single contract in year 3 with the economies of scale that come with a large remediation program and with only one mobilization and one de-mobilization cost.

Sounded reasonable. It was not to be. We discovered corroded hot water piping in the ceiling space of an auditorium. If it ruptured, it would cause lots of damage. Of course, the piping was wrapped with asbestos that we had to remove to replace the pipe. We had noted that the ceiling was dirty and stained and had scheduled renewal in year 5. But as long as we had to take the ceiling down and put it back up to get to the pipe, the extra cost of new tile was minimal. It would have been crazy not to replace it—particularly in light of the board's emphasis on cosmetic repair.

That's a simple example. Packaging construction work— particularly when it's renovation and remodeling—has a huge effect on construction costs. And there's no practical way to assume the eventual packaging when you are doing condition assessment.

The contract packaging has a large affect on construction cost.

Most of us are comfortable in our belief that if we add up all the deficiencies and estimate a total cost of, say, $50 million for a renewal program, it will be about right. There will be compensating errors in large groups of numbers. But we all know that any individual sub-set of costs can be way off. One day I visited the facility director of one of the country's largest state-supported universities. He had been using condition assessment data to set budgets for specific projects. He was livid about the inaccuracy. He had blown budgets right and left. Part of the problem was a change in the construction market, part was a change in the scope of work, and part was different contract packaging than the assessors had anticipated.

The law of large numbers helps, but individual contract elements may vary enormously.

I advised him not to rely on condition assessment data for individual project budgets. The company that had done his assessment was a good company (we had joint ventured with them and knew that to be true). We probably would have done no better. A major renovation project calls for a careful estimate with known market conditions. A 20% contingency is not too high.

When we first started doing condition assessment, we thought the value would be efficient packaging of the construction contracts. We could look at all the deficiencies, combine similar kinds of work and achieve economies of scale that weren't possible without comprehensive data.

The savings in contract packaging for repair and renovation is many times the cost of a condition assessment.

We were right—up to a point. We saved money by packaging work efficiently. At one university, we lined up three years of roofing work and let one roofer simply march across campus with one crew that got better and better and cheaper and cheaper as they went along.

To help us bundle work, we developed a "project-builder" module for our FCI software that allowed us to pull items of work into a project and bundle up sensible assignments for trade contractors.

On projects where we were hired to manage the follow-on contract for repair, the savings from efficient packaging of construction contracts paid for the cost of assessment by the time we did only a small portion of the repair work.

Look at this math. Assume that the assessment cost is 10 cents a square foot for repair work that averages $50 a square foot. That's one-fifth of one percent. Then recognize that efficient packaging can save 10, 20, sometimes 50% of the construction cost. It's a no-brainer investment.

But despite this remarkable savings, we were surprised to learn that saving money by packaging construction work was not the primary motivation for our clients. They wanted our condition assessment data *to get money.* A large database of detailed estimates for repair work was convincing evidence to prove need and obtain funding. A school district wanted condition assessment data to present to the public to get the bonds passed; a state college wanted the data to prove need to a legislature.

But often, the most important value of a condition assessment is to get money.

We would document thousands of deficiencies in a database and print out reports that categorized them in multiple ways. Then we would assemble them in multiple, fat three-ring binders, put them in a wheelbarrow and use up 12 feet of our client's shelf space to house them.

The dark secret of this service is that few people ever used the volumes of data that we produced. They gathered dust. While we used the project builder on those assignments where we were asked to manage repair, I don't know of many clients or their AEs who paid any attention to it when we weren't hired.

For one thing, no one ever even tried to fix everything. They couldn't afford it. We might tell a school district they had $100 million of needed repair. Then they'd explain they couldn't pass more than a $50 million bond and some of that needed to be spent on new schools. So we would set priorities and fix what was most pressing.

After we had estimated the cost of repairing several hundred million square feet, we began to believe we could produce an accurate estimate with just a little information. If we could get plans, learn the age of the facility, get the repair history and maybe look at a few typical samples of the facilities, we could produce a number that was reasonably accurate for a fee of about 2 cents a square foot instead of the 10 cents we were using. There would not be a detailed database of deficiencies but the bottom line would be just as good. A lot of clients preferred that approach. (We irreverently nicknamed this the "drive-by" assessment.)

We learned that we could produce an accurate estimate with just a little information.

Then we also went to the other extreme. We learned how to do very detailed assessments that included clear design solutions that had highly accurate data for estimates. So we named these different approaches Level 1 (the 2 cent approach), Level 2 (the standard 10 cent approach) and Level 3 (maybe the 25 cent approach).

And we learned how to do highly detailed condition assessments.

These different approaches to budgeting are appropriate for different clients and different situations. However, in most cases, an owner is unlikely to be able to afford to fix everything so it's silly to spend time and money making detailed estimates of work that won't be done. The better approach is to do the drive-by assessment, and if they get the money, then do a Level 3 detailed assessment for the funded work.

Meanwhile, the scope of services for condition assessment was expanding and its importance was growing. For instance, many of our owners pointed out that facilities might not be broken or worn out, but they weren't adequate. For example, the light fixtures worked; there just weren't enough of them to produce an acceptable light level. Or the classrooms were too small. Or the facility lacked a security system or was out of compliance with life-safety codes, accessibility standards or green design.

Sometimes buildings have problems because they are inadequate, not because they are broken or worn out.

Therefore, the world of condition assessors had to develop a "functional adequacy" module for their software. An owner could stipulate criteria for functional adequacy. The criteria might be light level, required space, square feet of chalkboard, cat 5 outlets, a LEED standard, a building code—whatever. That way we could estimate the cost of meeting a requirement as well as fixing things that were broken.

And other categories of "adequacy" emerged.

Some clients wanted their facilities assessed for disaster preparedness (a hurricane in Florida or an earthquake in California) so they could assure their constituents they would be safe, meet new code requirements or negotiate favorable insurance rates.

Sid Sanders is one of our brightest and most imaginative clients. Sid ran the statewide University of Texas system and then was recruited to manage the giant building program for The Methodist Hospital System in Houston. Every time Methodist built a new building some functions would move out of existing facilities and the inevitable musical chairs of space use would follow in the old facility. There was a constant churn of interior functions. So Sid asked us to expand a Level 1 assessment to include a comprehensive matrix of existing facilities that indicated what spaces could be adapted for which functions and what the cost would be to adapt them to those different functions.

Condition assessment services will continue to grow and be an ever greater component of planning and budgeting. As owners consolidate and portfolios get larger, their managers lose firsthand knowledge of the facilities. They want data-driven, fact-based systems.

Value engineering

Value engineering is cherished by CMs and detested by architects and engineers.

The usual problem with value engineering is the timing. The classic dumb assumption is that it occurs after design, not before. But it should be done before design. Then it jump-starts design and saves time as well as money. But it takes a team that anticipates cost without having a complete design.

Done properly, value engineering is a process that finds the greatest value for the least cost. It's a collaborative process because the solutions typically require agreement from users, different design disciplines and constructors. The choices may involve building materials, systems, scope or functional arrangement.

Frank Whitcomb, formerly president of CRS's construction
management group, explained it with this light-hearted but clear
example:

> *"The leaded glass in my front door is getting loose because the
> weather stripping is too tight and everybody has to slam the door
> to make it close. The common solution is to put small steel braces
> behind the glass. That's the product solution. The system solution
> is to change the weather stripping. The management solution is to
> use the back door."*

Value engineering is good; when it is usually done makes it bad.
The reason architects and engineers hate the process is that it's
often done at the wrong time. The designers blast ahead without
collaboration with the builders. Maybe the owner has not yet
brought a CM on board. Or maybe the CM is unskilled in pre-
design services and simply doesn't know how to provide advice
until the design is done.

Architects and engineers tend to think of the building as a finished product. Builders think of the process. The collaboration is usually productive.

Even worse, CMs tend to see AEs as a good source of business.
So they're disinclined to say much to the AE about design—they
worry that the AE will think it presumptuous for the CM to
comment on design before it begins.

So the inevitable happens. At the end of design, the project is
over the budget. The CM makes value engineering suggestions.
The architect cuts scope, the design concepts are compromised
and the designers lose money making the changes. Momentum is
lost and personal relations between the AEs and CMs deteriorate.
The designer snidely refers to "value engineering" as "value
elimination."

The serial builders that work with a prototype can extract value
engineering efforts from the project workflow and apply them to
the prototype. Organizations like Marriott and Target examine
costs endlessly. Value engineering becomes a program, not a
project activity.

Value engineering becomes a program, not a project activity.

Many clients with large building programs build unique buildings:
MIT, the State Department Embassies or the GSA Federal
Courthouse Program. For these projects, cost control is more
difficult. Pity the poor university facility director at a prestigious
institution. The administration expects cost control. The
institution's board has hired an internationally famous architect.

The design is unprecedented. A famous researcher has a new grant that requires design modification. Major donors have their own ideas. The CM doesn't join the project until the project is well into design. Everyone has something to say about the project. Invariably, the project will run over the budget, value engineering will focus on cost reduction and there will be pain and recrimination for all.

Value engineering can occur at the program level.

Value engineering should be done *before* design—and to the extent that there are commonalities among the projects, it should be done at the program, not the project level. In a large program, the cost of value engineering before design can be amortized across many projects. The sophisticated serial builders value engineer everything they can rotate into the program as a standard.

Cost estimating

A Program Manager must have a capability —in-house or outsourced—to estimate designs as they develop.

Continuous estimating, before and during design, is crucial. Historical cost records and parametric or systems estimates set a reasonable and achievable budget. Detailed estimates using quantity takeoffs put price tags on alternative design concepts, keep the project within a manageable range, create confidence that the bids are fair and provide information for contract negotiation.

But estimating is tricky. Estimating is an engineering process. An estimator measures the quantities of building materials and multiplies the quantity times the material cost, adds in the labor cost to put the material in place, adds in the equipment cost, General Conditions construction costs,[1] overhead and profit.

The books written and the courses taught on estimating describe this classic approach. Yet the numbers that five different subcontractors produce, using the same process, will vary enormously.

When a project is bid to a general contractor, there may be a narrow competitive range when bids are opened. Owners and AEs who look at these bids are inclined to believe that there may be about a 7% variance in the results different estimators produce. It's far greater.

---

1. See Concepts of Project Delivery, page 190, for a description of these costs.

It's greater because all the GCs tend to use the lowest subcontractor bids for most of their estimate so most of the GCs have just about the same set of subcontractors. The parts of the GC's bid that produce the variation will be a few subcontractors that are unique, a few that have given the GC a favorable price and the GC's own estimate of General Conditions construction, overhead and profit.

If you take the lid off the subcontractor bids, you will see enormous differences. Trades that are labor intensive or weather sensitive will vary enormously.

Some program owners estimate in the CSI format from their architects and CMs at each stage of design and then compare it to actual construction costs. This helps manage the process and gives project managers comparable information from one stage to the next.

Large programs provide an advantage. Actual construction costs can be captured on projects and fed into the future estimates. This improves predictability. Organizations like Marriott examine their costs relentlessly and keep a database of lessons learned and use it from one project to the next.

SCHEDULE CONTROL

The same unpredictable forces that affect cost also affect schedule. Managing cost is almost inseparable from managing schedule. Shortages of materials that drive prices up also cause delays. A workforce that has grown with unskilled mechanics makes mistakes and misses deadlines.

Moreover, the same economic forces that cause shortages are apt to affect the owner's requirements. For instance, rapid economic growth in a community may cause labor and material shortages—and at the same time increase needs for classrooms in a school, beds in a hospital or market demand for a retail roll-out.

Scheduling design vs. construction
Few industries have given as much attention to scheduling as construction. Few industries need it more. And great scheduling tools, such as CPM and PERT, are commonly available. CMs and GCs develop remarkable skills in knitting together tasks,

Bids from GCs are fairly close because they use the same sub proposals. But the subs can vary substantially.

The same unpredictability that affects cost, affects schedules.

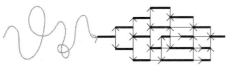

Construction is logical, sequential and production intensive. Design is decision intensive with repeated work and no limit on the amount of time that can be spent on a task.

As a designer develops the design, he or she discovers that many good ideas require doubling back to make changes in earlier work.

companies, materials and equipment into a tight, logical sequence of activities.

And few industries are as well suited to disciplined, analytical scheduling as construction. It takes so many bricklayers so many days and so many bricks to lay a brick wall. Increase the number of bricklayers and one can decrease the number of days. The foundations must be poured before building the wall and the windows are set after building the wall. It's a classic exercise in engineering logic.

The common mistake managers make is to try to bring the same engineering logic to scheduling design.

There are guidelines for the number of bricks that a mason can lay in a day. But the guidelines for the time required to design the wall are more controversial. Typically AEs set limits on design by dividing their fee by their person hour costs, setting staff levels and then setting deadlines. An old saw is:

> *"Designers don't finish, they just abandon the work."*

Many aspects of a design are studied more than once. Indeed design can be studied endlessly—and many designers are inclined to do so. In fact, the best designers are often the ones who hold on the longest and are the hardest to schedule.

A common error made by construction managers is to try to schedule design with the same techniques used to schedule construction. Construction is production intensive; design is decision intensive. Construction is sequential; design is iterative. Construction has defined needs for the resources of time, labor and materials; design only requires intellectual resources. The objective of a constructor is to do everything right the first time; a designer studies a problem over and over, refining at each step.

There isn't anything a designer can't spend more time on to make better. So the best architects are the ones who take more time and make a better design. There is an old joke:

> *"How do you find the architecture school on a university campus at night? It's the one with the lights on."*

So design is less predictable and more difficult to control than construction. But it sets cost, schedule and quality. Consequently, the most sophisticated Program Managers extract as much design activity as possible from the project workflow and put it into the program activities to make the delivery of projects more predictable.

Designers and contractors get irritated with each other. The designers get annoyed at the constructors because they're pestering them for drawings and decisions. And the contractors get annoyed at the architects because the architects want to keep studying the problem.

Different kinds of schedules

Master schedule
A master schedule shows the major design activities, points of approval, bid periods, bid review, fabrication and assembly times for major systems, major construction milestones and move-in activities. It shows how projects relate and how each major project participant interfaces with the others.

Design schedule
A design schedule integrates design review and approval activities. It identifies the decisions to be made, who must make them, the information required to make the decision, the time required to produce the information and who will do so. Although construction is constrained by the availability of labor and materials, design is always constrained by decision-making.

Short-interval schedule
Short-interval schedules may include an hour-by-hour schedule for a charrette or day-by-day activities for a two- or three-week period. During design, short-interval schedules cover activities between reviews. During construction, short-interval schedules are normally three-week rolling schedules.

Bid schedules
Bid schedules identify when documents will be available; when addenda will be issued; when pre-bid meetings will be held; and when bids will be due, opened and awarded.

Construction schedules
Construction schedules analyze strategies for interfacing design with construction sequencing, integrating activities of multiple contractors and coordinating delivery of owner-furnished

Design is the hardest part of a capital program to manage.

material. Some include labor-loaded schedules to measure progress or cost-loaded schedules to support payment requests or analyze change orders.

Occupancy schedules

Occupancy schedules integrate the users' move-in activities with the AEs, CMs and contractors. The schedules include distribution of furniture, fixtures and equipment to assigned locations, systems start-up and warranty documentation. No other phase is more critical to the client's final memory of the project.

QUALITY CONTROL

Here's a clear, unequivocal definition of quality:

> *Quality is conformance to requirements.*

Phillip Crosby explained that concept in his 1979 book *Quality Is Free: The Art of Making Quality Certain.* It's the best definition of quality I know of for this chaotic world of design and construction.

Quality isn't luxury, permanence, durability or beauty. It's conformance to requirements. Luxury, permanence, durability or beauty may be desirable and might be requirements—often they are. But not necessarily. If a building's functional purpose is well served by cost-effective insulated metal panels, and that's what's specified, it's bad quality to use travertine. So our job as a Program Manager is to help an owner define the requirements and then deliver them.

Project Definition is the foundation for quality control in a program.

Quality starts with requirements. And we've beat that drum as hard as we know how in the chapter *Program and Project Definition.* A quality control program has to begin with Project Definition.

We've stressed the importance of searching for repetition in the project workflow and rotating it into the program for continuous improvement. So that's the foundation for quality control in a program.

Much writing on construction projects describes quality control as making sure the plans and specifications are followed—good inspection in the field. That's certainly a form of conformance to requirements. But in a Program Management environment, we are constantly looking for ways to polish and improve—to redefine quality. And then to make sure the design responds precisely.

Quality control during design

So we start with Project Definition and the checklists that define requirements. But as a program unfolds, there are individual values that will help or hinder. Motivated design professionals will bring personal and professional biases, ambitions and inspiration to the table. The best will be the most difficult and will disrupt previous standards and accepted attitudes. Cherish the designers who challenge the standards, but be prepared to tell them to follow directions if they don't have a better idea.

Engineers and architects are taught to:

> *"Prefer your client's interests over your own, and, when the issues are clear, the public interest over both."* [2]

Professionalism means responsibility to the public good as well as the good of an owner. True professionals have divided allegiance.

But sooner or later, the project will be defined and it's the Program Manager's job to see that the design has it right. There are some basic tools:

A quality matrix
A quality matrix is a database that describes the project requirements and the required response from the design disciplines and consultants. It ensures that each requirement is assigned to the appropriate person or organization. It's the distribution of the requirements to the member of the extended project team best qualified to provide a solution for that requirement. It lets everybody know what they should be doing. It's useful to measure design progress—and it's notoriously harder to measure design than construction.

Constructibility, coordination and interference reviews
Constructibility, coordination and interference reviews examine the practicality of building systems and assembly methods. They review compatibility and check for physical conflicts, particularly

Challenge the standards, but stick with them if there isn't a better solution.

2. Carl Sapers admonishes students in his architecture professional practice classes at Harvard with this credo.

between mechanical and structural systems that often produce conflicts during construction.

Constructibility reviews find easy ways to build the building. They're typically done by a good construction superintendent or by estimators who have had field experience.

Here's an example: A school project we were designing had an unusually short schedule. We started design in August and promised it would be ready for students and teachers in 11 months. A crusty superintendent on our team suggested we change the foundation and slab details to allow us to erect the walls and roof before pouring the slab. He wanted to weather in the building as fast as possible so the trades could work in bad weather—and when we got the ground-in work done under roof, we could pour the slab under roof. Sure enough, it rained 28 days in January that year. No problem. We made the schedule.

Requirement compliance reviews

Requirement compliance reviews ensure that the functional and aesthetic requirements are being met. That's not only the owner's requirements. There may also be requirements for all the entitlement agencies.

Peer Reviews

A peer review can occur at any time in a project. Essentially it is a review of a design or construction activity by professionals with similar or greater credentials than the ones directly involved in the task. The review often uncovers large issues that are neglected or treated with less emphasis than what would be appropriate. Since we can all get too close to a problem or too fixed on our own solutions, it helps to have fresh eyes.

Quality control during construction

Construction inspection and testing are means to ensure conformance to the construction documents, code compliance and good craftsmanship. They include quality assurance (procedures to get things right the first time) and quality control (procedures to catch mistakes). Volumes have been written about these subjects so there is no need for repetition here.

Safety reviews by a Program Manager help to minimize accidents and litigation. They require contractors to prepare detailed safety plans. (But the requirements set by the Program Manager should take no action to relieve the contractor's responsibility for safety.)

However, construction inspection and safety reviews in a program are likely to be different than those in a single project. In a project, inspection by an on-site team inspector or a small group of inspectors requires a professional with generalized experience. A modest project will not support full-time inspectors for architectural, electrical, mechanical, civil, data distribution, safety, etc. But a program with multiple projects can have a team of roving specialists.

Quality: a management responsibility

In the public sector, the typical Program Management assignment is to control contractual performance: cost, schedule and scope—the *business* of building.[3] These clients don't often ask Program Managers to make better buildings. The assumption is that the architects will do that.

Too often, a Program Manager is charged with managing the business, not the quality of a building program.

In these Program Management assignments, the Program Managers usually deal with multiple architects—individual firms do individual projects. Good firms have good ideas, but it's uncommon for one firm to copy another or exchange ideas. There is little rotation. With a few exceptions, the public sector outsourced Program Manager doesn't set design standards, define and refine best practices or record lessons learned.[4] There's little refinement even when there are several design and construction cycles.

If there are multiple architects in a building program, it's uncommon for them to exchange ideas.

The problem seems to be most acute with public and institutional organizations pressured by politics or their constituencies to pass the work around to multiple taxpayers and campaign donors.

Also, some leaders are disinclined to get involved. They know construction programs are a hot potato. For example, in many states, one of the largest state expenditures is the prison program. In an election year, the challenger always criticizes the incumbent's management of prison construction. Public school building programs are also hotbeds for controversy. The most

3. A notable exception is the design excellence program at GSA.
4. A notable exception is the LAUSD lessons learned database (page 220).

common reason a school superintendent gets fired is not a poor educational curriculum. It's the cost and schedule overruns on a construction program.

These political pressures result in leadership voids. No one will take full responsibility for the success of the program.

An executive void is a recipe for failure.

On a school building program that I observed (unpleasantly close) the facilities manager had opposed the use of an outsourced Program Manager because he wanted to build his own staff. So he did everything possible to discredit the Program Manager. Soon the people on the Program Management team disliked him. The school superintendent was scared to touch the conflict. His lack of leadership left a dysfunctional relationship in place, slowed the program and created cost. It ended poorly.

In almost every case, these voids are recipes for trouble. On one poor-performing Program Management assignment, the Program Manager was not able to meet with either the school superintendent or the chairman of the building committee. The client contact was the facilities department that had been against the selection of a Program Manager from the first because they wanted to build their own staff. Again the superintendent was scared to touch the conflict and lack of leadership slowed the program and created cost.

We've seen too many organizations delegate project delivery to a facilities staff and emphasize only time, money and scope. They then hire a Program Manager to support the facilities staff. Neither has the responsibility to improve the performance of the facilities. They parcel projects out to individual architects—making it difficult to collect and implement best practices. The result is inconsistency in the final building products.

Happily, we've also seen the reverse. In both public and private organizations we've been impressed by strong leaders who felt that the design of the project and the performance of their buildings was a responsibility of top management. Most important, they understand that the users, AEs, CMs and builders have different goals, values and work habits. Somehow, without being experts in all those fields (no one ever is), they're able to knit together a cohesive and coherent team to make good buildings, on time and in the budget.

An Ability to Work with People

Leadership

Authority, Influence and Control

A Program Management team will be influenced by both stated and unstated values established by the organization and the program's leader. These values, both subtle and stated, will differ appreciably from one leader to the next. They will change if leadership changes, requiring adjustment among an established program team.

Leadership may come from executives, users, designers or construction agents—or from a combination. Each will have different interests—and some will be conflicting. Invariably, one of these sources of leadership will influence the program more than the others.

A Program Manager's authority can be either structural or influential. An in-house Program Manager, who holds the contracts with the project team, can have direct structural authority, but an outsourced Program Manager, who doesn't hold the contracts with the rest of the project team, will only have influential authority.

Influential authority will flow from the perception that the Program Manager supports the leadership goals—both written and unwritten.

A Program Manager must understand the culture and the values set by the program's leadership. If this chapter sensitizes you to the importance of this subtle matter and alerts you to the need for adaptability as leadership changes, it will have paid for the book and your time reading it.

Leadership shapes the program's culture: the landscape of written policies and unwritten attitudes. A set of services, values and procedures created for one program will not fit the next. Nor will it continue to fit the first if the leadership changes.

Program leadership may come from an individual who has another job within the owner's organization. Leadership may come from one of the owner's administrative executives, or it may come from a potential facility user. Or leadership may come from a designer. Or it may come from a construction agent: a Program Manager (either owner employed or an outsourced group) that has the responsibility to manage project delivery.

There are shifting balances of influence from all four of these sources, but one will likely dominate. The balance will influence formal policies and informal attitudes. It will affect decisions and define good and bad. It will shape the project's culture.

The two largest AE/CM companies in Houston, across the street from each other, had good but profoundly different values that affected decision-making.

Let me illustrate the affect of leadership on values. The first part of my career was spent with CRS—a company led by creative people from small towns who were building a national practice based on creative ideas. CRS was focused on aggressive growth and innovation. The way you shot down someone in a meeting was to say:

"There's nothing new about that."

CRS was so innovative that there were occasional failures. But other times there were striking successes.

When I moved to 3D/I, our founder, Vic Neuhaus, who had grown up in Houston, was well liked and was a personal friend of many of Houston's leaders. He had a great sense of responsibility. Avoiding project problems with his community of friends was on everyone's mind. Reliability was more important than innovation. The way you shot down someone in a meeting was to say,

"We haven't done that before."

Both organizations were well known, highly respected and successful. The differences weren't a matter of right and wrong. They were cultural differences that produced different kinds of success and different ways to measure the contribution of the organization's employees. The people who succeeded in each of the organizations understood the different values.

All the organizations we've worked for and all those we interviewed run their programs differently. They produce as many cultures as there are personalities among individuals and as there are missions among organizations. The differences are formally expressed and behavior is controlled through documents such as mission statements, policy manuals, procurement regulations, management plans and procedures.

There are as many differences in programs as there are differences in individuals.

But differences are also expressed informally, and they affect behavior through intangible values and traditions. There are subtle attitudes about risk, innovation, responsibility, work ethics and interpersonal relationships. Most of the latter will be unwritten and must be inferred from day-to-day interactions.

These attitudes affect the relative importance assigned to cost, schedule and quality. For instance, one organization may want to reduce the unit cost of construction to get more space from a limited public appropriation; another may want to shorten time-to-market for a competitive advantage; a third may want a unified aesthetic to strengthen an institutional identity or brand image—and so on.

Owners have vastly different convictions about the importance of buildings to their mission. Sometimes there is passion, sometimes indifference. A museum board will scour the earth for the right designer and spend scads of money on finishes while a factory owner will want a functional shell from an engineer.

The role of buildings in the success of owner organizations varies enormously.

Those convictions influence interaction among executives, users and facility groups in the owner's organization. They determine who makes decisions and sets direction.

This simple reality of who (or what group) leads the program has enormous consequences. Although we see programs as the act of governments, institutions and corporations, the differences are inevitably shaped by people—individual personalities with distinctive convictions, unique interests and personal styles. So

The personal convictions of the program leadership affect the program as much as the mission of the organization.

managing one design and construction program is never the same as another. The extremes are clear. Less clear are the subtle differences in values among similar programs. One healthcare owner will vary from the next. There will be variations among similar owners in government, education, retail and hospitality. Moreover, there will be variance during a program if the leadership changes.

Programs change when leadership changes. A smart Program Manager will get acquainted with the values of a new leader quickly.

Organizational values set subtle yardsticks that the owner's executives use to evaluate the performance of the people and organizations executing their programs. When the owner's leadership changes, the yardsticks change. Then the Program Managers who have been successful must change too or they will stumble.

A good program can get bumpy when leadership changes. How many times have you watched this scenario? A Program Manager develops a trusting relationship with a pleased owner. Then the owner changes management. A new executive brings a new set of values to measure performance. Usually, the new executive simply assumes everyone else holds the same values. But they aren't written and may not be spoken. Perhaps the old executive was worried most about quality. The new guy cares about cost and thinks everyone else should too. The old executive had a formal reporting structure. The new guy manages by walking around. Meanwhile, the team continues to operate under the old set of unwritten values. Problems ensue.

We can't begin to describe all the nuances of program culture. But we can outline some stereotypes and define some broad categories based on the groups who influence a program. They are:

1. Executives
2. Users
3. Designers
4. Agents

In choosing these categories, we expose ourselves to the sin of generalization. In this industry, there are always variations and exceptions. There are as many differences in program cultures as there are people running them.

So we know that the characterization of these four groups is oversimplifying a far more complicated subject. We admit the stereotyping. Nevertheless, let us forge ahead and characterize the likely tendencies of these four groups (and the inherent conflicts they might generate) for no other reason than to explain that a Program Management team must recognize and analyze a unique and individual set of influences on every project.

An interested CEO who has a passion for building will likely want a clear, strong response to the corporate goals and will drive on-course correction. There will be unilateral, non-bureaucratic decisions, and the yardstick is likely to be the bottom line, the opening date and conformance to corporate strategy.

Users will be more inclined to want functional efficiency and more space. They will probably form committees to think up requirements and let others worry about budgets. Their yardstick will doubtless be the facility's ultimate operational suitability.

Designers will be interested in aesthetics and building system quality. They may search for functional or technical innovations because their yardstick, in addition to a happy client, is recognition by peers in their profession.

Construction agents (in-house or outsourced Program Managers) will want definable requirements and reliable building systems because they will be measured by the yardstick of cost and schedule. They will want to minimize the ability of executives, users and designers to make capricious changes by establishing a stable process and will likely institutionalize bureaucratic procedures.

Of course, in any real-world construction program, there's influence from all four of these groups. But usually one group wields more power than the others. As the dominant group changes, so does the yardstick. The definition of "good work" is a variable that changes.

In some cases there may be several strong groups. For instance, at MIT we found strong users (often scientists with large research grants) who had considerable influence and caused continuous change during the course of a project. And MIT's administration was committed to high-design buildings and supported innovative architects. The designer and the user had more influence on decisions than the Program Manager. Schedules and budgets were not the significant drivers.

CEOs will be interested in the response to corporate goals; users will be interested in functional response; designers will be interested in aesthetics; construction agents will be interested in cost and schedule. Whoever has the most clout will elevate their interest.

A common situation that vexes a program team is a project that has shifting influences from executives, users, designers and agents as it progresses through design and construction. The result: change and delay as the project adjusts to different sets of values.

Human nature being what it is, these four groups instinctively see their own interests as "right" and the others as "wrong." And it's a very small step between thinking someone is wrong and thinking he or she is bad. As the team makes small decisions, driven by their value set, it's hard to keep some of the team members from having negative thoughts about others. Without strong leadership, a clear vision and good processes, these diverse interests may coalesce into warring camps. If so, it will be a difficult program.

But first, let's understand: no one, ever, anytime, is in complete control of a design and construction program. There's no emperor, no czar. And the dictators always fall. Even a dominant, hands-on CEO can't control it all. There's too much. The project leaders are always subject to oversight, approvals and permissions from boards, funding sources, legislators, regulatory agencies and the people who must get the job done.

Having said that, here are examples of these different leadership styles:

EXECUTIVES

Some organizations have a leader (CEO, general, superintendent or director) who understands how important buildings can be to the success of their enterprise, understands how to inspire the process, is interested in buildings and takes a hands-on approach.

There have been famous examples of leaders who have done just that: Steve Jobs (Apple Computer), Michael Eisner (Disney), Edgar Odell Lovett (Rice University), Sam Walton (Wal-Mart), Bill Marriott (Marriott Hotels) and Gerald Hines (Hines). They have all taken a passionate interest in their buildings. We talked to people from these organizations and present vignettes below to illustrate this kind of interest—and how it may vary.

When Steve Jobs was squeezed out of Apple in the 80s, he led the design of a UNIX-based personal computer. It didn't

©Roy Zipstein Photography, Courtesy of Apple Inc.

Steve Jobs' intense focus on design excellence influences both the products and facilities at Apple.

succeed, but the press described it as the world's most beautiful computer. When Jobs returned to Apple, he brought with him his commitment to design. He focused on the details of Apple products down to the graphics on the boxes they were shipped in. He selected some of the country's best design firms and managed them fiercely. Some of the Apple products are now in the Museum of Modern Art.

When Apple decided to open a chain of retail stores to showcase their products, Jobs drove the design concepts with his legendary passion for excellence. He worked with the design team regularly from concept to details. And he was exacting in the details— making adjustments and changes when it improved the result. Jobs was involved in store layout, door hardware, wood finishes and lighting. People worked long hours getting the first Apple store ready on time.

When Michael Eisner became Disney's CEO in 1984, he sought out the world's leading architects. From California to Tokyo, these firms brought award-winning designs to Disney hotels and office buildings.

Eisner assumed the role of final creative judge in building and theme park design. He scrutinized the most detailed architectural components intensely. To help keep the values of good architecture at the highest levels at Disney, he added New York architect Robert A. M. Stern to the Walt Disney Company Board of Directors from 1992 to 2003, and Stern designed several buildings for Disney.

Edgar Lovett and Ralph Adams Cram toured Europe together to conceive an aesthetic that would guide the identity of a new institution. It continues to do so. Pictured above is Lovett Hall, designed by Cram at the beginning of the 20th century and Baker Hall, designed by Robert A. M. Stern at the end of the 20th century.

We heard an amusing story about Eisner's commitment to design. We were told that in one meeting he became so enthusiastic about a project that he pulled himself up short, called Frank Wells, then Disney's President, and said:

"Frank, come quick, I'm spending too much money."

Edgar Odell Lovett was appointed president of Rice Institute in 1907, before it was built. Lovett had been a professor at Princeton and a member of the Princeton buildings and grounds committee. Cram, Goodhue & Ferguson were the principal architects for Princeton so Lovett returned to the people he knew. Lovett and Ralph Adams Cram toured Europe together and invented an architectural style that was an amalgam of

Campus Gothic and Mediterranean architecture. The unique style, unlike any other university in the world, reinforced Lovett's vision for a unique university. I am again quoting from Stephen Fox's history of Rice.[1]

> *"It was designed to represent the identity of a cultural institution that, because it was newly created, had no identity."*

Bob Workman told us that Sam Walton was hands-on in conceiving the Wal-Mart building program. He and Bob, who led BSW, a Tulsa-based AE firm, developed a process to accomplish almost all design at the program level, eliminating it from the project workflow. A team manages continuous improvement of the prototype. They develop and refine prototype modules. We were told that Wal-Mart makes about 150 changes a month to the prototype. BSW claims they can produce Construction Documents in less than a day for a unique facility assembled from the modules. It's unlikely that such an innovative process could have been put in place without an executive pushing it.

We were told that Bill Marriott frequently visits the mock-up rooms at Marriott headquarters. Like Jobs and Eisner, he is not afraid to make major corrections whenever he thinks they're necessary, and he's not afraid to make an executive decision. He discarded the name for a new brand that an internal group had spent months developing: he replaced "Maritel" with "Fairfield Inn." We understand that he is hands-on with the details of a prototype design: interior design, fabrics, colors, room layout and other interior materials. Then he is inclined to delegate the execution based on the approved prototype. But he will still get involved if he needs to.

A CEO has enormous prerogatives in making major changes to projects and program. One of the most spectacular examples was when Gerald Hines, early in his career, developed One Shell Plaza. SOM designed the building to be bush-hammered concrete. It would be Houston's tallest building—a real landmark for the city. The project rented faster and at higher rates than Hines had projected. So rather than pocketing the unexpected profit, Hines negotiated a massive change order to replace the bush-hammered concrete skin with travertine. It was a

One Shell Plaza was originally designed with a bush-hammered concrete skin. When it rented faster and at higher rates than anticipated, Hines changed the skin to travertine rather than pocket the profit. This commitment to quality contributed to Hines' spectacular success as an international developer.

1. Stephen Fox, *Rice University: an architectural tour*, Princeton Architectural Press, 2001.

commitment to quality that marked his development strategy for the future. Some would argue that because of this strategy, Hines has built more good architecture than any other organization in the world and has assumed an international reputation as a developer of high-quality buildings.

Leaders like Steve Jobs, Michael Eisner, Edgar Odell Lovett, Sam Walton, Bill Marriott and Gerald Hines understand their mission, usually because they set it. They have the authority to make changes, large or small, that reinforce their mission. They will adjust the budget, the schedule or the scope in the middle of the project if they think it's the right thing to do. Micro-management appears not to trouble them if they think the project can be improved.

Some of these organizations build their own in-house teams to design and manage the work. Others search for the best firms in the world to serve them. Usually, they do some of both and the executive leads the integration. These executive-driven building programs are intense. Most of the Program Management firms that work in these environments find it demanding but rewarding. There are crisp decisions, clear direction and high expectations for efficiency and performance. It's comparatively easy for a Program Manager to perform when the signals are loud and clear.

USERS

The salespeople that staff big-box retail facilities typically have little to say about the design of the store they operate. Neither do the customers. But in some organizations, the people who use the facilities have lots of clout. They will exercise a huge amount of control over the design.

In some programs, the users control the capital building program.

We talked to Paul Curley when he was Director of Capital Construction at MIT. He commented in words to this effect:

> *"When you're defining lab requirements with a Nobel Prize winner who has just received a massive grant or a major endowment, it's very difficult to tell them what your standards are and what you're going to give them. They're going to tell you what they want, and you're going to give it to them. Period."*

It's not just research universities like MIT. When we talked to Lionel Diaz, Director of Facilities at Maricopa Community College in Phoenix, he explained that there was little they could standardize because the presidents of each of the colleges in the network controlled design and wanted different things.

Several years ago, I consulted with a group of prestigious hospitals. They had been pressured by the modern economics of healthcare to band together to form a network. Each had been autonomous in the past and had developed an internal facilities department. Each managed design and construction programs differently. Our job was to advise them on how to knit these separate facilities groups into a cohesive whole, recommend economies of scale and choose best practices from each for universal application.

It wasn't hard to see how that could be done. But it was not to be. The doctors and research scientists using the hospitals were more powerful within the hospitals than the administrators who were searching for economies. So the facilities group had little clout. The doctors wanted their own facility group at their elbow—doing what they needed, when they needed it. They got what they wanted and economies of scale were nowhere to be seen.

The scientists and chemical engineers had ideas that improved the project every day. They also blew the budget.

On another occasion, we provided consulting for a large pharmaceutical research laboratory. The project was over the budget and the cost was growing steadily. It took little time to understand the reason. The client's scientists and chemical engineers had moved in with the project's design firm. They had good ideas every day. And every new good idea was a change order. Of course, all the scientists and chemical engineers thought they were improving the facility and that the changes were worth it.

We reported back to the chairman of the board who had hired us and gave him a simple message:

> *"Your staff is improving the project every day. So far it has produced a 20% increase in the project cost. Now you know the cause of the cost overruns. Maybe it's worth it. We don't know how to evaluate that. That's your job."*

We were a little worried with that plain talk, but the chairman agreed that the judgment call was their job. What we were able to point out was that giving the users free authority to make changes to the building program would not produce the cost control he was looking for but might produce a better operation.

Despite the budget and time inefficiencies, user control for some kinds of facilities is the right kind of control. While costs are apt to increase, the cost is part of achieving the organizational mission. For the highly specialized areas of research, healthcare and education, the user groups have much more specific knowledge of what they need and how the building should support those needs.

But one of the saddest things to see is a board or an administration that believes a Program Manager in a user-controlled group should produce the same change-free project and trouble-free process as an agency-controlled group.

Daniel Hudson Burnham (1846-1912) was an American architect and urban planner. He was the Director of Works (certainly a Program Manager) for the World's Columbian Exposition in Chicago in 1893.

DESIGNERS

In 1893, Daniel Burnham led a team of all-star architects that included Frederick Law Olmsted; Richard Morris Hunt; McKim, Mead and White; Adler and Sullivan; and Baron LeJenny to build Chicago's Great Columbian Exposition. Burnham was certainly an architect and did much of the design. But he was also a Program Manager. He managed the work from an on-site office and delivered.

The most extreme case of designer control we've ever seen was when we did a management study for an amusement company. They built unique entertainment projects—mechanical shows and rides. The building was an income-producing engine. A better building meant better income. The design group made changes until opening day—and then they shut down the ride and made more changes. There was only one criterion—the best they could do. They built a unique facility. They didn't like costly changes, but they accepted them because they believed the income from a good design would offset the costs. The design fee ran about half of the construction cost.

Contrast that 50% design fee with the fee of 1 or 2% for a site adaptation for a big-box retail prototype. But then families don't bundle their kids in a car and drive across the country to walk though a Wal-Mart.

Another striking example of designer control is at MIT. Victoria Sirianni led MIT's design and construction program during a

Stephen Holl's Simmons Hall at MIT was an innovative design that would not have been built without leadership and support from MIT's administration.

period of major expansion. She told me that when she took Stephen Holl's design for Simmons Hall to Dr. Charles Vest, then MIT's president, she told him that she was concerned that the building's design was so advanced that it might not work. Dr. Vest's reply was something like:

> *"It needs to work, but this is also the kind of place where pushing the envelope of design is important."*

I have great admiration for my alma mater for their efforts at the front edges of architecture. How many of us have had a client like that? (As a matter of interest, the design they were discussing was not the final. The final design was, believe it or not, more conventional.) Victoria went on to say:

> *"Pushing the envelope of design was very much in keeping with an institution that pushes the envelope of whatever it does."*

Paul Curly told us that Bill Mitchell, head of MIT's Media Lab, and Dr. Vest influenced architectural selection. When there's a famous designer with that kind of institutional support, the facilities Program Managers are bound to have a tough time maintaining budgets and schedules.

Perhaps that's the way it should be. As a prestigious university, MIT seeks to showcase architecture. (MIT was America's first school of architecture.) When MIT moved from Boston to Cambridge in 1916, they built a chain of fairly nondescript Federal style buildings. But beginning in the latter half of the 20th century, they began to build a string of trophy projects by Alvar Aalto, Eero Saarenin, Eduardo Catalano, I. M. Pei, Stephen Holl and Frank Gehry.

Since WWII, MIT has attracted leading architects for their building projects. Baker House was designed by Alvar Aalto in 1947.

MIT expects to be the best and expects their buildings to say so—to imply the world-class, leading-edge excellence of their programs, students and faculty. They advertise their institution with architecture, just as Steve Jobs does with his Apple stores.

Consequently, they hire famous designers and struggle through their building program on a project-by-project basis. They rotate very little. They achieve little program-wide efficiency and must deal with the inherent problems of unique design. But there are people at MIT who feel that the buildings created by these architects make it worthwhile. So do lots of other people.

Serial builders approach their projects differently—and they should. I don't care to learn about artificial intelligence at Wal-Mart nor do I want to buy tires at MIT. Different missions require different intellectual input. And different management strategies serve different value systems.

For some owners, architecture serves a functional need; sometimes it's a symbolic mandate. Form follows…well, whatever the leadership decrees. It's not a nice, memorable alliteration like "form follows function," but it's reality and it's usually right.

AGENTS

Many organizations have learned painfully that a building program can be a dark tunnel of horrors. Cost overruns, delays and litigation jump from the shadows and truncate careers. Frequently these organizations wisely recognize that they need a focused group of experienced people who have design and construction management as their full-time job. So they create an in-house division or outsource to a Program Management company to manage their programs.

The federal government tends to call these organizations "construction agents." They include the Corps of Engineers, the Naval Facilities Engineering Command (NAVFAC) and the General Services Agency (GSA). Agent organizations also include building departments in cities, counties and states.

The U.S. Corps of Engineers, NAVFAC and GSA are construction agents. Their objective is to meet defined goals, not make on-course corrections as a CEO, a designer or a user would.

Educational and healthcare institutions develop in-house facility groups often called something like "planning, design and construction management." Fortune 500 companies are more likely to call them "Real Estate Management." In addition to their responsibility to manage design and construction, some of these agent groups have real estate procurement, leasing and operational maintenance as their responsibility.

These agents represent organizations with executives who feel that the design of their buildings is not the highest priority in their organization's mission. The Secretary of Defense is not likely to be as concerned and involved in building design as Steve Jobs, Michael Eisner, Edgar Odell Lovett, Sam Walton, Bill Marriott or Gerald Hines. Although these agents are often employees of the owner's organizations, many owners outsource Program Management to a private organization that functions in an agency role.[2] So an outsourced Program Management company is, for the purposes of this discussion, an agent. And if I tend to dwell on this topic, it's because I've devoted much of my career to Program Management. It's also a role that I believe needs the most attention and holds the greatest promise for gain in the construction industry.

The typical assignment for an agent—a Program Manager—is focused on the *business* of building. Usually there is a defined budget, perhaps an appropriation by a legislature, a bond that has been passed or a line item in a board-approved capital plan. And there is a schedule. The Program Manager's job is to deliver a set of requirements for a list of projects, on time and on budget.

That's the yardstick used to measure their performance, so that's the yardstick they'll apply to the entire extended program team. Consequently, these agents are inclined to put the easily measurable metrics of cost, schedule and operational reliability above such fuzzy and hard-to-measure values as aesthetics and functional innovation.

Most construction agents are primarily concerned with the business of design and construction.

In many cases, this focus on the business of building will draw the criticism that Program Managers don't see the final buildings as important to their mission as executives, users or designers might. It's a fair criticism. While executives, users and designers are interested in the product, the agents are more interested in the process and the metrics of cost and schedule that are the yardsticks used to measure their success.

Too often the assumption is that the AE's responsibility is to make a good building and the construction agent's responsibility is to meet the schedule and the budget. That's too bad. The construction agent (a Program Manager) is in the crucial position to make good buildings.

Although there are notable exceptions, most owners don't put much pressure on an outsourced Program Manager to make better buildings. The assumption is that design is up to the architects, while the Program Manager is in charge of the budget and schedule. The agent is a control mechanism to keep the architect on track. Sadly, the mission does not include excellence in design; it's delivering the requirements as defined at the start—without hiccups. An outsourced Program Management group is highly unlikely to change from bush-hammered concrete to travertine in the middle of a project as Hines did. Functional

2. The 2006 FMI/CMAA Seventh Annual Survey of Owners reported that internal staff did Program Management 34% of the time. When these organizations outsourced, the companies they chose were construction management firms (30%), Program Management firms (20%), design firms (10%) and other (6%).

innovation or aesthetic symbolism takes a back seat to cost and schedule control.

In many of these assignments, the Program Managers manage multiple architects—individual firms do individual projects. Good firms have good ideas, but it's uncommon for the firms to share those good ideas. So each AE reinvents the wheel. The result is inconsistency—some buildings are good, some are not so good. Those of us who provide Program Management services need to correct this flaw in our practice.

The problem seems to be most acute with public owners, pressured by the politics of their constituencies to pass the work around to multiple taxpayers and campaign donors. In some cases we've seen public organizations engage in the height of senselessness and hire multiple Program Managers.

So, too often, the economies of scale are missed. For many years, we provided Program Management assistance to the Defense Commissary Agency (the organization that builds commissaries at military installations). In the late 1990s, we held a large meeting with consultants to discuss ways to improve the program. An architect who had done considerable work for DeCA sat across from me. I asked him:

Economies of scale are often missed.

> *"If the design fee to design one commissary is X, what is the fee for 10 commissaries?"*

He quickly responded, with a slight vein of irritation in his voice:

> *"10X!"*

That makes no sense. Later DeCA turned to a set of adaptable prototypes, reduced design cost and reduced errors.

I don't believe it was grasping avarice on the part of the architect. He was part of a good firm we had worked with on several projects. He simply believed, as many architects do, that each project should be an original creation. But for a serial builder that needs hundreds of similar buildings, that doesn't seem reasonable.

Happily, we've also seen the reverse. In organizations both public and private, we've been impressed by agent organizations who felt that the design of the project and the performance of their buildings was a core responsibility. So there is an extraordinary opportunity for improvement if the Program Manager collects the good ideas, distributes them and builds on them.

In-house construction agents are frequently more successful at setting standards and achieving improvements in design quality. Barbara White Bryson, Associate Vice President of Facilities Engineering and Planning at Rice University, commented:

> *"We don't want to straightjacket design, but we don't want to have to stock more than one size of paper towel for the bathrooms either."*

Construction agents typically define the process to keep users at bay after design approval.

But with some exceptions, it has been rare for an outsourced Program Manager to set design standards, define and refine best practices, develop continuous improvement and record lessons learned. The mission to make better buildings is not part of their scope of work. The private sector companies that provide these outsourced services and the owners that employ them should learn from these effective owner organizations.

Good construction agents typically document a process to define, estimate and approve requirements. After design approval, they try their utmost to keep the users at arm's length. They lack the authority to change from bush-hammered concrete to travertine after the building is designed or change the lighting and work all night two days before an opening. They're roundly criticized for change orders and cost overruns so they detest on-course corrections.

INFLUENTIAL VS. STRUCTURAL LEADERSHIP

An in-house Program Manager will have more structural authority than an outsourced firm.

Just as there are different kinds of leaders, there are different forms of leadership.

Some leaders—a president, a CEO, a chairman, a general, a superintendent—have structural control. There are clear lines of authority. The boss affects compensation, promotions and recognition. Other leaders simply influence others to do the right thing by example or persuasion. Some of the greatest leaders of history (Martin Luther, Mahatma Gandhi or Martin Luther King) did not have structural authority.

An in-house group of Program Managers has a good bit of structural authority because they select and contract with the extended project teams.

But an outsourced Program Manager doesn't usually hold the contracts with the designers and constructors or control their selection. The designers and constructors are selected by the same board or executives that select the Program Managers. And sometimes there is a little destructive competition between the Program Manager and the designers for the owner's approval.

Typically managers tend to use one of three forms of control:

1. Direct control through contractual or organizational authority
2. Indirect control through documented goals, objectives and procedures
3. Indirect control through example and personal persuasion.

Number 1 is structural. Numbers 2 and 3 are influential.

An outsourced Program Manager that only understands structural leadership will have a tough time. The authority of an outsourced Program Manager is weaker than that of an in-house Program Manager. Although there is implied authority because the holder of the contracts—the owner—has delegated authority to them and because they may be able to approve pay requests or evaluate performance, most of their leadership must be influential and they must learn influential leadership techniques.

Influential leadership works—often better than structural leadership. Successful AEs and constructors are typically led by people who have leadership qualities themselves and have a good bit of confidence in their own judgment. They will perform better with clear goals and procedures than autocratic direction.

Some of the world's greatest leaders have been influential leaders.

So most outsourced Program Managers will wisely firm up their control muscle with procedures and persuasion. They will document flow charts for program workflow and procedures manuals so people know how to perform. They persuade by documenting goals and values.

And as far as that goes, even though in-house Program Managers have structural authority, they will be wise to use all the influential techniques that they can muster. A culture of motivation, shared goals, of collaborative achievement and a sense of higher purpose will produce far better results than an authoritarian environment. People will work for money but they will fight and die for an idea.

Structural leaders are wise to use influence too.

So Program Managers may give direction but they must shore up their authority by establishing procedures, painting a vision and simply explaining the right thing to do.

Finally, our job is to forge teams with trusting relationships and shared goals. Legal agreements define tasks and terms; they're important. But relationships power the train.

Nevertheless, it's not enough for just the leaders to be good communicators and relationship builders. The leaders must create an environment where all team members freely communicate with others on the program.

No design and construction program goes exactly as planned. Rarely has the entire team worked together previously. Building strong relationships based upon each individual knowing that he or she will be treated fairly is essential to meeting the goals of time, cost and quality. When a hitch emerges, it's usually personal relationships between individuals that fix it.

Management effectiveness goes on steroids when managers develop a reputation of helping others succeed. If a Program Manager produces a culture where there is mutual support within the extended team for the idea that "no one is allowed to fail," then their authority will be great.

People and Project Teams

*If people want to help each other, the program will be far more successful.
If people dislike each other, they won't help and the program will suffer.
Collaboration is indispensable.*

*Creating a collaborative culture is a management art. It doesn't just
happen. Planning the attitudes and relationships among people is at least as
important as structuring the procedures and contracts among organizations.
It's more important in programs than in projects because it takes more
organizations and more people to deliver a project.*

*Program Managers have a wonderful opportunity that project managers
don't have. A Program Manager can build continuous, lasting, collaborative
relationships over multiple projects, weeding out the people and organizations
that cause conflict and rewarding the team players with promotions and more
work.*

Learning to be good with people is neglected in curriculums and
ignored by contracts. Yet it's a crucial management skill.

Of course, technical and legal knowledge is a prerequisite for
managing design and construction. We are taught those subjects

in school and on the job. We need to know how building systems are assembled and who puts them together; we need to know how long it takes so we can build schedules and fit people and organizations together; we need to know what things cost. And we need to know what contracts should say and how to track, document and enforce them. We've been taught this stuff and we should never quit learning more.

Project management has traditionally relied on these technical and legal underpinnings. Our concepts of structuring team performance have been based on organizational authority, precise contracts and legal recourse for non-performance. We've viewed those techniques as the proper tools of management. We've seen our job as the technical and legal challenges of design and construction and have neglected the soft matters of attitude and morale.

Collaboration—the application of more than one intellect, more than one body of experience and more than one viewpoint—is not an optional luxury for a program; it's a prerequisite necessity.

Yet we've watched technically competent teams fail to collaborate and have difficulties with the other organizations on a program. And we've seen plenty of owners who mismanaged their consultants and contractors and caused miserable program cultures. We've seen teams that operated like Swiss watches and others that became dysfunctional. We've watched highly competent people fail because they couldn't work together.

If members of a project team want to help one another, they'll help the project. Management philosophies that invoke the soft but essential spirit of teamwork and collaboration lead to better buildings. These are things that we can manage—and must. What could make more sense? People do things, not organizations.

Collaboration doesn't just happen. It must be managed.

We've operated under the assumption that project discord was a problem of unreasonable clients, dysfunctional bureaucracies, personality conflicts, unpredictable technical glitches or simply a lack of interpersonal skills.

In other words, we didn't think collaboration was something to manage. It simply happened or it didn't happen. Individual behavior was important, however, a person was simply endowed with good interpersonal skills—or not. That's wrong. Good personal relationships, crucial for collaboration, don't just fall in place because we staff a program with technically competent people. Collaboration is something that we need to understand, manage and improve.

Yes, some people are naturally endowed with these interpersonal skills and some people are just naturally difficult. But everybody can improve. We have a lot to learn about both individual and organizational behavior. We need to understand the basic mechanics of interpersonal relationships, the predictable behavior of groups on project teams and the forces that influence the actions of men and women who work together during periods of stress. We need to learn how to create and manage collaboration—to understand the architecture of teamwork. And these things we *can* study and learn about.

A construction program is made up of the cumulative, integrated, collaborative acts of individuals who work together. So our skill in understanding behavior and managing people is as important as our technical knowledge of design and construction.

It's clear, sometimes painfully clear, that technical knowledge isn't enough. However, there's a close relationship between technical competence and personal relationships. Inevitably, a technical failure will cause finger-pointing and conflict. Conversely, personality conflicts hinder collaboration and cause technical failure. One leads to the other. It's a nasty reciprocal relationship.

Too many people still carry stereotyped images of the unquenchable-ego architect, the by-the-numbers engineer, the unscrupulous contractor, the junk-yard-dog construction manager, the idealistic but impractical environmentalist and the demanding owner. All the players see the project from their professional corner and from their self-interest. Each has a hard time understanding the other disciplines and respecting the other values. The reality is that all are vital, and nothing shuts down collaboration faster than professional arrogance.

Stereotyping causes conflict.

Our industry has begun to scratch the surface on this matter. The late 20th century saw the rise of Partnering. Sometime in the 90s, Lester Edelman, then Chief Counsel for the U.S. Army Corps of Engineers, told me that after the Corps started using Partnering, their claims dropped 25%.

Partnering helps.

Partnering is not a bad place to begin. It focuses on opening channels of communication, installing systems to resolve problems and defining project goals for those who must work together. Clients, colleagues and competitors tell me they make more money, do better work and have fewer change orders. Employees tell me they enjoy their work more. It appears that the numbers-bound, bare-knuckled, mud-on-the-boots construction industry has discovered that this soft stuff is a good idea.

But too often, projects have held a single Partnering session and then have slid back into traditional adversarial patterns. It works better when the original session is followed by regular leadership meetings that implement the concepts outlined in the Partnering session.

Partnering has been a good project tool. But programs have a wonderful opportunity to build long-term relationships. There is the opportunity to co-locate teams, conduct multi-disciplinary workshops on program issues and develop long-lasting, trusting relationships. However, Partnering has to be a priority. If it is unmanaged and unmonitored, the relationships will be sporadic and unpredictable.

Every program is unique with unique individuals, problems, challenges and missions. But there are interpersonal behaviors and relationships that are invariably consistent. These behaviors are like weather. You don't know when it will rain next month— but you know it's highly likely that before the month is over, it will.

Programs benefit enormously if there's the right culture of mutual support. Managing culture, attitudes and interpersonal relationships is just as important as the technical challenges of scheduling and estimating. And these things can be managed. It takes just as much skill and requires at least equal attention.

We have learned that nothing, absolutely nothing, will help a program succeed more than everyone wanting everyone else to succeed. That makes good projects and happy clients.

Of course, we won't figure out how to eradicate all conflict. If we could, we could make world peace. But if we understand some of the common problems and predictable reactions, we can make progress.

And it's a lot more fun. So here are some of the things a manager might think about in dealing with the project team:

Following are 13 program realities—issues that influence human behavior and collaboration on design and construction programs.

Understanding them will help managers improve program performance.

There's a hierarchy of allegiance

Integrity is a prerequisite for a trusting relationship—and trusting relationships are necessary for a successful design and construction program. Success is considerably more likely when groups work openly and honestly, with candor and transparency. Nothing oils the machinery of a design and construction program more than trust.

As individuals, we know how to treat other individuals. We learned how in Sunday school, in kindergarten, at our parents' knees. And when we grow up, we have our spouses, good friends and colleagues to chastise us for misbehavior. We understand integrity at the person-to-person level.

But there's a hierarchy of allegiance. We all tend to be more supportive of the groups close to us than to more distant groups.

A design and construction program has a hierarchy of companies. People naturally are inclined to put their group in front of a larger group. A company's project manager may take an aggressive approach to pricing a change order to benefit his or her own company rather than the owner. Indeed, most of the companies—including the owner—will tend to put their allegiance to their own organization first, corroding trust.

In his book *Diplomacy*, Henry Kissinger observes that throughout the history of the world, nations felt no compunction about warring, lying and cheating for the good of their people or for the glory of empire. He points out that Woodrow Wilson confounded international diplomats with the doctrine that nations should treat other nations with the same morality that is expected of individuals.

We can behave like mini-nations and believe that our allegiance belongs to our own group first and that in dealing with other groups it's acceptable to use cunning and craftiness for financial or political advantage. But loyalty to our own group can undermine the need for integrity on a project team. Loyalty is an admirable quality—but integrity trumps it.

The actions of the individuals and companies (clients, designers and constructors) leave a long trail in many memories. There

We all tend to be more supportive of the groups close to us than to more distant groups. But nothing oils the machinery of a design and construction program more than trust.

will be many chapters ahead. Everyone will be better served by Wilson's doctrine: treat other groups with the same integrity that we expect from our friends.

In a program of many projects, the Program Manager has the opportunity, and the responsibility, to weed out people who give unfair allegiance to their own company.

Feelings are reciprocal

Try this. Tell someone something nice you heard about them. Tell them who said it. They will probably respond with something nice about the person who gave the compliment. A conversation like this is almost universal:

> Comment: *"Bill said you were hard-working and good at your job."*

> Response: *"That was nice. Bill is a good guy. He works hard too."*

So that's a rule for a Program Manager. Repeat compliments. When someone says something nice to you, it feels good. But it feels great when you hear it was said to someone else when you weren't around.

Now here's the important point. Groups respond like individuals. Project teams respond to praise.

It works another way too. Go to a project team meeting. Repeat a criticism from the client. Then listen to the team list the client's flaws. And the unfortunate thing is that the list-making won't be aimed at solving problems. It's a defensive function to shore up self-esteem by saying:

> *"They're criticizing us, but look how bad they are."*

Or it might be more childish:

> *"Well, we did it, but they did it too."*

We want satisfied team colleagues. How do we measure that? Well, we can look in the mirror, we can test our own feelings. Most of the time we can measure our colleague's satisfaction with us by how much we like them. If we think we are working for nice people, we can be pretty sure they're happy with us. If we hear our people grousing about someone else's dumb behavior, we can guess that person feels the same.

We want satisfied team colleagues. How do we measure that? Well, we can look in the mirror. Our feelings are probably reciprocated.

Laura Ingalls Wilder, who wrote Little House on the Prairie, said something like:

> *"People appear to us according to the light we throw upon them from our own minds."*

She could have added that light is reflected and influences how you appear to other people.

Feelings are reciprocated. What a simple thought. If you don't like people, they will sense it and then they won't like you. Soon you will focus on their bad acts and begin the list-making. So will they. A downward spiral starts.

It can happen in any one of the organizations. The owner can get cross with a consultant or a contractor, or a consultant can feel slighted or mistreated and corrupt their organization with bad talk. Then it becomes contagious.

I don't know how to fix this problem. When someone is ugly to me, I simply can't go stand in the corner and tell myself that I like them. But I can make some suggestions.

We can find something genuine we like about a person, talk about it, compliment them on it and see if we can't build on it.

We can skip list-making and identify the problem. It may be a technical problem or it may be personal. Maybe the critic feels unsupported. If that doesn't work, a good manager will get someone else to take over the relationship. Some of our best people have done so. My colleagues had to replace me on a job once.

Set a policy on a program: *"Bitch up, praise down."* The leaders ought to hear the complaints. And the leaders need to encourage good performance with regular recognition.

Meanwhile, we can avoid spreading contamination. We can keep our bad thoughts to ourselves and see if we can't encourage others to do the same. That's most true for our leaders. Their negative comments can pollute the team. Then morale will suffer, we will do bad work and get more criticism.

There's a corollary. We can spread positive comments and create good feelings. The best way to create an atmosphere where everyone wants us to succeed is for us to want them to succeed. Good feelings are just as contagious as bad feelings.

A friend is someone you enjoy being with and can count on when you need help. What could be more important at work? But there are differences between social and professional friendships. We accept social friends as they are. But in a program, if someone isn't performing, you must say so.

Friendship is neglected

Normally we think of friendship in a social sense: a friend is someone we enjoy being with and can count on if we need help.

But what could be more important at work? A network of project friendships is like a computer's operating system. It runs in the background, making things work—until it crashes. Then nothing works.

I remember Gene Lupia's retirement dinner. (Gene was the general in charge of civil engineering for the Air Force.) Gene said friendships kept him in the Air Force, solved problems and made things work. He talked about the great friends he had made in his career and what they had meant to him.

Gene's speech should be published and put on bookshelves next to works by Peter Drucker, Tom Peters and the rest of the management gurus. With all the management tomes written over the years, I know of none (until Jack Welch's book) that talked about friendship as a management concept. But of course it is. It makes life more rewarding and helps produce excellence.

We should be friends with each other, with our clients, with our consultants, with our contractors—with the extended project team. We need to stress civility, mutual support, candor, integrity and, you know, all the Sunday School stuff.

But there are major differences between a business and a social friendship. And it's important for all the people on a project team to realize the differences. Here are some that come to mind:

A business friendship doesn't require a social friendship outside of work. Indeed, some of our public clients have reservations about socializing with us. We must respect that. Furthermore, some of our employees want to keep their personal lives separate from their business relationships. So we must respect that too.

Another important difference between a social and a business friendship is this: we can ask our social friends for a favor, but although we may be friends with our clients, we can't ask for favors or unfair advantages in our work for them.

So if personal friends become clients, we must scrupulously avoid imposing on our friendship. Furthermore, if we represent a client, we must decline gifts or favors from people who want to do business with our client.

Finally, here's the most important difference. In a social relationship we can tacitly accept our friend's flaws. A personal friendship requires accepting our friends as they are—we choose them for what they are. And a good way to end a personal friendship is to decide our friend needs a makeover.

But on a project, there's a constant need to improve performance. We can't accept flaws that hurt the project. Professional friendship carries with it an important requirement to accept and give criticism. Friendship and criticism are not mutually exclusive. Constructive criticism is a form of support: it's a job requirement too.

Groups function like structures

It's a corny metaphor, but teams of people function much like structural systems.

Too much load on a structure will cause tension among the parts, deform the system and the system will fail. Teams are the same. Unachievable goals or heavy criticism are loads that create stress and demolish teamwork.

When things are going well, it's easy for teams to function. But when there are problems, our subconscious ego-protection systems naturally lead us to see the problems as the fault of others.

So finger-pointing and list-making reign. Collaboration, the structure of teamwork, fails.

Even the best teams, faced with continuous criticism, may collapse. And some ordinary teams, with the right encouragement, perform wonderfully.

Groups function like structural systems. They work best with a load—the right load. Not too much, not too little. That means leaders must know how much load is required.

I don't want to overwork the metaphor, but here's a corollary. Many structural systems require a load to perform as intended. Arches may not stand without weight. Pre-stressed beams may need a load to accept their designed alignment.

The same is true for teams. Teams need work to function well. Ambitious goals build teamwork. Achievement cements it.

So Program Managers must have the wisdom to adjust the team for the load. If the team is staffed inadequately, performance will crack. Conversely, if there are more people than jobs, people will compete for the same tasks. That hurts relationships too.

Nobody is in control of a design and construction program. Collaboration is the only path to success.

Nobody's in control

Thousands of people and hundreds of organizations come together to build a project. Nobody controls it all. While each organization may have a command structure, all must deal with groups that they can only influence—not control.

Program Managers are pretty far down the food chain. If it's an in-house group, the organization's primary business will be preeminent. But even the owner's organization will be controlled by a board or shareholders. And the Program Management group will have to answer to entitlement agencies.

If it's an outsourced group, there will be even less authority. Our ability to shape the outcome rests on our expertise, the trust placed in us and our credibility.

If we are an outsourced group, we report to our client. But our client's staff is not in complete control; they have administrators, boards and user groups. There may be citizen oversight committees, fine arts commissions, municipal agencies, regulatory agencies and code authorities. Associations for architects, engineers, contractors and labor may have interests. The media will watch and report.

But success—of the project and of the client—is heavily influenced by the attitudes of all these groups. When 3D/I, CRSS, Gilbane, Fluor Daniel, Brown & Root and Turner started the Emergency Bed Program for the Texas Department of Criminal Justice ($180 million of design and construction in six months), Warren Dean[1] said:

> *"With this enormous challenge, we need a policy: nobody can be allowed to fail."*

It was a clear thought and that policy served us well. Everyone had to help everybody else perform if the project was to succeed. These fierce competitors became great collaborators and we were all extraordinarily successful. And, of course, the project was successful

If everybody wants us to succeed, our chances will sure improve. And remember, feelings are reciprocated. Others are far more likely to want us to succeed if we want them to succeed.

1. Warren was then president of CRSS Constructors. He later became Group Vice President of Jacobs Engineering Group Inc.

Problems polarize organizations

One person can polarize an entire chain of command.

Several years ago, one of our project managers reached me at the Atlanta airport late on Friday and said:

> *"Our client wants you in his office Monday morning or we're fired."*

Of course I showed up. Most of their brass was there. I had never met them. But I took a scolding for about an hour.

I had spent the weekend getting up to speed on the project. Our project team explained in great detail that the problems were caused by our client's ineptitude. Of course, our client's project manager explained to his management that the problems were all our fault.

After being scolded for an hour, I started asking questions that revealed some of the owner's project manager's failures. I could see the owner's board chairman getting steamed. Finally he looked at me and said:

> *"You're really slick. Your questions are aimed at showing that it isn't your fault."*

At that point I got steamed too. But before I could say anything, Ron Schappaugh, who led our Program Management group said:

> *"He's slick, but he isn't slimy."*

Everybody cracked up. That broke the ice. After the laughing subsided, we got down to undressing the problem. Obviously, the truth was that there were missteps on both sides. Eventually we got things on track, but we had a lot of personal relationships to fix and it cost everybody time, money and anguish.

Unfortunately, it wasn't a unique event. Here's the anatomy of a classic project blow-up. Something goes wrong. It always does. No project escapes problems. It could be external events, a bad management decision or a mistake by the project team. Maybe the problem has been caused by us, maybe the client's team. Never mind who caused it, we'll all contribute our share before the project is over. Everybody knows there's a goof. The demons of job security and ego protection awaken. A project manager explains to his or her management why it's the owner's fault. A biased description of the goof escalates up the chain of command.

The demons of job security and ego protection awaken. A PM explains to his or her management why it's the client's fault. A biased description of the goof escalates up the chain of command. The same happens on the owner's side. Soon the leaders of the two organizations hate each other and have never met.

As it travels through the management structure, people spin the facts a little and attach their own list of past grievances.

Meanwhile, the same process goes on in the owner's organization. Their project people polarize their management structure. The principle of reciprocal feelings kicks in. Soon the leaders hate each other—and they've never met.

Project conflicts are inevitable. But there sure is a good way to minimize them. We must build trusting, brass-to-brass and staff-to-staff relationships with our clients and our sister companies on the program. If we do that, we can fix these problems when they occur. And we have to build those relationships at the start of a project— before the problems occur.

Teams get competitive with the owner

Often a Program Manager works with an owner's in-house facilities group. More often than not, the facilities department is disappointed that their administration hired an outsourced Program Manager instead of adding staff and promoting from within. Furthermore, the employees in the in-house facility group may worry that all their jobs might be outsourced as the program develops.

Meanwhile, the outsourced team may think they will elicit the approval of their own company management if they increase their scope of work. So they embark on a misguided mission to show the client's administration that they can do a better job than the client's in-house facility-group.

I've never seen that succeed. It's a recipe for failure.

If the facilities staff feels that the outsourced Program Manager is getting competitive, they will reciprocate. Nobody wins that game. A Program Manager's job is the client's success. Program Managers will always do better if they make heroes out of all the client's employees. Then they will be invited back next time the client needs help and, meanwhile, the client will tell their friends.

But most important, it's crucial for the program team to recognize that success is tied to the indivisible success of our client's staff.

In design and construction programs there are rarely independent winners.

Too often, outsourced Program Management teams get competitive with their clients.

Compensation causes jealousy

Inevitably, owners have compensation structures and work policies that are different than those of the firms they hire. The owners may be governments, institutions or Fortune 500 companies, but there will always be differences.

And if an owner hires multiple Program Management companies to help them, it's likely that each of the Program Managers will have different compensation policies. Furthermore, the AEs, CMs and subs will all be different too.

Some may have better benefits but a lower base. Some will have more holidays, but less flexibility for time off. If one company is loose on working hours and some employees come in late, others will notice. But if they work late to compensate, they may not notice.

The problem emerges because on a program, people will eventually learn how everyone else is compensated. Then everyone will be inclined to focus on the best components of each compensation package and become jealous.

Furthermore, private sector consultants will bill their labor cost with a multiple for overhead and profit. The owner's staff may see that number and equate it to their own salary and feel it to be an egregious injustice. Few institutional or public organizations make their employees aware of the overhead burden that exists. Many don't even know.

There's nothing like sunlight to dry up problems. The leadership of all the prime organizations should explain the inherent differences between the compensation structures. They must encourage the owners to explain to their staff that they have overhead too.

And the differences in work policies must be addressed. I've seen programs where the entire program team adapted to the owner's hours, holiday schedule and other working conditions. And I've seen programs where everybody did their own thing, maintaining their own policies. That can work too if everybody understands that the program policy is for everybody to work their own company rules.

However, sometimes all that doesn't work. Then the leaders have to just tell their project teams to get over it.

Multiple companies on a program mean multiple compensation packages. Eventually people will learn how others are compensated. Some will focus on the best components of each compensation package and become jealous.

When a new company joins the team, the people will feel like immigrants from a foreign country who don't know the language, the culture or the territory.

Bureaucracy frustrates everybody

Any owner with a continuous building program is a bureaucracy. And it's likely that private sector Program Management companies have their own bureaucracy.

Bureaucracies have classic problems: red tape, confused signals, lethargic change, gatekeepers, turf battles, power struggles—and frustration. People spin facts to protect themselves or support their interests. Middle management may make poor decisions or treat others poorly to look good for their boss. Often the leaders don't fully know what is going on and make poor decisions that frustrate the rank and file who see the problems clearly.

Then there will be a set of rules. They will be different than any other set of rules. A new company that starts working with an owner's bureaucracy will come from an environment with different rules. They will be inclined to see their own rules as right and anything else as wrong.

An owner's staff will know their procedures better than the Program Management company or other consultants that they retain. So when a new company joins the team, the people will feel like immigrants from a foreign country who don't know the language, the culture or the territory. And they will be inclined to disdain the new procedures.

We all accept our own bureaucracy because we understand it— and we get frustrated at other bureaucracies. We're tempted to show irritation at an owner's bureaucratic glitches, and vice versa. Typically we see our own procedures that we understand as good and see others as bad. And if our owner has bad procedures, it gets awfully close to making the owner seem bad.

First, a Program Manager must learn to take an objective view. There's more than one way to do things well.

Meanwhile, the Program Manager should spend time with our client trying to improve the bureaucracy. Some Program Managers have had great luck with process improvement teams staffed with their people and their client's people. They contribute the best ideas from some of their other clients; meanwhile, the client explains their thinking. Then the team improves the bureaucracy and adapts new ideas to the program. Nothing builds teamwork better than winning as a team.

We're most critical when we're guilty

I've spent many hours (most of them happy) racing sailboats. One day I realized that I got grumpy at the crew when I made a strategic blunder. I got mad at others when I was mad at myself. Same thing happens at work. I get cross at my colleagues when they tell me I'm wrong. I get even crosser if they prove it.

Here is a little test to demonstrate what can go wrong on a project. Pick someone you know and then lie in wait until they make a mistake. Then jump on it. Be mean, pick something obvious. Then tell them all about it. If you want to do it up brown, do it in front of a lot of people. I'll bet you'll hear a long, loud string of your own mistakes.

When someone drops a ball and feels guilty, the common reaction is to be critical of others.

You would probably respond the same way. And so will our clients. So will our JV partners and our subcontractors. And so will the agencies that we must work with. When another organization (owner, JV partner, builder—whatever) we work with knows that they aren't performing well, they feel guilty and become critical of us. It's simple human nature.

In my consulting assignments, I'm often expected to find fault with a design and construction operation. I did that a few times. It rendered my work useless. People got defensive instead of wanting to improve. I've learned to concentrate on improvement, not mistakes.

So if a Program Manager is criticized, the Program Manager gets defensive (feelings are reciprocal) and makes a list of the critic's faults. And in a design and construction program, when someone wants to start list-making, there's never a shortage of mistakes to add to the list.

So let me pose a hypothetical situation. Our client makes a mistake. It causes a problem. Our clients are just like the rest of the world, they get cross at us, just like I got cross at my sailing crew. So what do we do? Do we sit down and explain to our clients that it is really their fault? And if we do that, does it make the client feel guiltier and crosser? And do they then find more ways to criticize us? You bet.

If that happens, the project starts a tail spin. The team culture deteriorates, people don't like work, the technical results suffer, people complain. It will take unusually good leadership to fix it.

Design and construction problems aren't like wine. They don't improve with age.

Problems grow with time

One day, we were discussing a glitch in one of our projects. Someone suggested that we delay a decision—that we wait and see. Joe Scarano, an old friend and the leader of our Southern California practice, said:

"It's not wine. It won't improve with age."

Usually construction problems, unattended, are more like an open bottle—they get increasingly sour with time.

One of the reasons problems don't get solved is that people at the grass roots don't escalate them to the brass. They feel it's a sign of weakness or inability to do their job. Most project managers want to control their turf: they don't want the brass meddling in their projects. And when there's a problem they don't want to admit to their boss that they can't handle it.

Too many people struggle with problems instead of asking for help. If our client's representatives caused the problem, we are reluctant to go over their heads to their boss. We are afraid we will destroy our working relationships. Sometimes their brass caused the problem. Not understanding the details of the project, some higher-up may have given unreasonable or autocratic instructions. And, of course, the reverse is true. Sometimes our brass caused the problem. In these cases, the project managers can't fix the problem. They just live with it.

So the problem festers. Team members in both organizations are defensive and tell *their* bosses that the *other* company caused the problem. By the time the issue becomes intolerable and the brass must get into it, everyone is mad at one another and the project organization is unstable. The issues have become emotional as well as technical, and working relationships deteriorate. Remedies are arduous. At worst, they're litigious.

Good leaders will make sure that project teams feel secure about asking for help. I remember clearly a time when Barry Nixon (our Program Manager on DeCA) had a project glitch. He called Gary Boyd (our group leader) on Friday night. Gary called me and we were at Langley Air Force Base Saturday morning. Our client was impressed with our response. Of course Barry had been a successful PM here for 20 years, so he didn't feel insecure about asking for help.

We need to have agreements with our client to escalate problems up our corporate ladders quickly. And we need to develop brass-to-brass relationships before the problems occur so we can solve them in an atmosphere of trusting professional friendship.

Conflict tolerance is rare

It's natural for us to want the esteem of our colleagues. So sensing that disagreement carries a shadow of disapproval, we may be reluctant to argue. We don't want to be unsupportive or appear to mount a personal attack. We want to be liked so we shy away from conflict and criticism.

And there's always an underlying reluctance to disagree with the boss. He or she might get mad at you and hurt your career.

Yet among project team members, working for a common purpose, there's an obligation to speak up when you disagree. If you don't, and if you are wrong, you lose the opportunity to be persuaded to a wiser point of view—or if you are right, you lose the opportunity to enlighten another.

Or, worst of all, you lose the moment of innovation that comes when collaborative people toss ideas back and forth and build progressively to a conclusion that nobody would have thought of alone.

Among colleagues on a project team, it's not fair to disagree and not say so.

Many years ago, George Kassabaum (the K of HOK) said to me:

> *"Chuck, just because someone disagrees with you doesn't mean they're evil or mounting a personal attack. They may just see the truth differently than you."*

When I taught architecture at Rice University, I realized that some of the best students were the most contentious. Since then I've frequently seen that people who care most about their work fight hardest for their point of view—sometimes passionately. They create conflict *because* they care.

So if we want people who care about the job, we need to have a conflict-tolerant culture. Our project leaders need to encourage their teams to speak with candor.

Yes, we must not embarrass people in public. But we need thick skins. And team members must feel no fear in speaking up. Indeed, they must be told that they're obligated to do so.

Among colleagues on a project team, it's not fair to disagree silently—to lie back in the weeds and not express concerns. It prevents collaboration. And the worst sin is a slow roll: to disagree with a leader, stay silent and not follow direction.

A new idea is fragile

Rejecting someone's half-formed idea before it matures hurts teamwork. Parents are proud of their kids, even though the kids may need lots of development and tender love and care. A good way to alienate the parents of a new idea is to dismiss the idea while it is young and tender.

A new idea is like a child—not very productive but perhaps with great potential. So we have to coddle and cherish new ideas.

Nowhere is this condition more common than when we are trying to build collaboration between architects and builders. From the day young men and women enter architecture school, they're taught to be creative, original and to design unique things. Plagiarism is a sin. But contractors have to build what architects design—and guarantee the result. So contractors are intensely inclined to stay with the "tried and true," a second cousin to plagiarism in the architects' view.

I heard an architect say that a very good contractor he knew "spent more time thinking of why things don't work than figuring out how to make them work." Small wonder. It's the contractor who is responsible. Contractors lose money, send people back to fix things and struggle in vain with bad ideas that seemed like good ideas at the time. Naturally their first reaction is to search for the flaws in design ideas. And boy, do we need that kind of thinking.

So what do we do about this? Here are my thoughts:

We need to convince architects that they need to appreciate the contractors' knowledge. They need to listen closely when contractors warn us of flaws. The last thing we want is a contractor who follows our instructions and then says, "I knew it wouldn't work."

> *"Faced with the choice between changing one's mind and proving that there is no need to do so, almost everybody gets busy on the proof."* ....*John Kenneth Galbraith*

But we need tenacity. If all we ever did was to stay with the "tried and true," we'd never push the envelope.

Architects need to recognize that the builders are concerned with reliability and are circumspect about design innovation. Builders also need to listen and see if a frail idea can mature. If the first impression a builder gives to architects is that they are trying to hurt their child, they won't build teamwork. Builders need to get their ego on the positive side. If after study, they are convinced that it's not a good idea, they have to kill it.

Meanwhile Program Managers need to understand these basic differences between architects and builders and play marriage counselor.

A Look Ahead

A little history is woven throughout this book. I kept referring to the past to remind myself that these techniques of management and strategies of project delivery undergo constant change. So as I write about today's processes, I'm haunted by the belief that by the time you read this, there will have been more change. New and better ideas will replace today's thinking. I'll need to update this material pretty soon.

Rather than leave my thoughts to age and become obsolete, I will walk on thin ice again and make some observations about how the industry will evolve, or more accurately, how it is evolving.

Specialization will continue. More individuals and more companies will participate in a program. Buildings will be smarter, safer, sustainable and secure, and they will require more knowledge components from the professions and industry. Competition will drive manufacturers to more research and development and building products will be more sophisticated. The industry will continue to globalize and products will come from many countries.

It's likely that the U.S. will continue economic growth. Prosperity will spread internationally. More owners, including serial builders, will seek design excellence. The opportunity for architects working with continuous building programs will be to spread more innovative ideas across multiple projects—and to do more research and amortize its cost against a multi-building program.

Twenty-first century architects won't be dealing with the limited construction technology of Frank Lloyd Wright, Mies van der Rohe, Antonio Gaudi, Adolf Loos, Alvar Aalto and Le Corbusier. Innovative managers and the architects they choose already face an inexhaustible fountain of emerging technology that exceeds the comprehension of a single individual. They will not be able to master these technologies by themselves. Success will come to managers, architects, constructors and manufacturers who learn collaborative skills, pool their knowledge and share wonderful accomplishments.

There is a golf game called a scramble. It usually entails a foursome. Each player hits a ball, but then everyone plays the best ball. Because at least one of the players will hit a good shot, a team of ordinary club players will shoot below par and beat the best touring pro.

So it will be with design and construction. There will always be rewards for individual brilliance, inspirational leadership and innovative ideas. But the collaborative team will most often win.

There will be more companies involved in a program, but the number of first-tier subcontractors may not increase. The 50 to 100 subs that a prime constructor must work with already stretches any reasonably imagined span of control. But the sub-subs will proliferate and some subcontractors will become similar to general contractors with a tier of subs. More subs will be design-builders or CMs for their specific body of work. There may be some bundling of subs and actually fewer first-tier subcontractors.

Much of the technical knowledge of design and construction has already migrated from the traditional design professions to the manufacturers and specialty subcontractors. So the role of architects and engineers will increasingly be to evaluate and integrate industrialized building systems and components designed by the producers. The master builder will be a large team, sourced internationally.

It will be more and more crucial to find ways to contract with these companies and extract their knowledge before construction documents are complete. Program Managers, either as an outsourced company or as part of an owner's organization, will find ways to contract with specialty subcontractors and manufacturers to participate in the design in a reliable and responsible way. Some will be selected with lump-sum bidding, others with Bridging or any of the other selection methods that we've discussed. They may use horizontal procurement like HEB does for bar joists or Starbucks does for fixtures and equipment. These approaches will provide cost feedback earlier in the process—increasing the reliability of the project delivery processes and providing the wonderfully useful opportunity for technical input from manufacturers and subs.

Owners will staff internally to manage their increasingly consolidated portfolios, but they will also augment their staff with talent and techniques from the best of firms that provide design, Program Management and construction management services.

Information technology—the Internet, collaboration software and BIM— will play an increasingly critical role, soon becoming a prerequisite for practice. Manufacturers will have their products and systems in electronic form so what has traditionally been a manufacturer-produced shop drawing will be incorporated into a comprehensive, integrated set of Construction Documents. The CDs themselves will be both 4-D and electronic reports from a database that includes extensive alphanumeric information. Contractors will become experts at the use of computer simulation tools. Building construction will be simulated and tested before it moves out to the field. Prints can be made in the construction trailer for specific tasks on a daily basis and the racks of paper plans will shrink.

The challenge of integrating knowledge from a global assemblage of design professionals, constructors and manufacturers will be enormous. So will the rewards. The collaboration—the accumulation of intellectual capital from this multi-industry, multi-national, multi-profession collaboration— will be wonderfully satisfying to architects, engineers and construction managers. And we will make better buildings.

Appendix

As we assembled the thoughts for this book, Jesse, Miriam, Jim and I gained invaluable insight from conversations with individuals throughout the building industry who spoke to us about their programs. I'd like to thank the many people who were generous with their time and candor for their contribution to this study. They include:

Dr. William Akers, Professor Emeritus of Chemical Engineering and former Vice President of Administration, Rice University

Andy Anway, President, Amaze Design

Mike Bailey, Director of Facilities and Planning, Placentia-Yorba Linda Unified School District

Phillip Bernstein, Vice President, AEC Solutions Division, Autodesk

Mark A. Bodenschatz, Director of Design and Construction, Office of Physical Plant, Pennsylvania State University

William Bonham, Division Director, Facility Construction and Space Management, Texas Building and Procurement Commission

Joseph Borgert, Manager of Architecture, Property Development, Target Corporation

Boyce Bourland, Facilities Program Manager, Defense Commissary Agency

Charlie Brady, Associate Director for Engineering, Office of Facilities Planning and Construction, University of Texas System

Steve Brandt, Strategic Account Manager, Trane

Bill Breyfogle, Director of Construction and Support Services, Minnesota State Colleges and Universities

Raymond Brochstein, Chairman, Brochsteins Inc.

Deborah Brochstein, President and CEO, Brochsteins Inc.

Barbara White Bryson FAIA, Associate Vice President, Facilities Engineering and Planning, Rice University

Brad Burdic, National Manager, Johns Manville

Art Chen Jr., Director of Facilities Programs, Foundation for California Community Colleges

Jim Cowell, Deputy Chief Facilities Executive, New Construction, Los Angeles Unified School District

Paul R. Curley, Head of Capital Construction, MIT

William Daigneau, Vice President of Operations and Facilities Management, University of Texas MD Anderson Cancer Center

Donald Dana, Executive Vice President, Corporate Properties Group, Wells Fargo Bank

Megan Davis, Director of Finance, Land and Buildings, Stanford University

Warren Dean, Group Vice President, Jacobs Engineering Group Inc.

Michael Dell'Isola, Vice President, DMJM

David Dixon, Associate Director for Project Management, Office of Facilities Planning and Construction, University of Texas System

Dennis Doran, Senior Consultant, FMI Corporation

Stephan Fairfield, President/CEO, Covenant Community Capital Corporation

Ed Feiner, Director, Washington D.C. office, Skidmore, Owings & Merrill; former Chief Architect, General Services Administration

David Faulkner, Retail Development Management, Inc.
Raymond Floyd, Management and Efficiency Expert, former Worldwide Manager of Manufacturing, ExxonMobil Chemical
Dean Fox, Major General, Air Force Civil Engineer, United States Air Force
Stephen Fox, Adjunct Lecturer, Rice University
Bob Fraga, AIA, Director, Office of Contracting, Smithsonian Institution; former Manager, Facilities Portfolio, United States Postal Service
Edd Gibson, Professor and Garry Neil Drummond Chair, University of Alabama
George Gottuso, Senior Project Officer, New Jersey Schools Construction Corporation
Stephen Hagan, Project Knowledge Center, Property Development Division, General Services Administration
Clifford Ham, Senior Project Architect, Judicial Council of California, Administrative Office of the Courts
David Harris, President, National Institute of Building Sciences
John Harris, Executive Vice President, Conceptual Construction, Hines
George Heery, Chairman and CEO, Brookwood Program Management
Ray Herman, President, Herman/Stewart Construction
Gerald D. Hines, Chairman, Hines
Bob Hixon, Project Executive, Capitol Visitor Center
William Hoy, ALA, Senior Vice President, B.F. Saul Company; former Senior Vice President, Design and Project Management, Marriott International
Bruce Kendall, Deputy Chief Facilities Executive, Modernization and Repair, Los Angeles Unified School District
Bruce Knaphus, President, Kepco+ Inc
Steve Knisley, JMJ Associates
Jim Koutris, Vice President Project Management, Marriott International
Barry Kumar, General Services Administration
Bert Landry, Chief of the Design and Construction Division, Defense Commissary Agency
Ray Landy, President, DMJM
Jerrold Lea, Vice President, Conceptual Construction, Hines
Claude Le Feuvre, Parsons Infrastructure & Technology Group, Inc.
Susan Lipka, Executive Director, Capital Planning & Management, University of Texas MD Anderson Cancer Center
Stephen Makredes, Director of Construction, Property Development, Target Corporation
Robert Masch, Team Manager for Southern California, Kaiser Permanente
Wright Massey, Brand Architecture
Jim McConnell, former Chief Facilities Executive Los Angeles Unified School District
Guy Mehula, Chief Facilities Executive, Los Angeles Unified School Disrict
John Messervy, Director of Capital and Facilities Planning, Partners HealthCare System
Doug Nelson, Director, Property Development Division, National Capitol Region, General Services Administration
Christopher Noble, Noble & Wickersham LLP

Courtney Peterson, Director of Purchasing Programs, Foundation for California Community Colleges
Linda Phillips, General Services Administration
Charles Pollard, Senior Architect, Design Division, Houston Airport System
Thomas Regan, Dean, College of Architecture, Texas A&M University
Bill Reynolds, Group Vice President, Facility Alliance, HEB
David J. Rodd, University Architect, Rice University
Rick Rusk, Chief, Real Estate Services, Project Management Branch, State of California Department of General Services
Sid Sanders, Vice President, Facilities and Construction, The Methodist Hospital System
Carl Sapers, Adjunct Professor, Department of Architecture, The Graduate School of Design, Harvard University
James Sartain, Assistant Director, Manager, Design Division, Houston Airport System
Amanda Scarano, Production Executive, Irish DreamTime
Stan Scott, Assistant Director for Project Controls, Office of Facilities Planning and Construction, University of Texas System
Bob Seeger, Senior Vice President and Chief Architect, Wells Fargo Properties, Inc.
Les Shepherd, Acting Chief Architect, General Services Administration
Victoria Sirianni, Chief Facilities Officer, MIT
Scott Simpson, President and CEO, The Stubbins Associates
Bill Sims, AIA, retired Senior Vice President, Walt Disney Imagineering - Florida
Dennis Smith, Superintendent, Placentia-Yorba Linda Unified School District
Marc Steadman, Vice President of Construction, Property Development, Target Corporation
Jeff Stephens, President and CEO, BSW International
Ujwala Tamaskar, Manager, HQ Design and Construction, USPS
Douglas P. Tomlinson, Assistant Vice President, Project Management and Engineering, Rice University
Larry Toy, President, CEO, Foundation for California Community Colleges
Jerry Trevino, Architects, Defense Commissary Agency
Jan Tuchman, Editor-In-Chief, Engineering News Record
Rich Varda, Senior Vice President for Store Design, Target Corporation
Perry Waughtal, former Chief Financial Officer, Hines
Glenn Weiblen, Defense Commissary Agency
Kathryn E. West, Director of Real Estate Operations, Partners HealthCare System
Robert Workman, Chairman and CEO, BSW International

The Author

Chuck Thomsen consults with clients who have building programs. He is an advisory director of Parsons, Chairman of the Board of the Rice Building Institute and a member of the board of FMI.

Chuck joined 3D/International in 1982 and led the company, first as president, then as chairman, until it merged with Parsons in 2006. Previously, he spent 18 years with CRS where he started one of the country's first construction management companies and became president and CEO of the parent company.

He has worked on hundreds of projects in 20 countries and has personal experience with nearly every form of project delivery in all three basic roles: designer, constructor and manager.

Chuck is the first person to be elected a Fellow in both the American Institute of Architects (AIA) and the Construction Management Association of America (CMAA). He was elected Chancellor of CMAA's College of Fellows in 2007.

He has a master of architecture from the Massachusetts Institute of Technology and a bachelor of architecture from the University of Oklahoma.